RESOURCE BOOK AND INSTRUCTOR'S GUIDE FOR PASSING THE GED PROGRAM

REVISED

GLENCOE

Macmillan/McGraw–Hill

New York, New York   Columbus, Ohio   Mission Hills, California   Peoria, Illinois

GED • GED • GED • GED • GED

Text Acknowledgments

69 "The Eighteenth Amendment . . ." Carol Berkin and Leonard Wood, LAND OF PROMISE: A HISTORY OF THE UNITED STATES. Scott, Foresman and Company, 1983, pp. 586–87.

72 "According to one observer . . ." Gerald M. Pomper, "The Presidential Election," THE ELECTION OF 1976. pp. 74–75.

86 "Plants become quite . . ." Irwin L. Slesnick et al., BIOLOGY. Scott, Foresman and Company, 1985, p. 311.

94 "When Gracie had a migraine . . ." George Burns, GRACIE: A LOVE STORY. New York: G. P. Putnam's Sons, 1988, pp. 21–22.

94 "War is always attractive . . ." Philip Caputo, A RUMOR OF WAR. New York: Ballantine Books, 1977, p. xiv.

Illustration Acknowledgments

59 "United States: Population Changes, 1970–1980." Dr. Joan Schreiber and Kathleen Kain, REGIONS OF OUR COUNTRY AND OUR WORLD, Indiana Edition. Scott, Foresman and Company, 1985, p. 115.

61 "World Hunger." T. Walter Wallbank et al., HISTORY AND LIFE: THE WORLD AND ITS PEOPLE. Scott, Foresman and Company, 1984, p. 716.

62 "The 10 occupations with largest projected absolute growth from 1984 to 1995." Bureau of Labor Statistics, U.S. Dept. of Labor.

65 "How the federal government spends its money." Office of Management and Budget.

72 "Annual Precipitation in Riyadh, Saudi Arabia." Dr. Joan Schreiber and Kathleen Kain, REGIONS OF OUR COUNTRY AND OUR WORLD, Indiana Edition. Scott, Foresman and Company, 1985, p. 304.

76 "Survival in Captivity." From "Comparison of Longevity Among Vertebrates" chart from "Why Do Turtles Live So Long?" by J. Whitfield Gibbons, in BIOSCIENCE, Vol. 37 No. 4, April, 1987, p. 262. Reprinted by permission.

Cover Photo: W. Cody/Westlight

Send all inquiries to:
GLENCOE DIVISION
Macmillan/McGraw-Hill
936 Eastwind Drive
Westerville, OH 43081

ISBN 0-02-802018-9

2 3 4 5 6 7 8 9   MAL   99 98 97 96 95 94

Contents

What Is GED Instruction?

More than 1 in 5 adults over the age of 18 in the United States never completed high school. That fact surprises many who hear it; some even doubt the statistic. It is no surprise, however, to adult educators, many of whom have devoted their professional lives to helping such adults complete their education and, in the process, prove to themselves that they *can* learn.

The Tests of General Educational Development — commonly called the GED Test — were created to give adults just that opportunity, without actually returning to high school. Passing the GED Test means receiving a state-endowed GED certificate, a credential accepted by most businesses and colleges as the equivalent of a high school diploma. The GED Test is even referred to by many as the "high school equivalency test." GED instruction, then, enables adult learners to "pass the GED" and earn their GED credentials.

What's on the GED Test?

The GED Test covers five different areas of an average high school curriculum. In fact, it is actually a battery of five tests:

    Writing Skills Test
    Social Studies Test
    Science Test
    Test of Interpreting Literature and the Arts
    Mathematics Test

With the exception of the essay section of the Writing Skills Test, the tests are composed of five-option multiple-choice questions.

Although the GED Test comprises five content areas, it is by and large a test of skills, not knowledge. Reading, writing, math, and thinking skills are the focus of the test questions. These specific skills are usually seen as belonging to a hierarchy of general cognitive skills. The GED Testing Service has adapted Bloom's taxonomy of these cognitive levels and designed the test around the following general skills. While recall of knowledge may sometimes be necessary to help answer a question, it is never the sole skill tested by an item; one or more of the following need also be applied.

Comprehension is, of course, understanding what is read, seen, or heard. *Literal comprehension* is understanding information that is directly stated or shown. Paraphrasing and summarizing ideas are examples of literal comprehension. *Inferential comprehension* — higher on the cognitive scale — is understanding information that is merely implied — "reading between the lines," so to speak.

Application is taking information and using it in a new, somewhat different situation.

Analysis is dissecting a whole piece of information to understand its ideas and their relationships. Determining causes and their effects, differentiating between facts and opinions, and dissecting an author's technique are all instances of analyzing information.

Synthesis, on the other hand, is pulling together discrete ideas to produce a whole. Writing an essay is a good example of synthesizing.

Evaluation — highest of the GED cognitive levels — involves judging the merits of arguments, the strength of supporting evidence, the role of values in making decisions, and so on. Evaluation skills are sometimes called critical thinking skills.

Higher-level skills necessarily involve lower-level ones. For example, to evaluate a conclusion, one must first be able to comprehend the information and then analyze the separate pieces of evidence used to support the conclusion. Questions throughout the Glencoe GED program books have been labeled to identify the level of cognitive ability they are testing.

The Goals of GED Instruction

The higher-level skills are often less developed in adults entering a GED class—whether they are advancing from a pre-GED class or walking in off the street for the first time. The reading abilities of these adults usually range from seventh to ninth, and writing abilities likely lag farther behind. Reading levels of materials on the GED Test itself tend to range from eighth to twelfth. (The testing service does not use readability scales *per se*. Instead, it relies *both* on the judgment of educators as to whether a particular selection is written at "a level appropriate for a high school senior" *and* on the performance of GED examinees when they are given the selection to read in field tests.)

The goal of GED instruction is, at the very least, to bring an adult's skills up to a level sufficient to *pass* the GED Test. (Individual states determine what is a passing score, not the testing service itself. In most states, an examinee must achieve an overall average standard score of 45—corresponding roughly to a percentile rank of 31 when compared to the scores of a high school–senior norm group—and score no less than 35—an approximate percentile rank of 7—on any one test.) Yet some GED programs—or individual teachers—seek to do more in their classes than simply "teach to the test." They try to give adult students a rounded high school–level education and to instill in them a value for learning.

Glencoe's GED program can be used to achieve both goals.

The Glencoe GED Program

The GED class is marked by variety—adult students of various ages, at a variety of levels, and with a variety of learning styles. For that reason, Glencoe offers variety in its GED program to help you meet the goals of GED instruction.

The comprehensive general volume *Passing the GED* is geared to those students who need only basic, brief review before working with GED-level questions. The five *Springboards for Passing the GED* make up a series for students who need intensive instruction and practice in the content and skills found on the GED Test. And the *Practice Books for Passing the GED* offer intensive practice with GED-type multiple-choice questions as a good warm-up for the test.

The Glencoe GED program was developed with a clear idea of what is on the GED Test and of what is needed by GED students. Official materials from the GED Testing Service—*The Item Writer's Manual, The 1988 Tests of General Educational Development: A Preview, The Official Teacher's Guide to the Tests of General Educational Development*, and the *Official GED Practice Tests, Forms AA, BB, CC, and DD*—as

well as correspondence with editors from the GED Testing Service were essential in devising content outlines and the scope and sequence for the books in the Glencoe program. The charts on pages 128–137 classify the items on the GED Practice Tests and list the pages in the program where the skills required to answer those items are taught.

In addition, as consultants, reviewers, and even writers, GED teachers and other adult educators offered their expertise and insights into the needs of their students at every stage of the program—from development to production. The following adult educators were especially instrumental in formulating or producing different components of the Glencoe GED program.

Kathryn Boesel-Dunn
Columbus Public Schools
Columbus, Ohio

Teresa A. Brecht
South Suburban College
South Holland, Illinois

Toby G. Cannon
Cohn Adult Learning Center
Nashville, Tennessee

Charmaine M. Carney
Hawkeye Institute of Technology
Waterloo, Iowa

Mary S. Charuhas
College of Lake County
Grayslake, Illinois

Lee Chic
Sequoia Adult School
Redwood City, California

Gail Dowling
Vermont Institute for Self-Reliance
Calais, Vermont

Cynthia A. Green
Lincoln Instructional Center
Dallas, Texas

Esther Gross
Petit Jean Technical College
Morrilton, Arkansas

Theodore M. Harig
Ellsworth Correctional Center
Union Grove, Wisconsin

Chuck Herring
GED Institute
Seattle, Washington

Linda L. Kindy
Little Rock Adult Education Center
Little Rock, Arkansas

Claudia V. McClain
South Suburban College
South Holland, Illinois

Ed A. Mayfield
Fayette County Adult Education Center
Lexington, Kentucky

Valerie Meyer
Southern Illinois University
Edwardsville, Illinois

Pat Mitchell
Dallas Independent School District
Dallas, Texas

Laura Morris
Center for Community Education
Tallahassee, Florida

Evelyn H. Nunes
Virginia Commonwealth University
Richmond, Virginia

Ann Kuykendall Parker
Cohn Adult Learning Center
Nashville, Tennessee

Jill Plaza
Reading and Educational Consultants
Palatine, Illinois

Gail Rice
Adult Basic Education Program
Palos Heights, Illinois

Karen Samson
Chicago State University
Chicago, Illinois

Yvonne E. Siats-Fiskum
Gateway Technical College
Elkhorn, Wisconsin

Sheldon Silver
Truman College
Chicago, Illinois

Robert T. Sutton
Central Piedmont Community College
Charlotte, North Carolina

Joan Wallace
Adult Education Program
Elgin, Illinois

Passing the GED

Glencoe's *Passing the GED* is a comprehensive volume offering content and skill review coupled with extensive test practice in each of the five subjects found on the GED Test battery:

Writing Skills
Social Studies
Science
Interpreting Literature and the Arts
Mathematics

The book is geared to the GED student who needs a "refresher" course in most of the content and skills on the GED Test, perhaps instruction in just a few, and practice with GED-type test items. As such, it was developed with those qualities especially suited to independent study at the high school level by the adult student.

The high school–level content and skills in the book are those found on the GED Test, according to the GED Testing Service and its *Item Writer's Manual* and *Preview* of the 1988 Test. For example, the charts on pages 128 – 137 classify the items on the Official GED Practice Tests, Forms AA, BB, CC, and DD, and show where those skills are discussed or practiced in *Passing the GED*.

What's in *Passing the GED?*

A returning student is often an anxious one, especially if the student was conspicuously unsuccessful in his or her first experience with school. The introductory material in *Passing the GED* addresses this anxiety immediately by informing students about the GED Test and state requirements for passing it and by offering encouragement and motivational and study aids. An explanation of the format of the book and how to use it is given, followed by valuable test-taking tips.

The Pretests

The Pretests are a set of five multiple-choice tests about half the length of the tests on the GED battery, together with an essay assignment. They can be used to predict performance on the GED Test and thereby determine a course of study for each student. An Answer Key and a set of Diagnostic Charts at the end of the Pretests help do just that. The charts indicate which instructional subtopics in *Passing the GED* correspond to the different types of questions in the Pretests. The charts also group the questions according to Bloom's taxonomy of cognitive skills. Instructions for using these charts are on pages 9– 10. You'll find guidelines for administering the Pretests to students later in this section and copies of the diagnostic charts on pages 153– 157.

The Five Sections

Each of the color-coded strips on the ends of the pages identifies a major GED content section:

Purple   Interpreting Literature and the Arts
Gold   Writing Skills
Green   Social Studies
Red   Science
Blue   Mathematics

Interpreting Literature and the Arts is first because it helps strengthen reading skills that form a foundation for study in the other content areas. Writing Skills follows. This sequence allows students to practice the reading and writing skills they've developed when they study the Social Studies and Science sections.

Each section opens with a page that gives information about that content area and its GED Test. Then tinted Overview pages preview the kinds of questions found on the test and explain how to arrive at the answers.

Following the section opener and Overview are the instruction–test practice pages—the core of the book. Tinted columns signify instruction; white, practice test items. Most often the inner columns are tinted instruction, and the outer are white test practice with items that test the skill or involve the content taught in the inner column of the page. For that reason the students should first read the inner tinted column on a page and then go to the outer white column. If, however, a particular skill requires more instruction than just an inner column would allow, tinted instruction runs over into the next column or columns. And the outer white test practice columns may include items that review skills or content discussed in previous tinted columns.

The tinted instruction columns use the following components to present information and offer practice.

Warm-up Following discussion of a particular skill or content area, a short exercise gives students practice in using what they have just learned. Writing assignments, questions, summaries, and computation problems are examples of the kinds of exercises the Warm-ups provide.

Warm-up Answers The answers to a Warm-up are given at the bottom of the tinted column in which the Warm-up appears, so students can locate them easily. If a writing assignment or open-ended question is part of the Warm-up, a sample answer is given so that students have a model with which to compare their answers.

Coming to Terms Technical vocabulary is not directly tested by the GED Test. It is unnecessary for students to memorize long glossary lists of definitions. When knowledge of a term will be helpful to students, the term is in boldface type in the instructional material, defined in context, and then reviewed in a Coming to Terms. Such a presentation more closely reflects what students will encounter on the test—determining the meaning of words using context clues.

A Test-Taking Tip Within many of the tinted columns are individual tips on how to approach specific kinds of questions found on the GED Test. Students need not memorize these practical suggestions; they are also intended as motivational aids that bring the GED Test into focus.

Need a Hint? Whenever a practice test item in the white column is particularly demanding, a white block in the tinted column will help steer students in the right direction with a hint or suggestion. This component is especially helpful for those items that require a step-by-step thinking approach.

Answers

Answers to all practice test items in the white columns are given at the end of that particular section, along with explanations of why the answers are the correct ones. Students should check their answers once they have finished the two outer columns on a spread. Such routine checking will help them realize if they are having difficulty in a particular area.

In addition, a two-letter abbreviation has been added to the end of each answer explanation throughout *Passing the GED*. These abbreviations correspond to four of the cognitive levels in Bloom's taxonomy—comprehension, application, analysis, and evaluation—described on page 1 of this book. They can be used to help you or your students determine which types of questions are giving students the most

---

BEHAVIORAL SCIENCES/PSYCHOLOGY

Principles of Learning Learning takes place throughout the entire course of a person's life. It can be as simple as a baby's first drinking from a cup or as complex as you acquiring new skills for the GED Test. Psychologists define learning as changes in behavior resulting from experience or practice.

The simplest kind of learning is based on **stimulus** and **response**. A stimulus can make a person respond in a certain way, such as when a sudden loud noise makes someone jump.

In the early 1900s, the Russian psychologist Pavlov performed a classic experiment in learning. He trained dogs to salivate when they heard a bell. To do this, Pavlov rang a bell whenever he gave the dogs food. A dog's natural response to food is salivation. Since the dogs heard the bell whenever they were fed, they began to associate the sound with food. Eventually, the bell alone could produce the salivation response in the dogs.

☑ **A Test-Taking Tip**
Several questions on the GED Social Studies Test are similar to items 5–7 on this page. These items ask you to classify information. Make sure you understand the classifications before you choose an answer for each item.

Coming to Terms

stimulus something that produces behavior
response reaction to a stimulus

✎ **Warm-up**
Psychologists discovered that an animal in a maze learns the beginning and end points of the maze more easily than the parts in the middle. If this were also true of the way humans learned, what would happen when a child is introduced to the alphabet?

_____

_____

Sample Warm-up Answer
The child would learn the first and last letters of the alphabet more quickly and easily than those in the middle.

Items 5–7 refer to the following information.

Psychologists who study learning have discovered some general rules to help a person learn.

(1) Stagger—work in short practice sessions separated by long breaks.
(2) Imitate—imitate an expert.
(3) Practice—try the task yourself rather than just watch someone do it or listen to someone explain it.
(4) Evaluate—have your performance evaluated immediately.
(5) Parcel—divide the task into steps or parts.

Each of the following statements describes a learning situation. Choose the rule that is applied in each situation.

5. Sam practices the hardest lines of the musical score first. Which rule is he following?

(1) stagger   (2) imitate   (3) practice
(4) evaluate   (5) parcel

① ② ③ ④ ⑤

6. Right after Mercedes practices a lay-up in basketball, she asks the coach to tell her how she can improve. Which rule is she following?

(1) stagger   (2) imitate   (3) practice
(4) evaluate   (5) parcel

① ② ③ ④ ⑤

7. Charlie plans to study half an hour before and after dinner for his Spanish test. Which rule is he following?

(1) stagger   (2) imitate   (3) practice
(4) evaluate   (5) parcel

① ② ③ ④ ⑤

271

trouble. A key to these abbreviations has been provided at the bottom of each answer explanation page.

Minitests

At the end of each content section are from three to five short tests consisting of GED-type multiple-choice questions and, in the case of Writing Skills, essay assignments. These Minitests can be used as extra practice or reviews throughout a student's work in *Passing the GED*.

The Posttests

The Posttests are two sets of tests similar in content, format, and number of questions to those on the actual GED Test. Once students have completed their individual study plans, they can use the first of the two sets to gauge how they would do on the GED Test itself. The Diagnostic Charts on pages 678–679 will help students determine which instructional section subtopics they need to review.

Specific suggestions for administering both Posttests are given on page 11, and directions for using the Diagnostic Charts are given on page 9.

Readability

The reading levels of the passages used as stimuli for questions on the GED Test tend to range from eighth to twelfth grade, and the practice test items found in the white columns and on the Minitests and Posttests of *Passing the GED* fall within this range as well.

The text in the section openers, Overviews, and tinted instruction columns, on the other hand, ranges from fifth to eighth grade level. These levels aid comprehension of content, especially in such areas as science and mathematics, where students are likely already to be apprehensive. And the friendly yet adult tone of *Passing the GED* gives the book a "non-textbook," nonthreatening feel—an appealing quality to GED students.

Writing Across the Curriculum

The essay component, a new addition to the GED Test beginning in 1988, caused concern and even doubt on the part of many adult educators. Writing skills are lacking in the population as a whole, including many of those with college degrees. Teaching GED students to write, some teachers contended, was asking the impossible.

Yet communicating one's thoughts in writing is a useful and gratifying skill to possess in the world as well as in school. Teaching a person to write well has always been a worthwhile and generous endeavor. Since 1988, with the essay requirement on the GED Test, it has become essential in GED classes.

The Writing Skills section in *Passing the GED* develops strong writing and editing skills in GED students to prepare them for the GED Writing Skills Test. But writing is not limited to the Writing Skills section alone. In the Warm-up exercises of the Literature, Social Studies, and Science sections, students are asked to write in complete sentences. They may need to write answers to questions about information in the tinted columns, summaries of what they've read, explanations about certain events, or support for certain conclusions. Such exercises not only develop writing skills but also aid student comprehension of content material.

You can take full advantage of this thinking-writing connection by requiring even more writing of your students. You'll find specific suggestions for including writing in your classroom under "Using the Instruction–Test Practice Pages" on pages 10–11 of this guide.

The Roles of the Teacher

A GED course of instruction—though seeking to complete a student's high school education—is not a high school course. Adult students, even *young* adult students, are not high school students. Therefore, a GED class should not necessarily be structured as a high school class would be.

Passing the GED was developed with the special nature of the GED class in mind. In fact, *Passing the GED* is in many respects a "teacher's aide." It can help you fill the various essential roles that a GED teacher is called upon to play.

Diagnostician Even if your school or center has already administered placement tests to determine the general level of students, you may want to assess the more GED-specific level of their abilities in the areas of writing, social studies, science, interpreting literature, and math. The Pretests in *Passing the GED* can help in this assessment. Students' scores on the Pretests are a general indicator of how they would perform on the GED Test. Specific suggestions for giving the

Pretests are found under "Administering the Pretests" on pages 9–10.

In addition to diagnosing the current level of performance of your students, knowing the ultimate goal of each student is important. Some students may simply want to hold their GED certificates in their hands someday. Others may want to go on to study science at the community college. Still others may want from you as full and rounded an education as possible to make up for what they consider earlier, wasted years. You can photocopy the questionnaire below and ask each of your students to fill it out. Keep the questionnaires on file with your other assessments. Diagnosing both the current level of performance and the goals of each student will help you with the next role of a GED teacher.

Planner Once you know a student's current level of performance and goals, you usually want to plan the best course of action for him or her. At the end of the Pretests are an Answer Key, an Essay Scoring Checklist, and Diagnostic Charts to help you fulfill this role of planner. The Diagnostic Charts indicate which instructional subtopics of *Passing the GED* the student should emphasize in his or her course of study. The charts are also duplicated on pages 153–157 of this *Instructor's Guide*.

Motivator The role of motivator is important in any classroom, but that is especially true in a GED classroom, for GED students often need help with self-motivation and perseverance. You'll find some useful suggestions for motivating your students on pages 37–38 of this guide in the section "Teaching GED Students Effectively."

Resource person A resource person helps people by giving them the materials and information they need to succeed. *Passing the GED* is one resource students can use to succeed, but they will also need you for guidance and other resources.

Passing the GED was written as a one-on-one encounter with the GED student. As a *facilitator,* you can help students interact with the book. Make sure they do the Warm-up exercises before looking at the answers at the bottom of the page. Be sure they answer the white column test practice items before checking the answers at the back of the section. You can also facilitate small-group discussions about the practice test items themselves—how to approach them and the steps involved in answering them.

Passing the GED was written specifically to an audience of one—the individual student. You are likely to find that many of your students will be able to study independently with some initial "consulting" help from you. As a *consultant,* you can be ready when adults working independently need advice or additional information.

Name _____

To help me plan your studies, I'd like to know why you signed up for this class. Please check the reason or reasons below. You can check as many reasons as you like.

I signed up for this GED class in order to
- [ ] pass the GED Test
- [ ] learn about social studies, science, literature, math, and writing
- [ ] be able to go on to college
- [ ] get a better job
- [ ] get a promotion
- [ ] help my children with their schoolwork

If you have any other reasons for enrolling in this class, please write them here.

_____

_____

_____

The role of *instructor* is the most traditional role of the teacher as resource person. And even though *Passing the GED* was written mainly as an independent study resource, at times instructing the whole class or a group of students will be useful. This is especially true when the students have shown they are having difficulty with a particular concept. You can go over the appropriate tinted and white columns with the students, add your own examples, and then assign additional practice, such as the exercise sheets at the back of this book.

Troubleshooter A GED teacher needs to be alert to "trouble"—to misunderstanding or incomplete understanding on the part of a student. You can monitor students' comprehension as they work through *Passing the GED* by checking their answers to Warm-up exercises and asking questions of your own. In addition, the Performance Charts on pages 138–142 of this guide will help you spot probable problem areas. You'll find an explanation of how to use these charts on page 11.

Assessor The final role a teacher usually plays in a GED class is that of assessor. You can take a final assessment of the performance level of your students by using the two sets of Posttests and their accompanying Diagnostic Charts in *Passing the GED*. Guidelines for administering the Posttests are given on page 11, and the Posttest Diagnostic Charts are included on pages 153–157.

Using *Passing the GED*

Following are some general suggestions for teaching with Glencoe's *Passing the GED*. They expand on how you can use the text to help you fill your role as a GED teacher.

The introductory material is a resource for easing student anxiety about taking the GED Test and returning to school—a setting many students associate with failure or at least consider threatening. You'll especially want to go over the section "Using This Book" with the class. "Twenty-Four Tips for Passing the GED Test" will be helpful to students both as they begin their GED study and as they complete it—and are ready to take the test.

Administering the Pretests

To alleviate anxiety, explain to students the purpose of the Pretests—to show them how they would be likely to perform on the GED Test itself if they were to take the test today.

The Pretests can be self-administered by each student. If the books in your class are intended to be reused, or if you would like to create a realistic standardized-test experience to see how a student performs in such a situation, you can photocopy the appropriate answer sheet from pages 143–144 for use with the Pretests. The time allotted for each Pretest is given on the direction page at the beginning of that particular test.

With the exception of the essay section of the Writing Skills Pretest, each test can also be self-checked by the student. If your center or school already has a system to score student writing holistically, you can use that system to evaluate the essays. If no such system exists, you can use the Essay Scoring Checklist on page 63 of *Passing the GED* to evaluate each essay and identify possible problem areas. It is advisable *not* to read and correct the Pretest essays in the traditional way. Such teacher criticism at this point will only reinforce many GED students' misconception that good writing is "not making grammar and spelling mistakes" rather than communicating one's ideas successfully. (The characteristics and valid uses of both teacher criticism and holistic scoring are discussed in detail in Glencoe's *Teaching Adults to Write Essays: A Brief Guide for the Teacher of Writing*.)

Diagnostic Charts

Diagnostic Charts to help you and your students develop more focused study plans have been included at the end of the Pretests and Posttests in *Passing the GED*. The charts have also been reproduced for your use on pages 153–157 of this *Instructor's Guide*. After the students have taken the Pretests, they can use the charts, along with the Answer Key for each test, as study aids.

For example, suppose that a student took the Science Pretest and found that she missed questions 10, 12, 14, 15, 16, 18, 23, 25, 26, 27, 28, and 32. (On the Science Pretest Diagnostic Chart on page 62 of *Passing the GED*, the total number of questions in the Pretest relating to each subtopic is listed as the denominator of a fraction in the column headed "Total Number Correct.") After locating the missed question numbers on the chart, she writes the total number of questions that she answered *correctly* for each subtopic in the "Total Number Correct" column. In our imaginary student's case, low scores of 4/11 and 2/6 make it immediately apparent that the student had the most trouble with questions about Biology and Physics. High scores of 6/6 for Earth Science and 8/9 for Chemistry indicate that she had relatively little trouble with these types of questions. You could encourage this student to concentrate on the indicated instructional material on pages 340–359 (Biology) and 379–386 (Physics) of *Passing the GED*.

The Diagnostic Charts also further identify the questions by cognitive level based on Bloom's taxonomy, discussed on page 1 of this guide. Given the sample set of missed questions, our student demonstrates greater skill with comprehension and evaluation questions and has more difficulty with application and analysis questions. Diagnosing the cognitive levels that give your students the most trouble can help you select sample questions for in-class presentations. Since answer explanations in *Passing the GED* have been identified by cognitive level, you will find it easy to guide your students in paying closer attention to the answer explanations for questions of the skill level or levels that give them the most difficulty.

Using the Instruction–Test Practice Pages

Once students know what they most need to study, they are ready to begin the "meat" of the book—the individual content sections and the instruction–test practice pages they contain. Following are general suggestions for using these pages in your classroom.

Independent study Visit many GED classes, and you'll find students working at desks or tables by themselves. *Passing the GED* was developed especially for this kind of independent study in a classroom setting. A student can work through the tinted instructional columns at his or her own pace, answer the Warm-up questions and test practice items, and check the answers in the text. Such independent study frees you to be available to answer questions, elucidate points, work with individuals or small groups who need more intensive instruction, and read students' sentences, paragraphs, and essays for the Writing Skills section. Independent study does not mean, however, that a student has little or no need for a teacher. Some GED students experience difficulty in working on their own because they never really learned how to learn. Important learning skills include good study habits; time-management ability; the ability to set definite, reachable, incremental goals; self-questioning skills; and note-taking skills. The lack of such skills hinders a student's ability to learn effectively.

Initially, students will need your advice on how much material should be studied each session. Determine a good learning pace. As time passes, begin asking each student how much he or she will try to cover in a session. Have the students take on more responsibility for their learning, but also be available as a "paid consultant" to advise if a student is taking on too much or too little.

Pair work Pair work can be especially useful when students are working in the Writing Skills section. They can read each other's Warm-up sentences and paragraphs, discuss the writing, and perhaps even "edit" each other. Having students work in pairs can also be helpful with the Mathematics section; if necessary, pairs can drill each other on the basic facts to increase fluency or verbally work through the steps of solving the word problems in the white test practice columns. Again, using pair work frees you to work more intensively where such help is needed.

Class instruction When the majority of students in your class need work on a particular skill, or when you merely want to add some variety to the class, you may want to teach the class as a whole in the more traditional way. You can use the appropriate tinted instructional columns in *Passing the GED* as you would a basic text. In certain cases, you may also want to use supplementary materials, such as maps for a social studies lesson on reading maps. Discuss the information presented, ask questions to test comprehension, add your own examples, underscore important points, ask for summaries, and so forth.

Discussion Higher-level thinking skills—analysis and evaluation—are the focus of many of the items on the GED Test. As a break from normal classroom routine, you may want to divide your class into small groups and have them discuss a specific problem and the steps involved in solving it. (Making students think about thinking is the objective of such a discussion—more so than the solution of the problem.)

A few key criteria for any good discussion follow.

1. Make sure the topic under discussion is single and clear. The topic, however, should not be a yes-or-no question or a clear-cut right-or-wrong issue but one that involves thought and support.

2. Set a time limit.

3. Choose someone in each group to record ideas, or list ideas on the board yourself if the whole class is discussing the topic.

4. Make sure everyone participates.

Writing Writing is most often thought of as an objective of instruction, but it is also an excellent method of instruction. Whether students are studying independently or as a class, constantly remind them to write.

You can ask students to write down what they already know about a certain topic (for example, state and local governments under Political Science in the Social Studies section) before they begin reading about the topic. Have them take notes on the material in the tinted instructional columns. They can also write summaries of the information. Have students write their answers to the Warm-up exercises in complete sentences if possible. And ask them to write explanations of the answers they picked to the multiple-choice practice test items.

A notebook would be a handy place for each student to keep all his or her writing. It could also be used to hold the student's sentences, paragraphs, and essays written as assignments for the Writing Skills section. Using writing as a teaching method in this way not only helps students understand what they are reading; it also improves the writing skills needed on the GED Writing Skills Test.

Other suggested teaching/learning activities You'll find specific suggested activities for each of the GED content areas in the descriptions of the individual *Springboard* books that appear later in this guide. Many of them can be adapted for use with *Passing the GED* in your classroom. In addition, the reproducible exercise sheets at the back of this book can be copied and given to students who need practice in particular areas. You can create similar exercise sheets of your own.

Monitoring You can monitor students' work on the instruction–test practice pages by routinely checking their answers to the Warm-up exercises and their writing notebooks (if assigned). In addition, both you and the student can keep track of performance on the practice test items in the white columns with the charts on pages 138–142. Make copies of the charts for your students. As a student checks the answers to the items in a particular column, he or she should circle the numbers of the items answered incorrectly. Monitor these Performance Charts. Noting clusters of errors will help

you spot probable trouble areas. You can determine the content/skills tested by the circled items by checking the running heads on their pages. Individual or group instruction, together with assigned additional practice (for example, the exercise sheets in this book), can overcome the trouble.

Using the Minitests

The Minitests at the end of each content section can be used as a reinforcement once the section is completed, as a warm-up before the first Posttest is taken, or as a review between Posttests. Since there are at least three Minitests for each section, you can assign at least one Minitest for each purpose.

Administering the Posttests

Once an individual has worked through the instruction–test practice pages of the content areas, have the student take Posttest A. Try to create a standardized-test experience that is as realistic as possible—a quiet room, a proctor to time the test, and so on. You may want to photocopy the Posttest answer sheet from pages 145–147 for each student to use.

When the student has finished, he or she can check the answers and read their explanations in the book. The Essay Scoring Checklist on page 63 of *Passing the GED* will help you evaluate the essay if your school or center has no holistic scoring system of its own. Help the student use the Diagnostic Charts on pages 678–679 to determine which sections of instructional material to review. Directions for using these charts are given on pages 9–10 of this *Instructor's Guide,* and copies of the charts themselves are on pages 153–157. It would also be a good idea to discuss the answers with the student. This discussion will help you see which kinds of questions the student tended to miss. Based on the Diagnostic Chart results, you may want the student to reread certain section Overviews, review certain instruction–test practice pages, or use the Minitests for a particular section before going on to Posttest B. If a student does well on Posttest A, you can save Posttest B for a warm-up right before the student goes to take the actual GED Test.

The *Springboard for Passing the GED* Series

Glencoe's *Springboard for Passing the GED* series is a five-book program offering complete preparation for the GED Test. Each book corresponds to a test on the GED battery:

Springboard for Passing the GED Writing Skills Test

Springboard for Passing the GED Social Studies Test

Springboard for Passing the GED Science Test

Springboard for Passing the GED Test of Interpreting Literature and the Arts

Springboard for Passing the GED Mathematics Test

The *Springboard* series was developed with input from both GED Testing Service materials and adult educators in the field. High school–level content and skills taught in each book were taken from the testing service's own *Item Writer's Manual* and *Preview* of the 1988 GED Test. In addition, more basal reading, writing, and math skills have been included at the suggestion and with the help of GED teachers and other adult educators. A complete scope and sequence of skills for each book is given in the description of the book in this guide.

By including a wide range of skills, Glencoe's *Springboard* series can be used to prepare students to succeed well beyond the GED Test, not merely pass it.

What's in a *Springboard?*

Many adult learners are understandably anxious about their latest "academic endeavor." Knowledge of what lies ahead is one sure way to begin alleviating such anxiety. To that end, each *Springboard* begins with a description of the GED Test and of the specific subtest that is the focus of the book, as well as an explanation of the book itself and how to use it.

Recognizing and confronting anxiety are also essential to overcoming it, and students are helped to do just that with "Test Anxiety: How to Cope with It." A final section of general tips for test success wraps up each *Springboard*'s introductory material and leaves students motivated, encouraged, and ready to begin.

The Skills Surveys

Adult learners vary in skills among and within themselves. One student may show greater proficiency across the board than another in the same class; one student may have polished skills at one cognitive level but lack them at another; a third student may be skilled in one content area, such as reading, but deficient in another, such as math.

The Skills Survey in each book of Glencoe's *Springboard* series is a diagnostic tool you can use to help you determine each student's level of skills —which are present, which are lacking. A chart at the end of the Skills Survey answer section identifies the skills tested by the survey items and the lessons where those skills are taught. These "skill charts" are very similar to the Diagnostic Charts included in the Pretests and Posttests in *Passing the GED,* and they are reprinted on pages 158–167 of this *Instructor's Guide* for your convenience. An explanation of their use is given on pages 9–10. You can use the charts to help you and the student pinpoint the lessons on which he or she should especially focus. In addition, each answer explanation in the *Science, Social Studies,* and *Literature and the Arts Springboards* Skills Surveys is labeled with a two-letter abbreviation that identifies the question as belonging to one of the cognitive levels described on page 1 of this guide.

You'll find more detailed guidelines for using the Skills Surveys later in this section.

Lesson Components

The lessons in all five books contain the following components to ensure a logical progression from skill introduction to achievement and review.

The title of each lesson and a short introduction explain the skill that will be taught.

Here's an Example does just what its name states—it gives a specific example of the skill just explained. Students are shown how the skill applies to a

reading passage, a math word problem, or another appropriate stimulus.

Try It Yourself gives students the opportunity to try their hand at the skill using a new stimulus. Then the book carefully "walks through" the process in a step-by-step explanation, so the student can check his or her understanding and application of the skill.

Warm-up offers a chance to practice the skill more extensively. Students *write* their answers to questions and can check their work at the bottom of the page. This written self-check involves students in their learning and gives them more responsibility for it.

Very often students require a special "boost" to reach the GED level. **On the Springboard** gives them the lift they need with an intermediate-level stimulus and question—a ladder or, better yet, a springboard between the lower-level Warm-up and the GED level of skills. The Springboard questions are multiple choice, as the GED Test questions are, but with only three options instead of five. Directly after On the Springboard, students are told where to check their answers. They receive congratulations for correct answers and the re-

---

Simplifying Numbers

If you are asked to simplify a number with an exponent, you must find the answer for the repeated multiplication. If the base is 10, you can write down the answer at sight.

$$10^2 \text{ means } 10 \times 10 = 100$$
$$10^3 \text{ means } 10 \times 10 \times 10 = 1,000$$

If you are dealing with the base 10, the exponent tells how many 0s come after the 1 in the answer. If the base isn't 10, you will have to multiply out or compute the entire problem.

Here's an Example

■ Simplify 3^3.

Step 1 Write out what the exponent means

$$3^3 = 3 \times 3 \times 3$$

Step 2 Compute the answer.

$$3 \times 3 \times 3 = 27$$

So when you simplify 3^3, you get 27. Sometimes the base is negative, as in $(-3)^3$. Then you have to remember the rules about multiplying signed numbers. Write out the repeated multiplication.

$$(-3)^3 = (-3) \times (-3) \times (-3)$$

Multiply the first two numbers and you get $(-3) \times (-3) = +9$ (both numbers multiplied are negative, so the answer is positive). Now multiply $+9$ by the last (-3) and you get $(+9) \times (-3) = -27$ (positive times negative gives negative).

If the exponent is 1, it means that the base appears only 1 time. $3^1 = 3$, $10^1 = 10$, $(-5)^1 = -5$, and so on. Sometimes the exponent is zero, as in 2^0, 5^0, $(-8)^0$, and so on. Any number with an exponent of zero is equal to 1. For example, $2^0 = 1$; $5^0 = 1$; $(-8)^0 = 1$; and so on.

☑ A Test-Taking Tip

One quick way to check multiplication and division work with signed numbers on the GED Mathematics Test is to count the negative signs. An even number (2, 4, 6, and so on) of negative signs always gives a positive answer. An odd number of negative signs gives a negative answer.

Try It Yourself

■ Simplify 3^4. _____

Did you first write what 3^4 means? $3^4 = 3 \times 3 \times 3 \times 3$. Then did you compute the answer? Since $3 \times 3 \times 3 \times 3 = 81$, the answer is 81.

Now try another.

■ Simplify $(-5)^2$. _____

Did you write $(-5)^2 = (-5) \times (-5) = +25$? Multiplying two negatives gives a positive answer. Always keep the negative base in parentheses so you don't get confused with the signs. Look carefully at the difference between $(-5)^2$ and -5^2. The first one means this.

$$(-5)^2 = (-5) \times (-5) = +25$$

The second one means this.

$$-5^2 = -(5 \times 5) = -25$$

✎ Warm-up

Simplify.

1. $6^2 =$ _____
2. $(-4)^3 =$ _____
3. $(+7)^3 =$ _____
4. $10^5 =$ _____
5. $(-2)^4 =$ _____
6. $(-10)^2 =$ _____
7. $-4^2 =$ _____
8. $(0.3)^3 =$ _____
9. $+2^6 =$ _____
10. $(½)^2 =$ _____

Warm-up Answers
1. 36 2. -64 3. 343 4. 100,000 5. 16 6. 100
7. -16 8. 0.027 9. 64 10. ¼
Did 10 give you trouble? Since ½ is the base, it is multiplied by itself. You can tell that the whole fraction is the base because it is all in parentheses.

EXPONENTS 149

ward of moving up to the GED level. They receive encouragement and directions on what to review if their Springboard answers were incorrect.

Each lesson ends with **"The Real Thing."** Here students are asked to apply the lesson skill at the GED level with GED-type multiple-choice questions. Specifications in the GED *Item Writer's Manual* were followed carefully to ensure that both "The Real Thing" stimuli and questions are similar to those found on the actual GED Test. The first one or two questions involve the lesson skill; then several more GED-level questions review skills from previous lessons. "The Real Thing" offers real reinforcement to students, showing them that they are indeed moving toward the GED Test with each lesson they complete.

In addition to the standard lesson components described above, two "floating" components appear in lessons throughout each book. **A Test-Taking Tip** offers a helpful suggestion about how to answer a specific kind of question on the GED Test. It isn't really necessary for students to learn or memorize such tips. They serve as small incentives, intended to bring the GED Test into focus periodically as a real and reachable goal.

Technical vocabulary in Glencoe's *Springboard* series is limited to just those words and phrases that students *need* to know. (The GED Test itself is careful not to demand knowledge of much content-related vocabulary.) When a technical term is used in a *Springboard,* it is set in bold type, defined in context, and then reinforced in a **Coming to Terms** immediately following that section. Students who want to review the meaning of any term can find the term in the Index of the book; both it and the number of the page in which its Coming to Terms appears will be in bold. This system eliminates a long glossary, which many students mistakenly believe they need to memorize.

Built-in Practice and Review

At the end of each main section are annotated answers to the questions in On the Springboard and "The Real Thing." The explanations give students a further self-check; they can make sure they answered a question correctly for the right reasons. A Keeping Track chart helps them record their progress throughout the lessons and note which skills might best be reviewed before going on.

The Extra Practice at the end of each section offers still more GED-level stimuli and questions, reviewing

all the skills learned in the section. As in the Skills Surveys, the Extra Practice answer explanations for three of the five *Springboard* books—*Literature and the Arts, Science,* and *Social Studies*—have been labeled according to Bloom's taxonomy of cognitive levels. You may find these labels useful in determining the types of questions most often missed by your students. Students can keep track of their Extra Practice scores on the Progress Chart on the inside back cover of the book.

The Posttests

Once students have worked through the lessons of a book and reinforced their skills with the Extra Practice sections, they are ready to take the first of two Posttests modeled after the actual GED Test. Each Posttest follows the specifications of the *Item Writer's Manual* of the GED Testing Service in content, skills, and the number and kind of multiple-choice questions asked.

Students can check their answers themselves by reading the annotated answer explanations at the back of the book, record their scores on the Progress Chart

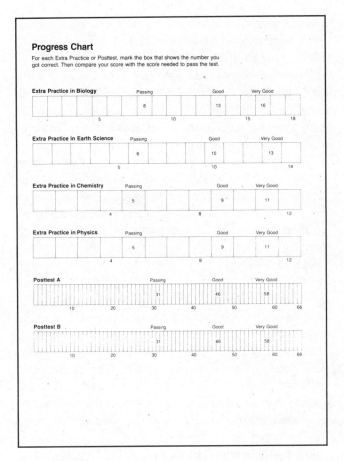

on the inside back cover, and, if need be, use the skill chart as a diagnostic tool to determine which sections of the book to review before taking the second Posttest. As in the Skills Survey and Extra Practice questions, the Posttest answer explanations have been labeled according to Bloom's taxonomy of cognitive levels, explained on page 1 of this *Instructor's Guide*.

Specific suggestions for administering the Posttests are given later in this section.

Readability

Instruction in the *Springboard* series is written at a relatively low level, ranging from fifth to seventh grade. The friendly, helpful tone of the text adds to its readability. This readability can accomplish two goals: better instruction of content and skills *and* better development of reading skills. That's because the more students can read and understand the material by themselves, the more their reading skills and stamina will be enhanced.

Literary, social studies, and science passages used as stimuli in the skill-building components—Here's an Example, Try It Yourself, Warm-up, and On the Springboard—increase in reading level throughout a lesson. On the other hand, passages used as stimuli in skill-testing components—"The Real Thing," Extra Practice, and the Posttests—are at higher levels, ranging from eighth to twelfth. These levels accurately reflect those on the GED Test itself.

Many adult educators feel that a student who reaches an eighth-grade level of reading stands a good chance of passing the GED Test. This growth in level is one goal of the *Springboard* series.

Writing Across the Curriculum

Teaching a person to write well has always been a worthwhile and generous endeavor. Since the 1988 GED Test, with its essay requirement, it has become essential in GED classes.

Glencoe's *Springboard for Passing the GED Writing Skills Test* is a comprehensive book for developing writing (not merely "English") skills in GED students. But writing in the Glencoe *Springboard* series is not limited to your writing classes alone. In the Warm-up exercises of the Literature, Science, and Social Studies *Springboards,* students are asked to write in complete sentences. They may need to write answers to questions about a reading passage, summaries of what they have read, explanations about certain events, or support for certain conclusions. Such exercises not only develop writing skills but also aid student comprehension of content material.

You can take full advantage of this thinking-writing connection by requiring even more writing of your students. You'll find more specific suggestions for including writing in your classroom under "Teaching Methods to Include in Your Lesson Plans" on pages 18–19 of this guide.

The Roles of the Teacher

The *Springboards* can and should be adapted for use with a number of learning environments and teaching methods. Even in a typical classroom setting, using the books in a number of ways can help meet students' differing needs and create classroom variety. You can use the *Springboard* series to help you fill the various essential roles that a GED teacher is called upon to play.

Diagnostician The first job a GED teacher often assumes is assessing the skills of his or her students. Even if your school or center has already administered placement tests to determine the general level of students, you may want to assess more specific, content-related skills and determine the specific needs of each of your students. Each book in the *Springboard* series has a Skills Survey for this diagnostic purpose.

By using the skill charts at the end of each survey and by talking with your students to determine why they answered the survey questions as they did, you'll have a better understanding of their level of thinking skills as well as their reading, writing, and math abilities. Specific suggestions for administering the Skills Surveys are found under "Using the Skills Surveys" on pages 17–18.

In addition to diagnosing the skills and needs of the students, knowing the ultimate goal of each student is important. Student goals can range from merely wanting to hold a GED certificate one day to acquiring as full and rounded an education as possible. You can photocopy the short questionnaire on goals that appears on page 8 and ask each of your students to fill it out. Keep the questionnaires on file with your other assessments.

Diagnosing both the needs and the goals of each student will help you with the next role of a GED teacher.

Planner Once you know a student's needs and goals, you can plan the best course of action to meet them. At the end of each Skills Survey in a *Springboard* is a chart showing the skill that was tested by each item and the lessons where that skill is taught or reinforced. Using the Skills Survey chart and the Table of Contents of the *Springboard*, you can tailor a learning plan to meet the specific abilities and desires of a student.

For students of lesser ability with a strong desire merely to pass the GED Test, your plan can be to teach and reinforce a minimum level of skills—those necessary to ensure a passing score. Content such as algebra and high-level skills such as evaluating scientific information need not be stressed.

For students of greater ability with a desire to go beyond a passing score, the whole range of content and skills found in each book can be part of their learning plan. Lessons dealing with higher-level thinking and writing are those you'll especially want to stress, for these skills carry import far beyond the GED Test and will help students progress in the world of work and the world of higher education.

Motivator Motivating students who often do not know how to motivate themselves or work toward a goal is an essential job of a successful GED teacher. You'll find useful suggestions for motivating your students on pages 37–38 of this guide in the section "Teaching GED Students Effectively."

Resource person It is perhaps the role of resource person that many teachers find particularly satisfying. A resource person helps people by giving them the materials and information they need to succeed. A *Springboard* is a resource you can use with your students to help them succeed.

Each *Springboard* was written as a discussion with the GED student. As a *facilitator,* you can help students take part in that discussion. Make sure they answer all in-text questions as well as exercise questions. You may even want to conduct guided reading of certain lessons by discussing with students the material before and after they read short pieces of the text. You can also facilitate small-group discussions about issues found in a social studies passage, say, or the theme of a literary passage.

Each *Springboard* was written specifically to an audience of one—the individual student. For that reason, you will likely find that some of your students will be able to study independently with some initial "consulting" help from you. As a *consultant*, you can be ready when adults working independently need additional information or advice. Independent study does not mean, however, that a student has little or no need for a teacher. Some GED students experience difficulty in working on their own because they never really learned how to learn. Important learning skills include good study habits; time-management ability; the ability to set definite, reachable, incremental goals; self-questioning skills; and note-taking skills. The lack of such skills hinders a student's ability to learn effectively.

Initially, you can advise on how much material should be studied each session. Determine a good learning pace. Tell the student what he or she will be learning about. As time passes, begin asking the student how much he or she will try to cover in a session and what methods he or she will use to study. Have the students take on more responsibility for their learning, but also be available as a "paid consultant" to advise if a student is taking on too much or too little.

As an *instructor*, you will be filling the most traditional role of a teacher and resource person. Instructing the whole class is useful when you are introducing students to a new area—fiction, for example, in *Interpreting Literature and the Arts* or biology in *Science*. At such times the section openers of the *Springboard* books will help you. Instructing the whole class or a group of students is especially useful when the students have shown they are having difficulty with a particular concept. You can review lessons in the *Springboard* with the students, add your own examples (and ask students to think of their own), and then assign additional practice.

The different teaching methods used in the role of resource person—discussion, independent study, small-group work, class instruction—are described in fuller detail along with others on pages 18–19.

Troubleshooter A GED teacher needs to be alert to "trouble"—to misunderstanding or incomplete understanding on the part of a student. You can monitor students' comprehension as they work through the lessons by checking their answers to Warm-up exercises and asking questions of your own. In addition, the Keeping Track charts that each student fills in at the end of

the answer explanations for each section will help you spot probable trouble areas, as will the Progress Chart—the Extra Practice "measuring sticks" on the inside back cover of each *Springboard*. Individual or group instruction, together with assigned additional practice (for example, the exercise sheets at the end of this book), can overcome the trouble.

Assessor The final role a teacher usually plays in a GED class is that of assessor. You can take a final assessment of the skills of your students with the Posttests in the *Springboards*—two in each book. Use the skill charts and cognitive level labels included with the answer explanations for each test to help you determine how well your students have developed specific skills. Guidelines for administering the Posttests are given on page 19, "Using the Posttests."

Using the *Springboards*

The *Springboards* were devised to be used in a variety of ways to meet the variety of needs in the GED classroom. Following are some general suggestions for teaching with the Glencoe *Springboards*.

Using the Skills Surveys

To alleviate anxiety, explain to students the purpose of the Skills Survey at the beginning of each book—that before one can start to prepare for the GED Test, one must know *where* to start.

Each survey can be self-administered by the student. If the books in your class are intended to be reused, or if you would like to create a realistic standardized-test experience to see how a student performs in such a situation, you can photocopy the appropriate answer sheet from pages 148–152 for use with the Skills Survey.

With the exception of the essay section of the Writing Skills Survey, each survey can also be self-checked by the student. However, if at all possible try to *discuss* each student's answers with the student. Ask why the student answered the way he or she did. Given the nature of multiple-choice questions, a student can get a right answer for the wrong reason (or can get the wrong answer for a reason other than lack of the skill the question was intended to test). Only by knowing the reasons for the answers can you truly know which skills a student has, which are present but need to be strengthened, and which are absent.

Social Studies Skills Survey		Class Performance			
Question number	Number of incorrect answers	Percentage (total in col. 2)		Skill	Lesson
		$\left(\begin{array}{c}\text{no. of items}\\\text{in col. 1}\end{array}\right) \times \left(\begin{array}{c}\text{no. in}\\\text{class}\end{array}\right)$			
1, 13	⊬Ш IIII	$\frac{9}{3\times10} = \frac{9}{30} = 30\%$		Inference	4
2, 7	⊬Ш	$\frac{5}{10} = 50\%$		Summarizing	14
3, 5, 19, 23	⊬Ш I	$\frac{6}{4\times10} = \frac{6}{40} = 15\%$		Restating information	2, 13

If your center or school already has a system to score student writing holistically, you can use that system to evaluate the essay section of the Writing Skills Survey. If no such system exists, you can use the Essay Scoring Checklist on page 25 of the Writing Skills *Springboard* to evaluate each writing sample and identify possible problem areas. It is advisable *not* to read and correct the survey writing sample in the traditional way. Such teacher criticism at this point will only reinforce many GED students' misconception that good writing is "not making grammar and spelling mistakes" rather than communicating one's ideas successfully. (The characteristics and valid uses of both teacher criticism and holistic scoring are discussed in detail in Glencoe's *Teaching Adults to Write Essays: A Brief Guide for the Teacher of Writing*.)

A chart at the end of the answer explanations for each Skills Survey lists the skills that were tested by the particular items and the lessons that teach and reinforce those skills. Together with the student, you can use the chart to create an individualized learning plan for the student.

You can also create class learning plans by noting which skills a majority of the students in your class need to learn or strengthen. The charts on pages 158–167 will help you tally class scores on individual survey items and pinpoint problem skills. Simply take each Skills Survey answer sheet, mark the items each student answered incorrectly, and then total the marks for each skill and find the class percentage. Above is an example from the Class Performance Chart for the Social Studies Skills Survey.

Teaching Methods to Include in Your Lesson Plans

Once you have a good idea of the needs of individual students and of the class in general, you can make lesson plans for the objectives of each session as well as for the materials and methods you will use.

In each lesson of each *Springboard*, the title and brief introduction name the skill that is the main objective of that lesson. Aside from the *Springboard* itself, you may want to use other materials: maps for a social studies lesson, for example, or money and coins for a math lesson. Following are general suggestions for different teaching methods you can use to meet the needs of your students and add variety to classroom routine.

Independent study   Visit many GED classes, and you'll find students working at desks or tables by themselves. The *Springboards* are especially adaptable for this kind of independent study in a classroom setting. A student can work through each lesson at his or her own pace, answer the Warm-up, On the Springboard, and "The Real Thing" questions, and check the answers in the student text. Keeping Track and the Progress Chart help both you and the student monitor learning. Independent study frees you to be available to answer questions, elucidate points, or work with individuals or small groups who need more intensive, personal instruction.

Pair and small-group work   A slight variation on independent study is to pair off students who are at similar levels or who need to work on the same skill(s). (Small groups of three or four may also be appropriate.) The students can work through a lesson together, check each other's work, and make up other questions to ask each other.

Pair work can be especially useful when working in the Writing Skills *Springboard*, for example, where students can read each other's sentences and paragraphs, discuss the writing, and perhaps even "edit" each other. Or it can be helpful when working with the Math *Springboard*; pairs can drill each other on the basic facts or verbally work through the steps of solving word problems. Again, using this method frees you to work more intensively where such help is needed.

Class instruction When a Skills Survey reveals that the majority of students in a class need work on one or more particular skills, or when you merely want to add some variety to the class, you may want to teach the class as a whole in the more traditional way. First, ask students what they already know about the skill or content to be discussed. Next, guide students' reading of the text. Ask them to read each paragraph or section of the lesson on their own; then, discuss the information presented, ask questions to test comprehension, add your own examples (and ask students for theirs), underscore important points, ask for summaries, and so forth. Working through higher-level thinking problems—such as evaluating the data in an experiment in the Science *Springboard*—is a good focus for this method of skill presentation.

Discussion As a teaching method, discussion nicely complements small-group work and class instruction. Issues discussed in the Social Studies *Springboard* and literary themes found in passages in the *Springboard for Interpreting Literature and the Arts* are especially good sources of discussion topics. So, too, are solving a specific problem and the steps involved in that solution. (Making students think about thinking is the objective of such a discussion topic—more so than the solution of the problem.)

A few key criteria for any good discussion follow.

1. Make sure the topic under discussion is single and clear. The topic should not, however, be a yes-or-no question or a clear-cut right-or-wrong issue but one that involves thought and support.

2. Set a time limit.

3. Choose someone in each group to record ideas, or list ideas on the board if the whole class is discussing the topic.

4. Make sure everyone participates.

Writing Writing is most often thought of as an objective of instruction, but it is also an excellent method of instruction. Whether students are studying independently, in pairs or small groups, or as a class, constantly remind them to write.

You can ask them to preview a lesson and then write their predictions of what the lesson will be about. Have them write their answers to all the Warm-up questions in complete sentences if possible. Ask them to write explanations of the answers they picked to On the Springboard and "The Real Thing" multiple-choice questions. And have them write summaries at the end of each lesson. They can also write summaries of the social studies, science, and literary passages they read in the *Springboards*. Using writing as a teaching method in this way not only helps students understand what they are reading; it also improves the writing skills so needed on the GED Writing Skills Test and in real life.

You'll find more specific suggested activities using these teaching methods for each content area in the descriptions of the individual *Springboards* that follow this section.

Using the Posttests

Once an individual has finished working through the lessons of a *Springboard*, have the student take the first of the two Posttests found in every book. Try to create a standardized-test experience that is as realistic as possible—a quiet room, a proctor to time the test, and so on. You may want to photocopy the appropriate Posttest answer sheet from pages 145–147 for each student to use.

When the student has finished, he or she can check the answers and read their explanations in the student text. As with the Skills Surveys, it would also be a good idea to discuss the answers with the student. This discussion, along with the use of the skill chart located at the end of the answer explanations, will help you see which kinds of questions the student tended to miss. Based on the student's score and the skill chart results, you may want the student to review sections of the book or use the Extra Practice sections before going on to Posttest B. If a student does well on Posttest A, you can save Posttest B for a warm-up right before the student takes the actual GED Test.

Springboard for Passing the GED Writing Skills Test

The philosophy underlying Glencoe's *Springboard for Passing the GED Writing Skills Test* is that writing is best taught as what it was invented to be: a means of communication. Those "rules" of English grammar and spelling that have traditionally been the main objective of instruction are merely the means to a greater end—the effective communication of one's ideas.

To be able to write is a satisfying and useful skill—helpful in the real world of business memos and letters; helpful in learning other skills and knowledge, whether in school or not; and helpful, of course, on the GED Writing Skills Test. In fact, the ability to write is a plus on *both* sections of the test: the multiple-choice "editing" part as well as the essay section. That's because the skills one develops in writing transfer more readily to editing than vice versa. In other words, even when teaching for a standardized test like the GED exam, it is more appropriate to teach a student to write well than merely to spot errors; the ability to do the former often encompasses the latter.

What's in the *Springboard for Passing the GED Writing Skills Test?*

The *Springboard* begins with introductory material about taking the GED Test in general and the Writing Skills Test in particular. You can use this introduction and the test tips it includes to ease your students into what may be for many an uncertain situation, especially if this is their first time back in an academic environment since they dropped out. If you intend for students to study or even just read sections of lessons independently, you'll want to go over "How to Use This Book" with the class. A special section called "Getting Ready to Write" addresses writing anxiety as well as the *power* that comes with learning to write.

The Skills Survey on pages 13–21 is a half-length GED-type multiple-choice test with a GED-level essay assignment. You'll find instructions for administering and scoring both sections of the Survey on pages 17–18 of this guide, "Using the Skills Surveys."

The first main instructional section of the *Springboard* is "Writing Sentences." The emphasis of these early lessons is on both communicating one's ideas by using sound sentence structure and the manipulability of that structure. The Warm-ups in this section offer a variety of sentence exercises—completing, expanding, combining, and generating one's own—plus a prewriting exercise on a personal and interesting topic. Sample answers are provided at the bottom of the page for the former.

In this section On the Springboard comprises a GED-type but intermediate-level paragraph with several multiple-choice questions testing the element of sentence structure taught in the lesson, plus an assignment to write at least several sentences about the topic from the Warm-up prewriting exercise. Writing teachers advise that even beginning or otherwise reluctant writers will write "pages" on a topic that piques their interest. Since getting students *writing* is important at this stage, no attempt was made in the Springboard assignment to stop the writer at a certain number of sentences, nor to have the student try to create a traditional five- or six-sentence paragraph. Getting ideas down on paper in a variety of acceptable and creative sentences is the main objective of this section.

"The Real Thing" ends each lesson with a GED-level item set of a paragraph and five multiple-choice questions. And Extra Practice ends the section with a GED-level paragraph and multiple-choice questions testing all the elements of sentence structure students have learned so far.

"Writing Essays"—the midsection of the *Springboard*—emphasizes the effective communication of ideas by expressing them clearly and organizing them into a coherent whole—first a paragraph, then an essay. Such organization and expression can come about only if the writer follows the process of writing: prewriting, writing a first draft, and revising.

Warm-ups in this section offer various prewriting activities. Once students have learned to prewrite by thinking of ideas and creating an organizational plan for them, On the Springboard gives them stimulating writing topics that ask about their personal experiences and opinions. "The Real Thing" essay assignment is always more general and impersonal, as a GED essay topic would be. Extra Practice ends the section with five such GED-level essay assignments.

The third and final instructional section—"Editing Your Work"—stresses the more traditional aspects of language arts instruction—grammar, usage, and mechanics—as a way to polish or "put a good face on" one's writing. In fact, editing is taught as the final step in the writing process that was introduced in the second section.

On the Springboard now comprises an intermediate-level item set, with several multiple-choice questions testing the lesson concept, and a personal topic to write about. "The Real Thing" brings students one step closer to their goal with a GED-level item set testing lesson *and* review concepts as well as a GED-level essay assignment.

Spelling Breaks are interspersed between the lessons of this section. Although some teachers insist that you cannot teach spelling, the Spelling Breaks do give common spelling rules and practice. More important, they give *responsibility* to the student for editing his or her own spelling and for working on personal spelling "demons" with the "Target Word List" in Spelling Break 1.

In the Extra Practice for this final section, all elements found on the actual GED Test come together: a paragraph with multiple-choice questions covering sentence structure (from section one) and usage and mechanics (from section three), together with a GED-level essay topic (covered in section two).

The two Posttests are, of course, similar to the GED Writing Skills Test in format and content, with both a multiple-choice section and an essay topic. Suggestions for administering and checking the tests are given on page 19 of this guide under "Using the Posttests."

At the back of the *Springboard* is a helpful Style Guide, similar to those used by professional writers and editors. Elements of usage, punctuation guidelines, and rules for capitalization are here in a handy reference tool that you may want to use yourself. In addition, the GED Spelling List—those words that may appear as spelling errors on the GED Test—are included and grouped for easier reference and study.

GED Content and Skills

The first section of the GED Writing Skills Test contains eight or nine individual paragraphs and fifty-five multiple-choice items that ask the examinee to correct or revise sentences in those paragraphs. Application of the following areas of standard English grammar, usage, and mechanics—and *only* the following—may be tested by the items:

Sentence Structure: coordination and subordination of ideas, sentence fragments, run-ons, comma splices, parallelism, placement of modifiers, and clarity of expression

Usage: verb forms and tenses, subject-verb agreement, and pronoun usage

Mechanics: capitalization, spelling (limited to a list of commonly misspelled words compiled by the GED Testing Service), and punctuation (limited to commas)

The charts on pages 128–129 of this guide identify which of the content areas above are tested by the items on the Official GED Practice Tests and the corresponding pages in the Writing Skills *Springboard* where those areas of content and skills are taught.

The second part of the GED Writing Skills Test requires an approximately 200-word essay on a given topic of general, common interest. Because the essay is scored holistically, key elements of a successful GED essay tend to be logical organization, support for a controlling idea, and clear expression. Mistakes in grammar and mechanics seriously affect the score only if they seriously interfere with the overall impression the piece of writing gives. (For a detailed explanation of holistic scoring in general and of the holistic system used to score the GED essay, see the GED Testing Service's own *1988 Tests of General Educational Development: A Preview, The Official Teacher's Guide to the Tests of General Educational Development,* or Glencoe's *Teaching Adults to Write Essays.* The elements that contribute to a sound GED essay and the *Springboard* pages where they are taught are listed on the Scope and Sequence chart on page 168 of this guide.

Scope and Sequence

The chart on page 168 reflects the entire scope and sequence of content areas and skills taught and reinforced in the *Springboard for Passing the GED Writing Skills Test.* Those printed in boldface are GED content and skills. Others are basal or corollary skills included on the advice of adult educators and writing teachers.

Suggested Teaching/Learning Activities

You'll find general suggestions for teaching with Glencoe's *Springboard for Passing the GED Writing Skills Test* on pages 18–19. "Teaching Methods to Include in Your Lesson Plans." Following are specific ideas for managing your writing class and suggestions for teaching particular concepts.

- Create two folders for copies of each student's writing—one folder for you, one for the student.
- Have each student begin a journal. Request that students write in their journals for at least ten minutes every day. (If time permits, you might give them ten minutes at the beginning of every class session.) Monitor the journal writing from time to time, but by and large the students should view their journals as their personal writing.
- Create a file of student work to use as examples in your class. Such work should usually be an example of *good* writing.
- To underscore the difference between speech and writing, tape-record a student telling a short anecdote. Then ask how the story would be *written.* Guiding the class sentence by sentence, write

the story on the blackboard or an overhead transparency, replaying the tape or portions of it as often as necessary. When finished, tape-record a student reading the written story; then play the two retellings back to back.

- Stress to students that *sample* answers are given for many of the Warm-up sentence exercises. There is almost always more than one good way to write a sentence. If a student is unsure whether his or her answer is acceptable, he or she should feel free to ask you. You might want to write a sentence on the board and discuss all the ways it could be written.
- No sample answers are given to the writing assignments on personal topics in the Warm-ups and On the Springboard. As students progress, pairs can work together and check each other by reading each other's sentences and paragraphs.
- Assign plenty of "real life" writing activities— notes to children's teachers, letters to the editor, business letters of complaint or request, personal invitations and thank-yous, and so on.
- Start a file of good writing topics. Share ideas with other teachers. Dozens of topics are already given in the Warm-ups, On the Springboard, "The Real Thing," Extra Practice, and the Posttests of the Writing Skills *Springboard.* You'll also find scores of other good writing topics in Glencoe's *Passing the GED, Practice Book for Passing the GED Writing Skills Test, Pre-GED Writing Skills,* and *Teaching Adults to Write Essays.*
- Integrate reading and writing as much as possible:
  - Have the class as a whole or in small groups analyze the writing techniques—sentence structures, organization of ideas, and so forth—of authors they read in literature class.
  - Ask students to write paragraphs and essays communicating their ideas about the themes of the literary passages they read.
  - Have students find the main idea, supporting details, tone, and so forth of one another's paragraphs as they would for the passages they read in literature.
- Ask volunteers to read their paragraphs and essays aloud.

Revising Checklist

- ☐ My controlling idea is clear.
- ☐ Every sentence and paragraph supports the controlling idea.
- ☐ My ideas are tied smoothly together with transitions.
- ☐ My essay has a clear beginning, middle, and end.
- ☐ Specific examples help support my details.
- ☐ A variety of sentence structures makes the writing flow and sound smooth.
- ☐ The structure of each sentence is correct and will be clear to my reader.
- ☐ I've used concise, precise, and standard words.

Editing Checklist

- ☐ Sentences are complete.
- ☐ Subjects and verbs agree.
- ☐ Verb forms are correct.
- ☐ The times of the verbs are consistent.
- ☐ Words are spelled correctly.
- ☐ Words are capitalized correctly.
- ☐ Each sentence has end punctuation.
- ☐ Commas are used correctly.

- If students need work on vocabulary development, games such as crossword puzzles, wordsearch puzzles, and Password may help. (Some students, however, dislike such vocabulary exercises and resent "wasting time" on them. If you have such a student, dictionary or thesaurus exercises would be more appropriate.)
- Take outlines or maps of ideas and, as a class, write paragraphs or essays from them. See pages 116–117 in the Writing Skills *Springboard* for examples of idea maps.
- Take finished pieces of writing—students' as well as published authors'—and outline the ideas or map them as a class.
- Take a paragraph and show how it could be expanded into an essay by making each of its sentences the main idea of its own paragraph.
- Take an essay and show how it can be condensed into a paragraph by taking the main idea of each paragraph and writing it as a supporting detail of one paragraph.
- Make copies of the Revising Checklist on this page for students to use when they revise their writing.
- Make copies of the Editing Checklist on this page for your students to use when they edit their writing.
- Make copies of some of the GED-type item sets in On the Springboard, "The Real Thing," and

Extra Practice. Give students a paragraph without its questions. Have them rewrite it, revising and editing as they see fit. Then give them the multiple-choice questions to see if and how they changed the areas that required changing.

- Assign the reproducible exercise sheets at the back of this book when students are having problems in these particular areas:

    sentence structures
    subject-verb agreement
    verb forms
    spelling plurals, possessives, and contractions
    capitalization
    punctuation
    paragraph organization
    topic sentences
    transitions
    irrelevant details

You can create similar practice sheets yourself.

You'll find many more activities for teaching sentence, paragraph, and essay writing; different ways to evaluate student writing; and an explanation of the pedagogical theory of teaching writing on which the Writing Skills *Springboard* is based in Glencoe's *Teaching Adults to Write Essays: A Brief Guide for the Teacher of Writing.*

Springboard for Passing the GED Social Studies Test

To teach social studies is to interweave information and skills, since knowledge in isolation is never a useful commodity. This is especially true in a GED social studies class because the sixty-four multiple-choice questions on the GED Social Studies Test mainly test the examinee's comprehension, application, analysis, and evaluation skills. Prior knowledge is never the sole objective of a test item; rather, the ability to understand and *use* social studies information is.

The Glencoe *Springboard for Passing the GED Social Studies Test* reflects this needed blend of content and skills. Unlike other GED books, the first half of the *Springboard* is *not* a detailed content section followed by a description of skills in the second half,

an arrangement that places undue emphasis on the knowledge of facts. Nor is that organization reversed, with a lengthy skills section followed by content, an arrangement that runs the risk of losing students with a dry, uninteresting opening.

Instead, the *Springboard* intersperses skills with content throughout the book. Students read a page or two of social studies information and then learn or review a particular skill that can be applied to that content. The information is about one of the five GED social studies areas—high school–level content but always related as much as possible to the real world in which adult students live.

What's in the *Springboard for Passing the GED Social Studies Test?*

The *Springboard* begins with introductory material about taking the GED Test in general and the Social Studies Test in particular. You can use this introduction and the test tips it includes to ease your students into your class. If you intend for students to study or even just read sections of lessons independently, you'll want to go over "How to Use This Book" with the class.

A special section called "Answering Questions Based on Graphics" addresses a problem area for many GED students—how to read maps, graphs, and tables. You can introduce your students to this skill by going through the section and discussing it with the class. Reading graphics is reinforced with the maps, graphs, and tables that appear in lessons throughout the book.

The Skills Survey on pages 15–23 is a multiple-choice test half as long as the GED Social Studies Test. Suggestions for administering and scoring the survey are given on pages 17–18 of this guide under "Using the Skills Surveys."

The major instructional sections of the *Springboard* correspond to the five major content areas on the GED Social Studies Test:

Geography
Behavioral Sciences
Economics
Political Science
U.S. History

Each lesson within these sections is split into two parts: content and skills.

The lesson title tells the general content topic; each black subheading underlined in green begins a subtopic. You may want students to preview each lesson before they begin reading by noting these subheadings and perhaps jotting down what they already know about the topics and questions they have about them. The introductory paragraph that precedes each subheading tells students what they can expect to learn in the following subsection. It also directs students to read the Warm-up question at the end of the section and use it to focus their reading. This strategy can be transferred to other kinds of reading as well as to the GED Test itself. Let students know that as examinees they can preview the questions before they read a passage on the test to help them know what information they should be looking for.

Once students have read each short subsection, the Warm-up gives them a chance to test their comprehension of the information by answering a question or two or by writing a summary of it. The objectives of these content sections, then, are to get students reading social studies information and to develop their comprehension skills.

The skill section of the lesson follows the last content subsection. Its green subheading underlined in black tells you the skill that is the focus of that lesson. Early lessons in the book sometimes include two or more related skills. The components Here's an Example, Try It Yourself, On the Springboard, and "The Real Thing" carefully lead the student from introduction of the skill through practice to GED-level testing. As students progress through the book and skills are recycled and reinforced, the lower-level components Here's an Example and Try It Yourself may drop out.

Both On the Springboard and "The Real Thing" are often two-part components themselves. The first part is a single item, offering a short bit of focused information and a single question about it that tests the lesson skill. The second part consists of a lengthier passage or more complex visual that contains extraneous content. The latter format gives students practice first in determining what information is needed to answer a particular question and then in finding that information.

The Extra Practice that ends each section of the book has GED-level passages and multiple-choice questions from that particular content area. You can assign the Extra Practice as reinforcement once a student has finished a section, as a warm-up before the student takes the first Posttest, or as needed review if his or her performance on Posttest A shows that further practice is needed in a certain content area. The skill chart at the end of each Posttest will be helpful in determining which Extra Practice questions to assign. Instructions for the use of these charts are on pages 9–10.

The Posttests are similar to the actual GED Social Studies Test in format and content. Suggestions for administering and scoring the two Posttests can be found on page 19, "Using the Posttests."

GED Content and Skills

The GED Social Studies Test tests five content areas—geography, behavioral sciences, economics, political science, and U.S. history—at four cognitive levels—comprehension, application, analysis, and evaluation. The charts on pages 130–131 of this guide list the skills tested by the items on the Official GED Practice Tests, Forms AA, BB, CC, and DD, as well as the corresponding pages in the Social Studies *Springboard* that teach or reinforce those skills. In addition, each answer explanation for the Skills Survey, Extra Practice sections, and Posttests has been labeled with a two-letter abbreviation that corresponds to one of the four cognitive levels mentioned above.

Scope and Sequence

The chart on page 169 of this guide shows the entire scope and sequence of skills taught in the Social Studies *Springboard*. GED skills are printed in boldface; other skills are basal or corollary skills included on the advice of adult educators.

Suggested Teaching/Learning Activities

You'll find general suggestions for teaching with Glencoe's *Springboard for Passing the GED Social Studies Test* on pages 18–19. "Teaching Methods to Include in Your Lesson Plans." Following are specific ideas for teaching particular concepts.
- Give students sets of relevant data—cost of living increases, population counts, and so on—and have them make line graphs, bar graphs, and pie graphs from them.
- Give pairs of students social studies graphs. The students can make up their own questions, exchange them, and answer each other's questions.
- Give pairs of students maps. The students can make up their own questions, exchange them, and answer each other's questions.
- As a class or in small groups, discuss some of the social issues talked about in the content sections or in passages in the skills sections. Empha-

size that students should try to give facts to support their opinions.

- Ask students to bring in newspaper and magazine articles about social studies topics that interest them. Discuss as a class or in small groups.
- Recognizing cause-and-effect relationships is always a key skill. As students read content sections and passages in the skills sections, have them make charts listing causes on one side and their effects on the other.
- Extensive knowledge of social studies terminology is not necessary on the GED Test, but for students who need practice with basic and essential terms, such as *democracy* and *population,* you may want to create a crossword or word-search puzzle. Clues should be definitions, and students must fill in or find each term being defined. (Be aware, though, that some students dislike such vocabulary exercises. For these students, a fill-in-the-blank context exercise would be more appropriate.)
- GED students often lack a sense of geography. Exhibit maps of the United States and the world at all times during your social studies class. Whenever any reference is made to a state, country, or region in any of the content areas—for example, to a Latin American dictatorship in Political Science or to the Confederacy in U.S. History—have a student locate that place on the map. Mark your own location on both maps so that it can be clearly seen. (You may also want to include a globe in this activity.)
- Compile newspaper editorials on social and economic issues of the day. (You might search for some yourself as well as asking students to bring in their own.) Discuss which statements are opinions and which are facts used to support those opinions.
- As a class, compile on the blackboard or an overhead transparency a list of problems your students see (for example, garbage pickup, the budget deficit, poor roads). For each problem or issue, have students figure whom they would write or talk to at which level of government—local, state, or federal—to help get the problem resolved.
- Have students watch the news on the economy and bring in economic articles and graphs. Dis-

cuss how the current state of the economy relates to the general concepts students are learning about the business cycle, economic growth, recession, and so forth.

- As you begin each history lesson, ask students to tell or write what they already know about that particular period of history. Also have them list any questions they would like to ask about the period. This activity will help you determine where to start in your presentation and clear up any misconceptions about historical events students might have. Once a lesson is finished, you might also want students to write summaries of what they have learned.
- Whenever a student answers a question orally or in writing, encourage paraphrasing rather than repeating words directly from the text. Ask, "Could you say that in your own words?"
- Whenever appropriate, ask a student to explain *why* he or she answered a question in a particular way. This tactic is especially helpful with inference questions. Ask, "How do you know that?" so that the student will need to pinpoint the clues he or she used to infer the necessary information.
- Analyze some of the GED-level test questions found in "The Real Thing" and Extra Practice with the class, especially those that require step-by-step thinking.
- Assign the reproducible exercise sheets at the back of this book if students are having problems in these particular areas:

    reading maps
    knowing U.S. states and regions
    reading tables
    reading line graphs
    reading bar graphs
    reading pie graphs
    general versus specific concepts
    classifying information
    using context clues to understand vocabulary
    cause-and-effect relationships
    point of view
    assessing data
    drawing conclusions
    distinguishing facts and opinions

You can also create similar practice sheets of your own.

Springboard for Passing the GED Science Test

The GED Science Test is similar to the Social Studies Test in that it is mainly an examination of comprehension, application, analysis, and evaluation skills, applied, in this case, to four science content areas. The ability to understand and use scientific information is key, not the knowledge of scientific facts.

For that reason, the organization and objectives of the *Springboard for Passing the GED Science Test* are similar to those of its "sister" *Springboard* for Social Studies. The Science *Springboard* intersperses skills with content throughout the book. Students read a page or two of scientific information and then learn or review a particular skill that can be applied to that content. The information concerns one of the four GED science areas—high school–level content but always related as much as possible to the adult world.

What's in the *Springboard for Passing the GED Science Test?*

The *Springboard* begins with introductory material about taking the GED Test in general and the GED Science Test in particular. You can use this introduction and the test tips it includes to ease students into your class. If you intend for students to study or even just read sections of lessons independently, you'll want to go over "How to Use This Book" with the class.

A special section called "How to Read Scientific Diagrams, Tables, and Graphs" addresses a problem area for many GED students. You can go through this section as a class and discuss it with students. Reading visual materials is reinforced with the diagrams, tables, and graphs that appear in the lessons throughout the book.

The Skills Survey on pages 15–22 is a multiple-choice test with one-third as many questions as the GED Science Test. You'll find suggestions for administering and scoring the Survey on pages 17–18 of this guide under "Using the Skills Surveys."

The major instructional sections of the book correspond to the four major content areas on the GED Science Test:

Biology
Earth Science
Chemistry
Physics

Each lesson within these sections is split into two parts: content and skill.

The lesson title tells the general content topic; each black subheading underlined with red begins a subtopic. You may want students to preview each lesson before they begin reading by noting these subheadings and perhaps jotting down what they already know about the topics and questions they would like answered.

The introductory paragraph that precedes each subheading tells students what they can expect to learn in the following section. It also directs them to read the Warm-up question at the end of the section and use it to focus their reading. This strategy can be transferred to other kinds of reading as well as to the GED Test itself. Let students know that as examinees they can preview the questions before they read a passage on the test to help them know what information they should be looking for.

Once students have read a section, the Warm-up gives them a chance to test their comprehension of the information by answering a question or two or by writing a summary of it. The objectives of the content section, therefore, are to get students reading scientific information and to develop their basic comprehension skills.

The skill section of the lesson follows the last content subsection. Its red subheading underlined by black tells you the skill that will be the focus in that lesson. Early lessons may include two or more related skills. The components Here's an Example, Try It Yourself, On the Springboard, and "The Real Thing" carefully lead students from an introduction of the skill through practice to GED-level testing. As students progress through the book and skills are recycled and reinforced, the lower-level components Here's an Example and Try It Yourself may drop out.

Both On the Springboard and "The Real Thing" are often two-part components themselves. The first part is a single item, offering a short bit of focused information and a question about it that tests the lesson skill. The second part consists of a lengthier passage or more complex visual that contains extraneous content. The latter format gives students practice first in determining what information is necessary to answer a particular item and then in finding that information among extraneous data.

The Extra Practice that ends each section of the book has GED-level passages and multiple-choice questions from that particular content area. You can assign the Extra Practice as reinforcement once a student has finished a section, as a warm-up before the student takes the first Posttest, or as needed review if his or her performance on Posttest A shows that further practice is needed in a content area before Posttest B is taken. The skill chart at the end of each Posttest will help you determine which content areas each student needs to review. Instructions for the use of these charts are on pages 9–10 of this guide.

The Posttests are similar in content and format to the actual GED Science Test. Suggestions for administering and scoring the tests can be found under "Using the Posttests" on page 19.

GED Content and Skills

The GED Science Test tests four content areas—biology, earth science, chemistry, and physics—at four cognitive levels—comprehension, application, analysis, and evaluation. The charts on pages 132–133 list the items from the Official GED Practice Tests, Forms AA, BB, CC, and DD, that test these skills and the corresponding pages in the Science *Springboard* that teach or reinforce the skills. In addition, each answer explanation for the Skills Survey, Extra Practice sections, and Posttests has been labeled with a two-letter abbreviation that corresponds to one of the four cognitive levels mentioned above.

Scope and Sequence

The chart on page 170 of this guide shows the entire scope and sequence of skills taught in the Science *Springboard*. GED skills are printed in boldface; other skills are basal or corollary skills included at the advice of adult educators.

Suggested Teaching/Learning Activities

You'll find general suggestions for teaching with Glencoe's *Springboard for Passing the GED Science Test* on pages 18–19, "Teaching Methods to Include in Your Lesson Plans." Following are specific ideas for teaching particular concepts.

- Give students sets of relevant data—weather statistics, animal population counts, level of pollutants, and so on—and have them make line graphs, bar graphs, and pie graphs from them.
- Give pairs of students science graphs. The students can make up their own questions, exchange them, and answer each other's questions.
- Give pairs of students scientific diagrams. The students can make up their own questions, exchange them, and answer each other's questions.
- Ask students to diagram something each is familiar with—part of a car engine, for example, or a blow-dryer.
- As a class or in small groups, discuss some of the scientific issues talked about in the content sections and in the passages in the skills sections. Emphasize that students should try to give facts to support their opinions.
- Ask students to bring in magazine and newspaper articles about scientific topics that interest them. Discuss as a class or in small groups. Help students distinguish between facts and hypotheses found in the articles.

- Recognizing cause-and-effect relationships is always a key skill in science. As students read content sections and passages in the skills sections, have them make charts listing causes on one side and their effects on the other.
- Students may want to create their own classification sets like those taught in Lesson 6. They can work in pairs and try to classify each other's examples of general principles or classes.
- Extensive knowledge of science terminology is not necessary for the GED Test, but for students who need practice with basic and essential terms, such as *hypothesis* and *cell,* you may want to create a crossword or word-search puzzle. Clues should be definitions, and students must fill in or find each term being defined. (Be aware, though, that some students dislike such vocabulary exercises. For these students, a fill-in-the-blank context exercise would be more appropriate.)
- As students begin a lesson, ask them to tell or write what they already know about that particular topic. Also ask them to list any questions they would like answered. This activity is useful in a class situation because it helps you determine where to start in your class presentation. It's useful for students reading independently, too, since it gives you a way to interact with them. In both cases, you can use students' responses to clear up any misconceptions they may have. Once a lesson is finished, you may also want students to write summaries of what they have learned. You can answer any questions they still have or direct them to resources where they can research the answers themselves.
- Whenever a student answers a question orally or in writing, encourage paraphrasing rather than repeating words directly from the text. Ask, "Could you say that in your own words?"

- Whenever appropriate, ask a student to explain *why* he or she answered a question in a particular way. This tactic is especially helpful with inference questions. Ask, "How do you know that?" so that the student will pinpoint the clues he or she used to infer the necessary information.
- In later skills sections where Here's an Example and Try It Yourself do not appear, you might ask students if they can think of their own examples of the skill (which they have already learned) before they go on to work On the Springboard and "The Real Thing."
- Analyze some of the GED-level test questions found in "The Real Thing" and Extra Practice with the class, especially those that require step-by-step thinking.
- Assign the reproducible exercise sheets at the back of this book if students are having problems in these particular areas:
  reading diagrams
  reading tables and charts
  reading line graphs
  reading bar graphs
  reading pie graphs
  general versus specific concepts
  classifying information
  using context clues to understand vocabulary
  applying information
  cause-and-effect relationships
  analogies
  distinguishing facts and opinions
  assessing data
  drawing conclusions
  testing hypotheses
  You can create similar practice sheets yourself.

Springboard for Passing the GED Test of Interpreting Literature and the Arts

Reading skills form the foundation for success on the GED Test. They are required to understand the information presented on the GED Social Studies and Science Tests, and they certainly play a role in the ability to edit the paragraphs on the GED Writing Skills Test and to understand the word problems on the GED Mathematics Test. And on the GED Test of Interpreting Literature and the Arts, the *skill* of reading as it is applied to literature and commentary, not the knowledge of great authors and their works, is the focus of examination.

Glencoe's *Springboard for Passing the GED Test of Interpreting Literature and the Arts* reflects this skills orientation. As much as possible, skills are presented as a means to an end—as a way to understand and appreciate a written piece of communication between author and reader. Instruction opens with emphasis on understanding the whole of what is read—the author's central message, the main idea. This emphasis is repeated in the opening lesson of each of the five sections in the book. Sections end with higher-level skills of analysis that enable a reader to appreciate the author's technique and style.

What's in the *Springboard for Passing the GED Test of Interpreting Literature and the Arts?*

The *Springboard* begins with introductory material about taking the GED Test in general and the GED Test of Interpreting Literature and the Arts in particular. You can use this introduction and the test tips it includes to ease students into your class. If you intend for students to study or even just read sections of lessons independently, you'll want to go over "How to Use This Book" with the class.

A special section called "Learn to Rely on Your Dictionary" discusses a few basic dictionary skills. You may feel that some of your lower-level GED students will benefit from reading this page.

The Skills Survey on pages 11–16 is a multiple-choice test with approximately one-half the number of questions on the GED Test of Interpreting Literature and the Arts. You'll find suggestions for administering the Survey on pages 17–18 of this guide under "Using the Skills Surveys."

Five major sections make up the instructional core of the book:

Popular and Classical Nonfiction
Commentary
Popular and Classical Fiction
Popular and Classical Drama
Popular and Classical Poetry

These divisions reflect the classification of passages on the GED Test on the basis of genre and status of work—popular (contemporary) and classical (of recognized enduring quality).

Each lesson follows the format and contains the components explained on pages 12–14, "What's in a *Springboard?*" The Extra Practice pages at the close of the five sections can be used for reinforcement as each section is completed, as a warm-up for the Posttests, or as review between Posttests. The skill chart at the end of each Posttest will help you determine which content areas each student needs to review. Instructions for the use of these charts are on pages 9–10. The Posttests themselves are similar in format and content to the actual GED Test of Interpreting Literature and the Arts. Suggestions for administering the Posttests are given on page 19, "Using the Posttests."

GED Content and Skills

The GED Test of Interpreting Literature and the Arts is largely a test of reading comprehension—60 percent of the questions test the literal and inferential understanding of selections from popular and classical literature and arts commentary. Application and analysis of the author's style and technique are the focus of the remainder of the test items. The charts on pages 134–135 of this guide list the items on the Official GED Practice Tests, Forms AA, BB, CC, and DD, the skills they require, and the pages in the *Springboard* where those skills are taught and reinforced. In addition, each answer explanation for the Skills Survey, Extra Practice sections, and Posttests has been labeled with a two-letter abbreviation that corresponds to one of the four cognitive levels—comprehension, application, analysis, and evaluation—explained on page 1.

Scope and Sequence

The chart on page 171 of this guide shows the scope and sequence of all the skills developed in Glencoe's *Springboard for Passing the GED Test of Interpreting Literature and the Arts*. Each GED skill is printed in boldface. Other skills are basal reading skills that have been included to help strengthen students' foundation in reading and aid their study in the content areas.

Suggested Teaching/Learning Activities

You'll find general suggestions for teaching with the *Springboard for Passing the GED Test of Interpreting Literature and the Arts* on pages 18–19, "Teaching Methods to Include in Your Lesson Plans." Following are ideas you can use for developing specific skills.

- Have each student begin a journal in a notebook. Students can record their thoughts and feelings about the themes of the literary selections they are reading. You might also want them to write answers to questions in their journals.
- To solidify this important skill, ask students for the main idea of each passage they read in Nonfiction and Commentary if they are not asked for it in the book. Have them state or write the main idea in a complete sentence. You may sometimes want students to summarize the main idea and major supporting details.
- Be sure students read the passage and answer the question in Try It Yourself before they read the explanation of how to reach the answer. You may want them to write their answers in the margins of the book (if it is their own) or in their journals.
- Remind students to use the purpose questions before passages in On the Springboard, "The Real Thing," and Extra Practice to focus their reading. Once students have finished reading a passage and answered the multiple-choice questions, have them write an answer to the purpose question.
- Ask students to explain their answers to questions. This tactic is especially useful for inference questions. Ask, "How do you know that?" so that a student must identify the clues that helped him or her infer, for example, the setting of a story or the motivation behind a character's behavior.
- Whenever a student answers a question orally or in writing, encourage paraphrasing rather than quoting words directly from the text. Ask, "Can you say that in your own words?"
- Integrate reading with writing as much as possible. As students analyze techniques that authors may use—for example, opening with an interesting incident or including a quotation—suggest that students try to use some of these techniques in their own writing.
- Student readers are especially prone to stopping at each unfamiliar word, so they often lose the train of thought and, therefore, the author's message. Strongly encourage the use of context clues. Make sure students realize that context includes the words *after* the unfamiliar word as well as before it. Tell a student blocked by such a word to read to the end of the sentence. If the reader still cannot determine the meaning, urge him or her to keep on reading. Tell students they

can jot down unknown words in their journals and look them up in a dictionary later—after they have finished reading the whole piece.

- If a student expresses an interest in a particular passage from the book, you can help him or her locate the source of the passage in the Acknowledgments and suggest that the student get the book from the library and read the entire work.
- Encourage students to read columnists in newspapers and magazines whose writing could be considered literary and whose work might even appear on the GED Test. Examples include Ellen Goodman, William Safire, Dave Barry, Carl Rowan, and Mary McGrory. Clip articles you come across that would be especially appropriate, and ask students to bring in their own. Keep them on file. With each article, you can distribute the reproducible exercise sheet "Thinking About the Nonfiction You've Read" on page 89 of this book for students to answer.
- Ask students to bring in commentaries they have read in newspapers, magazines, and TV guides. Distribute copies of the reproducible exercise sheet "Thinking About the Commentary You've Read" on page 90 of this book for them to answer. Or working in pairs, students can write their own questions about the commentaries, exchange papers, and then read each other's articles and answer the questions.
- Have students write their own commentaries on arts and entertainment they have seen, heard, or read: TV shows, movies, books, and so on. Students can exchange papers and analyze each other's writing for such elements as the main idea, supporting details, and tone.
- To build reading stamina, as well as a better understanding and appreciation of fiction, you might want to have on hand copies of several short stories that would be likely to appeal to your students. The following are just a few examples. Students can discuss the stories in small groups, or you can distribute the reproducible exercise sheet "Thinking About the Story You've Read" on page 91 of this book for students to answer.

"The Monkey's Paw" by W. W. Jacobs
"The Enormous Radio" by John Cheever
"The Gift of the Magi" by O. Henry
"The Tell-Tale Heart" by Edgar Allan Poe
"The Short Happy Life of Francis Macomber" by Ernest Hemingway

- Strongly encourage visualizing in students. Constantly ask them to describe the characters, settings, and action in the literary passages they read, even if the author does not explicitly describe them.
- Play a tape recording of a play as students read along. This activity can help students understand how they can "hear" a character speaking lines when they read.
- Assign roles and have students read drama excerpts aloud.
- When students read excerpts from plays, distribute copies of the reproducible exercise sheet "Thinking About the Drama You've Read" on page 92 of this book for them to answer.
- Have students read poems aloud so that they can better hear the rhythms of the lines and the sounds of the letters.
- When students read a poem, distribute copies of the reproducible exercise sheet "Thinking About the Poem You've Read" on page 93 of this book for them to answer.
- Encourage interested students to write their own poems.
- Song lyrics can be poetry, too. Allow interested students to write down the lyrics of some of their favorite songs and then determine the meaning, mood, figurative language, and so on.
- Assign the reproducible exercise sheets at the back of this book to give students practice in the following areas:
    getting the main idea
    inferences

You'll find more exercises for working with literature in Glencoe's *The Reading-Writing Connection: Writing Activities Based on Selections from Modern Literature.*

Springboard for Passing the GED Mathematics Test

Even with the inclusion of an essay on the GED Writing Skills Test beginning in 1988, the GED Mathematics Test continues to be the exam that causes the most concern among GED students and, therefore, their teachers. The *Springboard for Passing the GED Mathematics Test* addresses this concern. It was developed with those qualities that directly answer the needs of the GED math student:

- An incremental approach within lessons and within sections of lessons, to lead students slowly yet steadily to skill achievement
- An emphasis on word problems, to focus attention on the area that most students need work with but one they fear the most

- A friendly, helpful tone to the instruction, to aid comprehension and ease student tension

What's in the *Springboard for Passing the GED Mathematics Test?*

The *Springboard* begins with introductory material about the GED Test in general and the GED Mathematics Test in particular. You can use this introduction and the test tips it includes to ease students into your class. If you intend for students to study or even just read sections of lessons independently, you'll want to go over "How to Use This Book" with the class.

A special section on pages 4–5 called "Math Anxiety: Proving the Math Myths False" addresses this very real and very common obstacle to learning. You might want to read through this material with the class. Ask your students to share their previous experiences with learning math and their current feelings about the subject.

The Skills Survey on pages 10–13 is a multiple-choice test with one-half the number of questions that are on the GED Mathematics Test. You'll find suggestions for administering the Survey on pages 17–18 of this guide under "Using the Skills Surveys." When giving a diagnostic math test, it is most important that you *see* a student's work to know *why* he or she missed an answer, so have students number each problem on their scratch paper, and collect the scratch paper as well as the answer sheets.

The major instructional sections of the book are Arithmetic, Geometry, and Algebra. Arithmetic comprises basic computation skills as well as the GED Testing Service's content classifications of Data Analysis, Number Relationships, and Measurement. In addition, the thinking skills required to solve word problems are developed in lessons interspersed throughout the Arithmetic section. The initial lesson offers a system for solving word problems—a system that stresses the step-by-step thinking many GED students lack. Successive lessons take students through two-, three-, and four-step problems and the need to assess whether data is sufficient or extraneous.

The format and components of each lesson are explained fully on pages 12–14 of this guide, "What's in a *Springboard?*" As often as possible, the stimulus (marked by a box) in Here's an Example and Try It Yourself is in the form of a word problem, even if the focus of the lesson may be computation. Such a presentation gives math a meaningful, real-world orientation. Also, teachers report that students are better able to handle word problems if presented in this way.

Try It Yourself is a self-check for the student. A friendly explanation of how to compute the answer or solve the word problem follows the stimulus, and the answer itself is "buried" in text near the end of the explanation so that students cannot inadvertently see it before they have worked the problem themselves.

If a lesson comprises a number of skills, the final "Real Thing" will include review questions for all the lesson skills as well as two or three initial items testing the last skill taught.

Geometry, rather than Algebra, follows Arithmetic for two reasons: (1) it is a natural extension of the lessons on measurement that end the Arithmetic section, and (2) many students find the physical, real-world nature of much of geometry easier to visualize and therefore deal with than the pure abstraction of Algebra. The concept of a letter such as *x* representing an unknown, variable quantity is more comprehensible if a student has already dealt with a letter in a formula standing for a familiar visual dimension, such as *l* for length or *A* for area.

Those elements of coordinate geometry—which is itself a marriage of geometry and algebra—that require knowledge only of geometry are taught at the end of the Geometry section. Those that include algebraic concepts are taught at the end of Algebra in the final lesson of the book.

The Extra Practice at the ends of the sections can be used as reinforcement as each section is completed, as a warm-up for the Posttests, or as a review between Posttests. The skill chart at the end of each Posttest will help you determine which content areas each student needs to review. Instructions for the use of these charts are on pages 9–10.

The Posttests are similar in content and format to the actual GED Mathematics Test. You'll find suggestions for administering them on page 19 of this guide under "Using the Posttests." As with the Skills Survey, you'll want to look at the scratch paper with students' work as well as their answers to assess their skills accurately.

GED Content and Skills

In general the items on the GED Mathematics Test cover the application of mathematical knowledge in these content areas: basic arithmetic, data analysis (tables, graphs, medians, ratios), number relationships (signed numbers, exponents, scientific notation), measurement, geometry, and algebra. Reading and thinking skills are also tested in that they are inherent in solving word problems.

The charts on pages 136–137 of this guide list the items on the Official GED Practice Tests, Forms AA, BB, CC, and DD, the computation skills tested by the items, and the pages in the *Springboard* that teach those skills.

Scope and Sequence

The chart on page 172 shows the entire range of content and skills taught and reinforced in the *Springboard for Passing the GED Mathematics Test*. Specific GED content is printed in boldface. Other content and skills are basal or corollary to GED content.

Suggested Teaching/Learning Activities

You'll find general suggestions for teaching with Glencoe's *Springboard for Passing the GED Mathematics Test* on pages 18–19, "Teaching Methods to Include in Your Lesson Plans." Following are ideas for teaching specific content and skills.

- If several of your students are not fluent in the basic addition, subtraction, multiplication, or division facts, have them work in pairs with flash cards. Or have individual students work with calculators. A student can try to answer a basic fact such as 3 + 9 before pressing the equal-sign button.
- Have students copy the following "System for Solving a Word Problem" on index cards. They can use their copies as bookmarks and handy reminders of the steps to take when they are working with word problems.

A. Read carefully. Imagine or draw a picture.
B. Figure what information you need.
C. Decide which operation(s) to use.
D. Set up the problem. ⎫ once for one-
E. Compute. ⎬ step problem,
F. Check your arithmetic. ⎭ twice for two-
G. See if your answer   step, and so on
   makes sense.

- Have students write their own word problems—perhaps stemming from situations in their own lives. Students can exchange papers and work each other's problems.
- Create a file of practical, real-world information that students can use to solve problems on their own. For example:
  a. stock market reports for work with fractions
  b. current interest rates for savings accounts, NOW checking accounts, CDs, treasury bonds, and so on, for work with percents, decimals, and fractions
  c. telephone rates for work with decimals
  d. sports statistics for work with percentages (winning percentages), ratios (batting averages), averages (bowling averages), and so on
  e. grocery receipts for work with rounding
  Bring your own materials for the file, and invite students to contribute their own.
- Stress the importance of visualizing a word problem. Demonstrate how to diagram the information in a problem to help understand and solve it. You might want to have students select which of several diagrams correctly represents a word problem.
- If students have difficulty with a particular word problem because of the size of the numbers involved, suggest that they substitute very low, "manageable" numbers (such as 2 or 10) for the large numbers and then try to figure out the setup of the problem.
- Have students work on word problems in small groups or pairs. Ask them to list the steps needed to solve each problem.
- When solving word problems, students can sometimes use calculators to concentrate on the correct understanding and setup of a problem and eliminate the emphasis on computation.
- Give students sets of data and have them make bar graphs, line graphs, circle graphs, and pictographs from them. You may also want students to make up math questions about their graphs, exchange papers, and answer each other's questions.
- Make sure students try to solve the problem in each Try It Yourself before they read the explanation and answer. You can have them place a sheet of paper over the answer and solve the problem before removing the paper; you might want them to keep a notebook for this purpose.
- For review, have students routinely go back one or two lessons, cover their answers to the Warmup problems, and work the problems again.
- Have students make copies of the following memory aid on index cards to keep when working with numerical and algebraic expressions and identifying the setup expressions for word problems.

Parentheses
Exponents
Multiply
Divide
Add
Subtract

- *At most* only one quadratic equation appears on each form of the GED Mathematics Test. You may want to skip over this difficult content matter (Lesson 49) with those of your students who are having problems with algebra.
- Assign the reproducible exercise sheets at the back of this book when students are having problems in the following areas:
  fluency in the basic addition, subtraction, multiplication, or division facts
  fluency in adding, subtracting, multiplying, or dividing whole numbers, decimals, or fractions
  fluency in multiplying by multiples of 10
  rounding and estimating
  visualizing word problems
  choosing the information needed to solve a word problem
  identifying the operation(s) needed to solve a word problem
  identifying the setup of word problems
  setting up word problems themselves
  setting up percent problems
You can also create similar exercise sheets of your own.

The Practice Books for Passing the GED

For those students who need or desire extensive practice with GED-type test items, Glencoe's *Practice Books* meet that need. There's a *Practice Book* for each of the five tests on the GED Test battery:

> Writing Skills Test
> Social Studies Test
> Science Test
> Test of Interpreting Literature and the Arts
> Mathematics Test

Each *Practice Book* is divided into the content areas that appear on that particular GED Test. If, for example, a student needs more work with biology questions after studying the Biology section of either *Passing the GED* or the *Springboard for Passing the GED Science Test*, you can assign the Biology section of the *Practice Book for Passing the GED Science Test*. All the practice test items were created following the GED Testing Service's guidelines for content, skills, and format. Annotated answers at the back of each book explain *why* the answer to each multiple-choice question is the correct one.

In addition, each *Practice Book* contains two Posttests—full-length simulated GED Tests in that area. You can photocopy the Posttest Answer Sheets on pages 145–147 of this guide for use with the *Practice Book* Posttests. The student can self-administer and self-check all the Posttests except for the essay assignments on the two Writing Skills Posttests. An Essay Scoring Checklist has been provided for you to evaluate the Posttest essays (and the essays written for the Essay section of the *Practice Book,* if you wish).

An Answer Key and Progress Chart at the back of each *Practice Book* help the student figure his or her score and determine how it compares with a passing score on the actual GED Test.

Teaching GED Students Effectively

Knowing Your Students

"Know thy student" could be the first commandment of effective teaching, yet, as experienced GED teachers know, there is no typical GED student. A GED student can be anywhere from 17 to 80+ years old; male or female; white, African American, Hispanic, Asian, or Native American; unemployed or employed; poor or middle class.

This diversity is perhaps what makes teaching GED students the rewarding challenge it is. The key common characteristic that makes it possible is that GED students are, above all, *adults*. They have experienced life—with its frustrations, successes, tragedies, triumphs, embarrassment, pride, hate, love, boredom, and humor. Their experiences with childhood, schooling, parenting, marriage, work, worship, and community living have combined to make them unique adult human beings.

Reasons for dropping out Very often the GED student originally dropped out because of boredom or disinterest in school. The high school student saw no immediate connection between work in school and the eventual reward of satisfying, well-paying work in the real world. This difficulty in conceiving of and working toward more abstract, long-term goals is characteristic of many GED students. Chronic problems with school can often be traced to just this difficulty.

While that picture matches the common conception of the GED student, it is by no means the only one. Impending parenthood, a lack of family encouragement to finish school, the need to care for or financially support family members, even prison terms—these too are reasons many students left school.

Reasons for returning Unlike children, adult students have a personal reason for being in your class. GED attendance is rarely mandatory. While the reasons for returning to school are as diverse as students' personal traits, most GED students want to be users of education rather than just recipients. They usually enroll in a GED course because they want eventually to apply what they learn to their roles in the world of work, family, and community. In these adult roles, they face decisions, changes, problems, and opportunities in which they have discovered a high school education makes a difference.

The majority have job-oriented reasons for returning—to get a good job, a better job, or a promotion that is unattainable without a high school diploma. About a third say they would like to further their education beyond the high school level (again, usually to increase their employability). Some do return for the personal satisfaction of completing what they once left unfinished. Many also say they want to become better parents (perhaps helping their children with schoolwork), better-informed consumers (getting more for their money), or more active participants in their religious groups (reading sacred writings).

The common purpose lying behind each of these reasons for returning to school—the tangible goal each GED student is striving for—is the GED certificate signifying that the recipient has attained the equivalent of a high school education.

The two traits that characterize every GED student, then, are that he or she is an adult, and that he or she wants to pass the GED Test. The effective teacher keeps these traits in mind at all times to help reach and motivate students.

Motivating Students

A motivated student is, of course, a critical element in effective teaching. Motivation is especially important in the GED classroom because many GED students have had unsatisfactory experiences in school settings. They may be somewhat unsure of their abilities and even anxious. These feelings make motivation an important "job duty" of the effective GED teacher. Sincere friendliness and helpfulness, without condescension, can make a big difference to these students.

First impressions are important. Your own feelings about groups and people are shaped by your first encounters with them. The same is true of the adults in your GED class. More people drop out of adult education classes after the first or second session than do later in the course. So it is especially important during the first sessions to use techniques that encourage adults to persist.

To be effective, first sessions should be friendly. Some adults will be fearful of bad experiences in your class. They may be afraid of appearing stupid or being ridiculed. A friendly, supportive climate will help them feel welcome and comfortable. Adult students are appreciative of teachers who are informal, enthusiastic, and responsive.

Find out a little about each student's background, interests, and goals. (A questionnaire on page 8 will help you learn the educational goals of each student.) introduce students to one another, using any ice-breaking activities that you enjoy.

Make contrasts between students' earlier school experiences and your classroom. Perhaps as children students decided that a particular subject was boring or too difficult. Help them see that now the real issue is not the subject but themselves—whether they can open their minds and give the subject a fresh start.

For those who are especially fearful of returning to school, there are several reassurances you can give during the first session. Let your students know that even if they did not enjoy school before, they can succeed at it now. Perhaps their high school teachers did not understand how they learn best. Some of them may learn math from a fellow student better than from you, the teacher. Some may enjoy the stimulation of small-group discussion. Tell the class that you will take the time to help each student find out how he or she best processes information, memorizes, and learns.

Also tell such students that you will be happy to explain everything in as many ways as possible until they understand. For example, if they had trouble learning decimals, you will give them everyday problems involving money. They can learn at their own pace. No one is competing with anyone else in the class. Students need to be convinced that this is so.

Especially encourage students not to worry about being "stupid." Even highly educated persons find some ideas hard to understand, some problems hard to solve, some situations that make them feel "dumb." They have simply learned how to handle their frustration at not being able to understand or to solve a problem easily. If they don't see a solution right away, they come back to it later or perhaps discuss it with someone. The important thing is that they *don't give up.*

If there is time, let your students discuss their feelings about school. (You may want them to *write* about

their feelings first; then discuss.) They will discover that they are not alone in their doubts and fears. Then let them share what they hope to do once they pass the GED Test. End on a note of confidence that they will be able to reach their goals.

Motivating students does not cease to be important after the first class session. Being able to pace students' study is essential, for small but constant successes each week throughout the course constitute the most motivating experiences of all. The sense of achievement after hard work—especially learning something that a student thought he or she could not learn—makes continued hard work that much easier to do.

Occasional reminders of the GED Test—the purpose of your class and, therefore, the "light at the end of the tunnel"—can also motivate. Relate what students are learning to the GED Test as much as possible so that they do not lose sight of the purpose of their hard work.

Personal success stories can also be highly motivating. If you are an experienced GED teacher, you no doubt can tell your class about some of your former students and their successful experience with studying for and taking the GED Test. Even more motivating would be an occasional visit and talk by successful former students. Or you could ask such students to tell you an account of their GED success, write these stories on posters (accompanied by photographs, if possible), and hang them around the room. Such visual reminders would be constant encouragement to current students (and positive reinforcement for you!).

Integrating Concepts

School disciplines aside, the world is not a tidy arrangement of discrete fields of interest and activity but a conglomeration of these "content and skill areas." In the real world, for example, an economic activity intrinsically involves sociology, mathematics, politics, geography, psychology, ad infinitum.

The GED Test, despite its division into five content-area exams, seeks to test "comprehensive, integrated skills rather than isolated fragments of learning from individual disciplines" (quoted from *The 1988 Tests of General Educational Development: A Preview.* Washington, D.C.: The GED Testing Service of the American Council on Education, 1985). Many GED students, unlike ABE or pre-GED learners, often recall being previously exposed to material. They therefore need a refresher course in some content matter (especially in math and writing) and practice in reading skills (especially as they apply to literature, social studies, and science) and thinking skills.

But there is also a need for students to see how the discrete concepts and pieces of information that they remember relate to one another. In fact, many GED examinees are confused and disconcerted at the mix of items on, say, the GED Science Test. Not only have they studied writing, interpreting literature, social studies, science, and math separately, but they have also studied biology, earth science, chemistry, and physics as rigidly distinct blocks. The effective GED teacher focuses on the integration of skills and content and sees it as a course goal.

Perhaps "integrating sessions" can be routinely scheduled to present to the class the ways in which the skills and content that are being practiced and studied independently are related. Discussion is one good method to use for integrating. In small groups or as a class, have students think of all the ways they know in which certain concepts are related to each other. For example, How is psychology (physical needs, the need for safety, the need for approval) related to economics (the law of supply and demand, marketing and advertising concepts)? How can the method of evaluating the merits of a conclusion in a scientific experiment be applied to evaluating whether a candidate for political office is worthy of one's vote?

Reading and writing, aside from being skills tested on the GED examination, are also skills that can be applied to any field of study. As such, they are enabling skills; they help students learn about, understand, apply, analyze, and evaluate any kind of information they desire or need. Teaching and using reading and writing as enabling skills will also help students integrate the skills and content they are learning.

Matching Styles

Teaching Styles

Adults—regardless of their academic skills—will be very perceptive about your teaching style. They may not know what technique you are using, but they will know whether you are comfortable with it. It is important,

therefore, that you not try to be someone you are not. You and your students will benefit if you use a teaching style with which you are comfortable.

Your style is likely to be quite different from that of another GED teacher. It is based upon your own personality, the nature of the particular content you are teaching, how you perceive the role of the teacher, and what your students expect. You may not even know how to label your teaching style. If you consistently meet with success, you may not even need to know how.

Personality Your teaching style reflects your personality. If you are very outgoing, you may be comfortable with role-playing, open-ended discussion, and other techniques that another teacher would find awkward. If you like order in your classroom, you probably are more effective if you plan lessons to minimize diverse simultaneous activities in your classroom.

The nature of the content To a certain degree, the actual content of the course will influence your teaching style. Obviously, students studying for the GED Writing Skills Test should practice writing essays. The student who only reads about how to write or who hears a lecture on pronoun usage cannot be expected to master the skill.

Your perception of the teacher's role You are likely to have some definite ideas about the role of an effective teacher. If you venture far from those parameters, you probably feel uncomfortable—and less effective.

For example, you may feel you do your best teaching when you allow students to work at their own pace and come to you whenever they need help. If you feel strongly about this approach to teaching, you would probably be uncomfortable following a rigid pattern of assignments and quizzes.

Feeling uncomfortable, however, is no reason to drop a particular teaching method. Good teachers try new things and, as with anything new, they may feel uncomfortable at first. Perseverance on the teacher's part to find and use an effective method of teaching a particular skill to a particular student is just as important as perseverance on the student's part to learn it.

What students expect This is an interesting—and often frustrating—element for teachers to incorporate into their style. Adult students often have very definite ideas about what is appropriate in a teaching style. Many students expect to learn by the very methods that failed them in earlier attempts at formal instruction. Frequently, teachers who spend a lot of time devising creative ways to teach are startled to find that their students do not believe they are learning if they are having fun.

This is an area where a GED teacher needs to adapt style as the course goes along. Introduce and explain change to your students. Say, "Tonight we're going to try something different. You may learn something you thought you could not." Help students understand that there are many ways to learn effectively.

You can be an effective teacher using different techniques. Use whatever techniques work for you and your students. If you are effective, keep doing what you do best. If you feel you are not reaching your students as well as you can, or if you are a new GED teacher and unsure of how best to teach, think about your students' learning styles, and match your style as much as possible to them.

Learning Styles

There are as many ways to learn a skill or concept as there are to teach it. To identify students' learning styles, you can use information you get from the students themselves and especially your own observations. If your teaching has been in an area other than adult education, be prepared for a wide variety of learning styles among your students. Also be prepared for the fact that you will not magically be able to identify a student's learning style.

GED students learn in many ways, but they may have an impoverished repertoire of learning styles. They do not know what the options are. They may be unaware that past failures in school may have been due more to ill-matched learning styles than to a lack of ability on their part. Here are some dimensions of learning style of which students should become aware.

Global versus analytical Some learners have a holistic view of the world; they are quite good at getting the gist of things but lack the ability to go beyond the general picture. Other learners can have a difficult time seeing "the forest for the trees." They perceive and dissect every last detail but cannot understand the meaning of the whole.

Auditory versus visual versus kinesthetic Perception is key to understanding and, therefore, learning. Certain people learn best through a particular perceptual mode.

Some people are auditory learners; hearing information is the best way for them to retain it. Others are visual learners; seeing information written down or expressed in a diagram or graph enables them to understand and remember it. Still others are heavily kinesthetic learners; doing something manually or "going through the motions" of a skill is the best way for them to learn it—in essence, they "feel" when they have learned it.

For most people, a combination of perceptual modes is most effective. By hearing an idea, seeing it written on a chalkboard or overhead transparency, and writing it down themselves, students utilize their strongest mode and reinforce it with others.

Perceptual disabilities Auditory processing problems can make verbal information and instructions hard to understand. Visual processing can hinder reading ability, and motor problems can make the physical act of writing more difficult. Although such learning disabilities are found much more often in ABE or even pre-GED classes, student and teacher alike should be aware that they may be a factor in the GED classroom.

Independent study versus small groups versus teacher instruction The immediate environment in which a student learns best differs from individual to individual and from subject to subject. Students should be comfortable with the style of environment. A discrepancy can exist, though, between what students say they prefer and what may actually be the best environment for learning.

For instance, one student may insist he likes to study along only because he is afraid of being ridiculed by others. Another may say she prefers working in a small group, but she becomes easily distracted by the chance to socialize; the learning task at hand becomes secondary. Still other students prefer teacher instruction because it can be, in essence, the "easiest"—read "laziest"—way to learn. These students hope to open their minds and have the teacher pour the necessary information into them without overt work on their part.

Sometimes a student's preference changes as the course progresses. For example, some students may want to work alone at first and even do so fairly successfully, but after they make friends in the class and establish a rapport with you, they want more and more to work with a group.

These examples underscore the presence of other variables affecting learning style. As with teaching style, personality, course content, and expectations all help influence the way an individual learns best.

Personality Some men and women tend to be single-minded about solving problems. They can handle only one stressful issue at a time. All other areas of their lives and their immediate environment are neglected while they devote their attention to whatever is most pressing. These students have trouble focusing their attention, particularly in a group setting. To reach these students, you may need to provide a separate study area or make time for one-on-one teaching. As students' skills grow, you may be able to work these loners into a group-learning situation.

Other students are more extroverted; they learn best with a cooperative learning style. For these students, discussion may be an effective classroom tool. Students who describe experiences and express opinions in a small group can clarify their own ideas. Discussion also helps these learners relate new concepts to current understanding. For many students, talking about a topic helps clear up misunderstanding, identify relevant experience, integrate concepts, generate enthusiasm, and encourage the sharing of ideas. These contribute to students' retention of material.

The nature of the content Learning style may be mandated by the content itself. Individual drill and practice may be the only practical way to increase fluency in the basic arithmetic facts, for example. Seatwork may be required if you deal with a large number of students with widely diverse abilities. Some students may be able to read literature on their own but seek a group-study situation for solving word problems.

What students expect Many GED students have fixed ideas about appropriate learning styles. Because some students can be surprisingly rigid in how they want to learn, you will want to take this into consideration in planning your teaching.

Other students may be turned off by rigid, traditional styles or environments that do not have the flexibility to allow for their individual needs. If you have experience as an elementary or secondary school teacher, you may need to throw out many of the more traditional trappings of those settings: the teacher's desk, for example, or student chairs in rows. Perhaps tables surrounded by chairs or a lounge area with comfortable seating would be more appropriate for you and your students.

Match Styles

Obviously, it's best to take into account both your teaching style and your students' learning styles as you teach. Ask yourself how much you think the teacher should dominate, what pace students can successfully keep up, how you can use instructional methods (group discussion, seatwork, and so on), and what kind of feedback you get from your students. As you get to know your students, try to match your teaching style with their learning styles.

Most adults are capable of learning on their own. One of the most worthwhile goals of adult education is to help adults achieve self-direction in their learning. The old saying "Give me a fish and I eat for a day, but teach me to fish and I eat for a lifetime" is a good analogy for self-directed learning.

The students in your class will vary in their interest and ability regarding self-directed learning. Some will welcome independent study. Others may not yet be able to handle it because they want a great deal of structure from you.

One way in which you can help students become self-directed learners is to talk to them about the times when they have learned something on their own. You can talk about why and how they learned, as well as about the satisfaction they gained from the experience. You also might discuss with students how they can achieve some course objectives on their own. Involve them in the process of clarifying objectives, considering alternative ways of studying, organizing activities, and evaluating their progress.

Many students come to a GED class with unrealistic ideas about what they can accomplish in a given time. By involving students in planning, you also help them set realistic goals. As noted before, point out what they should know and be able to do upon completion of a unit of study. Expose them to other materials and experiences that can help them achieve their objectives. Help them structure their self-directed learning. For most students, this will help increase their interest and persistence in the course. More important, it will help prepare them to learn more independently in the future—when you and the structure of a class are no longer available to them.

Exercise Sheets

On the following pages are sets of exercise sheets for the content areas on the GED Test. These are just examples of the kinds of sheets that can be created to individualize instruction and practice.

All can be used independently by individual students, but you can also vary their use in your classroom. For example, a student needing practice with the basic arithmetic facts can use a calculator when working on those exercise sheets until he or she is ready to try a timed drill. Pairs of students can work together on such pages as "Writing Topic Sentences" and "Visualizing Word Problems" and compare sentences and diagrams with each other. And small groups of students can discuss the individual items on "Point of View" in social studies, "Testing Hypotheses" in science, "Thinking About the Story You've Read" in literature, and so on.

Writing Skills

Combining Sentences
Independent and Dependent Thoughts
Subject-Verb Agreement: A
Subject-Verb Agreement: B
Verb Forms: A

Verb Forms: B
Spelling Plurals
Plurals and Possessive Nouns
Possessive Pronouns and Contractions
Punctuation

Capitalization
Organizing Ideas
Writing Topic Sentences
Transitions
Irrelevant Details

Social Studies

Working with a U.S. Map—Regions
Working with a U.S. Map—States
Working with a World Map
Working with Tables
Working with Line Graphs

Working with Bar Graphs
Working with Pie Graphs
General and Specific Concepts
Classifying
Using Context Clues

Causes and Effects
Point of View
Assessing Data
Drawing Conclusions
Facts and Opinions

Science

Working with Diagrams
Working with Tables and Charts
Working with Line Graphs
Working with Bar Graphs
Working with Pie Graphs

General and Specific Concepts
Classifying
Using Context Clues
Applying Scientific Information
Causes and Effects

Analogies
Facts and Opinions
Assessing Data
Drawing Conclusions
Testing Hypotheses

Interpreting Literature and the Arts

Thinking About the Nonfiction You've Read
Thinking About the Commentary You've Read
Thinking About the Story You've Read

Thinking About the Drama You've Read   Inferences
Thinking About the Poem You've Read
Getting the Main Idea

Mathematics

Basic Arithmetic Facts
Basic Subtraction Facts
Basic Multiplication Facts
Basic Division Facts
Adding and Subtracting Whole Numbers
Multiplying and Dividing Whole Numbers
Adding and Subtracting Decimals
Multiplying and Dividing Decimals
Multiplying and Dividing with Multiples of 10
Adding and Subtracting Fractions

Multiplying and Dividing Fractions
Rounding Numbers
Estimating Answers
Visualizing Word Problems: A
Visualizing Word Problems: B
Choosing the Numbers You Need
Deciding Which Operation to Use
Choosing the Right Setup
Setting Up a Word Problem
Percent Problems

Combining Sentences

**Rewrite these paragraphs, combining some sentences so the paragraphs
read more smoothly. Be sure not to change the meaning.**

A. Many actors in early Western movies were real cowboys. Many
extras were too. They had worked on ranches. They had worked in
Wild West shows. They came to California. They had heard they
could get five dollars a day. They could get a box lunch. This pay
was for riding and roping in the movies. Hoot Gibson was one of
these cowboys. He had grown up in Nebraska. He had punched
cattle. He had competed in rodeos. He was a reckless stuntman.
He became a Western movie star.

_____

_____

_____

_____

_____

_____

_____

B. Today, people plant irises. They plant the irises in flower gardens.
People in Europe used to eat iris roots. This happened many years
ago. People believed iris root cured many illnesses. People also
chewed the roots. They chewed them to mask bad breath. They
gave pieces of iris root to babies. Babies teethed on the pieces. A
certain kind of iris root is used today. It is called orrisroot. It is
used in perfumes. It is used in powders. It is used in medicines.

_____

_____

_____

_____

_____

_____

Independent and Dependent Thoughts

Use the word lists to help you fill in each blank with the word that best relates the independent and dependent thoughts. Add commas between the thoughts where they are needed.

when
before
because
but

_____ the automobile was available many people rode bicycles. Now, adults are riding bicycles again _____ they are concerned about physical fitness. The many bicycle types can be confusing _____ you can find the one that is best for you. _____ you choose a bicycle you should think about how you want to use the bicycle.

so
and
if

_____ you want a sturdy bicycle for errands and short trips you will be happiest with a one-speed or a three-speed bike. However, some people want to take long rides up and down hills _____ they need a touring or racing bike. These bikes have ten or more speeds _____ they are lighter in weight.

whether
even when
although

The city bicycle is another type. _____ it has many gears like a touring bicycle it is sturdy like a three-speed bike. The all-terrain bicycle is even sturdier than the city bicycle. _____ you ride it on or off the pavement it will perform well. Its many gears give it power _____ it is going up steep slopes and through soft sandy areas.

Subject-Verb Agreement: A

A. Choose the word in parentheses that completes each sentence correctly. Write that word in the blank.

1. Professional ice hockey (be, is) _____ exciting.

2. Each of the players (wears, wear) _____ a protective helmet.

3. Hockey pucks (travels, travel) _____faster than 100 miles an hour.

4. There (is, are) _____ sometimes fights among the players.

5. The game (don't, doesn't) _____ stop for substitution of players.

6. The season (runs, run) _____ from October to April.

7. Four teams from each division (competes, compete) _____ in the play-offs.

8. The winning team (receives, receive) _____ the Stanley Cup.

9. Gordie Howe and Phil Esposito (was, were) _____ two great hockey players.

10. Wayne Gretzky (has, have) _____ won the Most Valuable Player award nine times.

B. Write two sentences of your own with *does* as part of the verb.

1. _____

_____

2. _____

_____

C. Write two sentences of your own with *doesn't* as part of the verb.

1. _____

_____

2. _____

_____

Subject-Verb Agreement: B

A. Choose the word in parentheses that completes each sentence correctly. Write that word in the blank.

When people (decides, decide) _____ to paint a room, they want to get started right away. However, there (is, are) _____ good reasons to do some preparation first. Grease on a kitchen wall (keeps, keep) _____ paint from sticking well. Washing the walls (gets, get) _____ rid of any dust or grease. Wiping with a mop (helps, help) _____ clean the ceiling. New paint also (doesn't, don't) _____ hold well to a shiny surface, like enamel. If the enamel is roughed up with sandpaper, new paint jobs (holds, hold) _____ better. Floor wax on the baseboards also (stops, stop) _____ paint from sticking. Wax remover (takes, take) _____ it off. Professional painters (removes, remove) _____ the rust from radiators and pipes with sandpaper or steel wool. A careful painter then (puts, put) _____ on metal primer. The painter should make sure each of these areas (is, are) _____ dry before starting to paint.

B. Write two sentences of your own with *get* as the verb.

1. _____

_____

2. _____

_____

C. Write two sentences of your own with *gets* as the verb.

1. _____

_____

2. _____

_____

Verb Forms: A

A. Choose the word in parentheses that completes each sentence correctly. Write that word in the blank.

Stevie Wonder (showed, shown) _____ his musical talent early in life. At 9 years of age, he played the piano, drum, and harmonica. Stevie had never (saw, seen) _____ the instruments he played; he had been blind since birth. His hearing, though, was very sensitive. If a coin was dropped, he (knowed, knew) _____ what it was by the sound it made. His sensitivity to musical pitch and rhythm helped him sing and play like a much older performer.

Ronnie White, a singer with the Miracles, (saw, seen) _____ Stevie do a concert for his friends. Ronnie quickly (got, gotten) _____ Stevie an audition with Berry Gordy, the president of Motown Records. Gordy immediately (give, gave) _____ Stevie a five-year recording contract. At age 10, Stevie was a professional singer, but he was also still a kid. He kept on doing the things he had always (did, done) _____. The new recording artist still (runned, ran) _____ around the neighborhood with his friends and rode a bicycle while his brother steered. He got by on a weekly allowance of $2.50. During this period, he (did, done) _____ concerts mostly on weekends. His remarkable talent continued to develop. By the time he was 12, he had (became, become) _____ a star.

B. Write two sentences of your own, using the verb form *saw*.

1. _____

_____

2. _____

_____

C. Write two sentences of your own, using the verb form *seen*.

1. _____

_____

2. _____

_____

Verb Forms: B

A. Choose the word in parentheses that completes each sentence correctly. Write that word in the blank.

On the Waterfront is a movie classic that first (come, came) _____ out in 1954. Frank Sinatra had (went, gone) _____ out for the leading role, but the director (give, gave) _____ it to Marlon Brando. Brando played Terry Malloy, a longshoreman who also (did, done) _____ errands for the head of the local longshoremen's union. The movie is about corruption and violence. Terry is an ex-boxer who (throwed, threw) _____ an important fight and ruined his career in the ring. He knows that the union boss that he works for now has (stole, stolen) _____ money from the union. Recently, Terry (brought, brung) _____ a friend, Joey, to a rooftop meeting, which resulted in Joey's death. Before long, Terry has (fell, fallen) _____ in love with Joey's sister, Edie. He has (chose, chosen) _____ to risk his life in the fight for an honest union. However, he feels that if Edie (knowed, knew) _____ the things he had (did, done) _____, she would hate him. A suspenseful story and powerful performances make *On the Waterfront* a movie that still (be appealing, appeals) _____ to audiences today.

B. Write two sentences of your own, using the verb form *did*.

1. _____

_____

2. _____

_____

C. Write two sentences of your own, using the verb form *done*.

1. _____

_____

2. _____

_____

Spelling Plurals

The word list below contains singular nouns. Find the plural forms of these words in the puzzle. The words may be written across or down. As you circle each plural form, write it underneath the singular form on the list. One has been circled to get you started.

ability	deed	library	potato	speech
ache	dollar	loaf	rhythm	title
aisle	emergency	moral	role	tongue
analysis	entrance	neighbor	roll	vein
answer	guess	nickel	sandwich	view
bargain	half	niece	sigh	week
bush	hero	pear	site	
company	judgment	policeman	soul	

```
R X E W B A L C O M P A N I E S R E X
A E M E R G E N C I E S I C I O P P S
D N D E E D S E Z S A E C K L U T A A
I T O K I Q N I S J R R K S E L D B E
N R P S Y T A G U E S S E S U S O I N
O A S P E E C H E S B O L F R O L L S
T N D O R S I B U S H E S R H P L I G
S C G T S A L O A V E S D H Y U A T O
I E Y A O A X R L E S O T E T Y R I R
G S E T I N I S A N D W I C H E S E Q
H E R O E S K A N E S N A B M B O S E
S T A E S W O L A C H E S A S T R A N
S U L S T E M F L I B R A R I E S V T
I G R A V R S O Y N T O N G U E S T O
T I T L E S U T S O A S H A L V E S R
E P O L I C E M E N L E S I B I R T E
S E R A N G S Y S G S T O N I E C E S
E R A I S L E S T R O L E S S W E A B
M O R A L S Q J U D G M E N T S Z U S
```

Plurals and Possessive Nouns

A. Choose the word in parentheses that completes each sentence correctly. Write that word in the blank.

A (person's, persons) _____ right to vote is an important right. Most U.S. (citizen's, citizens) _____ aged 18 or older can vote if they are registered. (Person's, Persons) _____ who have been convicted of certain crimes lose their right to vote. A few other groups of people do not have voting rights.

(Voter's, Voters) _____ must go to the correct polling place. A (voter's, voters) _____ polling location depends on where the voter lives. Each state is divided into (county's, counties) _____ or (ward's, wards) _____. These are further divided into (precinct's, precincts) _____. Voters must go to the polling place in the precinct where they live. Election (official's, officials) _____ check each name against the (precinct's, precincts) _____ registration list.

U.S. (citizen's, citizens) _____ vote by secret ballot. A secret (ballot's, ballots) _____ advantage is that voters don't have to worry about what (other's, others) _____ will think of their vote. Voters go into a curtained booth to mark their (ballot's, ballots) _____.

B. Write two sentences of your own using the possessive noun *company's*.

1. _____

   _____

2. _____

   _____

C. Write two sentences of your own using the plural noun *companies*.

1. _____

   _____

2. _____

   _____

Possessive Pronouns and Contractions

A. Choose the word in parentheses that completes each sentence correctly. Write that word in the blank.

1. If (you're, your) _____ like most Americans, you get two or three colds a year.

2. However, (it's, its) _____ common for children to get ten colds in a year.

3. Cold germs enter (you're, your) _____ body through (you're, your) _____ eyes, nose, and mouth.

4. People often catch colds by getting the germs on (they're, their) _____ hands.

5. Then (they're, their) _____ likely to rub (they're, their) _____ eyes.

6. A cold is uncomfortable, but (it's, its) _____ usually not serious.

7. When (you're, your) _____ suffering from a cold, you may also have a sore throat.

8. A cold sufferer's nose is usually running, or (it's, its) _____ stuffed up.

9. Many people feel that (they're, their) _____ helped by chicken soup.

10. Antibiotics don't cure a cold but do protect against (it's, its) _____ complications.

11. An ordinary cold runs (it's, its) _____ course in a few days.

12. A person (who's, whose) _____ older has fewer colds than a younger person.

13. (Who's, Whose) _____ colds last the longest? Smokers' colds tend to hang on.

B. Write two sentences of your own using the contraction _it's_.

1. _____

_____

2. _____

_____

C. Write two sentences of your own using the possessive pronoun _its_.

1. _____

_____

2. _____

_____

Punctuation

Copy the body of this letter, adding commas, periods, and semicolons where they are needed.

The Arwen Company
463 Crosley Parkway
Teagarden, PA

Dear Arwen representative:

I recently saw one of your products at a friend's house It was called the Sleeper and it plugged into an electrical outlet. By moving the dial you could get the sound of rain a waterfall or waves on a beach. My friend said it masked the sounds of street traffic therefore it helped him get to sleep and stay asleep. He bought it about three years ago from *Lindley's* a mail-order catalog. Do you still make the Sleeper? If you do let me know how I can get one. Please answer as soon as possible I would like to give it as a gift.

Sincerely,

D. D. Morrison

_____

_____

_____

_____

_____

_____

_____

_____

_____

_____

_____

_____

Capitalization

Copy the body of this letter, correcting the capitalization.

Charles Cochrane, Editor
NewsReview Magazine
145 East 35th Street
New York, NY 10016

Dear Mr. Cochrane:

I enjoyed albert winslow's article on opportunities in the state of ohio. However, I would like to point out a few errors that I noticed. First of all, cleveland is the largest city in the state, but it is not the capital, nor is it the location of ohio university. Also, the shoreline along lake erie is mostly rocky as he describes it, but there are some sandy beaches. His discussion of cincinnati's river festival should have mentioned that it takes place in august. His section on ohio's history stated that general anthony wayne built fort goodwill. The correct name of the fort was fort recovery. Finally, his list of u.s. leaders born in ohio left out president ulysses s. grant. I was glad mr. winslow liked ohio, but I think next time he should try to keep his facts straight.

Sincerely,

Henry Bishop
Canton, Ohio

_____

_____

_____

_____

_____

_____

_____

_____

_____

_____

_____

_____

_____

_____

Organizing Ideas

A. Use this outline to write a paragraph on the benefits of regular exercise.

    A. Have a good time
        1. Enjoy sport or activity
        2. Get together with friends
    B. Feel better
        1. Have more energy
        2. Feel more relaxed
    C. Look better
        1. Tone up muscles
        2. Burn off fat

_____

_____

_____

_____

_____

_____

_____

_____

B. Read the paragraph below. Then complete the map of the ideas in the paragraph.

Salespeople work in many different settings. People who do direct selling demonstrate their products in people's homes or try to sell over the phone. A retail salesperson works in a store. Wholesalers travel to many retail stores to offer their products to store representatives.

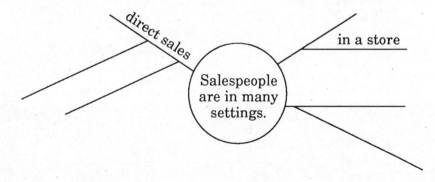

Writing Topic Sentences

Write a topic sentence on the blank lines for each paragraph.

A. _____

_____

Some people don't remember their dreams. They may think they
don't dream at all, but they do. Other people remember only a few
dreams, so they think they don't dream very often. In fact, adults
have three to five dreams in a night. Even babies show physical
signs of dreaming.

B. _____

_____

Wild animals are sometimes bought as pets because they are
unusual or beautiful. Then the new owners find that they can't give
a wild pet the living conditions it was used to. The animal may
cause severe bites and scratches when startled or angered. It may
have diseases that it passes along to humans or other animals.
Many of these wild pets die within two years.

C. _____

_____

Manufacturing companies and other businesses are continuing to
move to the Atlanta area. New hotels, office buildings, and
apartment complexes are being built in downtown Atlanta. The
population of the metropolitan area has passed two million.

Transitions

Use the word lists to fill the blanks in the paragraphs. Add commas where they are needed.

first
however
in addition
in that case
for instance

   Following a budget helps people keep from running out of money. _____ a budget helps people spend their money for the things they need or want most. _____ a person on a budget may eat a brown-bag lunch at work in order to buy a cassette tape. There are three major steps in budgeting.
   _____ estimate your income. If your only income is a regular salary, this step is easy. _____ you may have a job whose hours vary, or you may sometimes get extra money from a side job. _____ choose a past period of time to help you estimate your future income.

as a result
finally
for example
next
on the other hand

   _____ estimate your expenses. On one hand, you will have certain fixed expenses, such as rent or mortgage and a car payment. _____ you will have expenses that vary, depending partly on your choices. These expenses include clothing, food, and entertainment.
   _____ write down what you actually spend. This helps you adjust your budget. _____ you may find you are able to spend less for clothes than you have allowed. _____ you may be able to increase your allowance for entertainment.

Irrelevant Details

In each paragraph below, cross out the information that does not explain or support the main idea.

A. Many states in the United States operate some form of lottery to raise money. Players buy numbered tickets, hoping to win cash prizes. In some state lotteries, top winners receive millions of dollars, but most lottery winners receive much smaller amounts. Some people also win money in sweepstakes. Lottery ticket sales bring in billions of dollars to the states each year.

B. People have several mistaken ideas about bats. A bat isn't "blind as a bat." Bats can see well. Also, bats don't fly into people and get tangled in their hair. Neither do birds. Bats try to avoid people, and they can navigate very well. Some people are also very frightened of snakes and spiders.

C. The causes of stress can be emotional or physical or a combination of both. Losing a job is stressful, and so is getting married. Many people enjoy sports activities. Working or living in a noisy environment is also stressful. Smoking cigarettes and not getting enough sleep are two other contributors to stress. Some people are more easygoing than others.

Working with a U.S. Map—Regions

Use the two maps to answer the questions that follow.

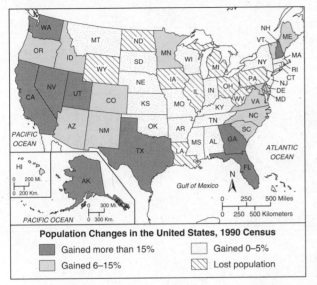

Population Changes in the United States, 1990 Census
- Gained more than 15%
- Gained 6–15%
- Gained 0–5%
- Lost population

1a. The North Central states are sometimes divided into the Great Lakes states and the Plains states. Which six North Central states are the Great Lakes states?

_____

b. Which six North Central states are the Plains states?

_____

c. How would you summarize population trends in the North Central states?

_____

2a. The South and Southwest are sometimes called "the sun belt." Name five states that are in the sun belt.

_____

b. What evidence is there on the map that people are moving to the sun belt?

_____

3. Which region lost the most population?

_____

4. Name three states in the interior West.

_____

5. Name the two states that are separated from the mainland.

_____

Working with a U.S. Map—States

Use this map to answer the questions that follow.

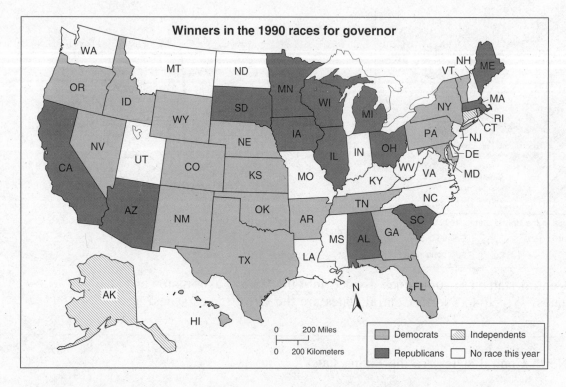

Winners in the 1990 races for governor

Legend: Democrats; Independents; Republicans; No race this year

1a. Which party won most of the governors' races in the western half of the country?

_____

b. Name six western states that voted for this party's candidate.

_____

2a. Which party won most of the governors' races in the North Central states?

_____

b. Name five North Central states that voted for this party's candidate.

_____

3. Only thirteen states voted Republican governors into office in 1990, but there were more than thirteen Republican governors in office in 1990.

_____

Working with a World Map

Use the maps below to answer the questions that follow.

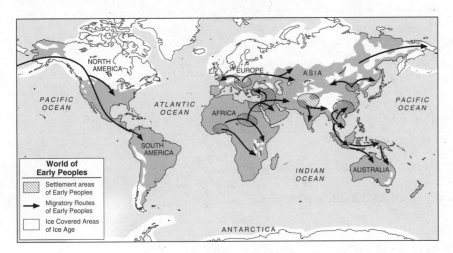

1. Describe the settlement areas of early peoples.

_____

_____

2. What was the origin of the groups who came down the coast of North America and into South America?

_____

3. Summarize the movement of peoples from southern Europe.

_____

4. List a major difference between North America today and North America at the time shown on the map.

_____

5. The areas shown as covered by ice during the Ice Age were not ice-covered continuously. The ice retreated and then returned over time. What information given by the map supports this fact?

_____

Working with Tables

The information in this table will help you with questions 1–6.

The Union and the Confederacy, 1861	Union	Confederacy
Number of States	23	11
Population	22,339,989 (71%)	9,103,332 (29%)
Industrial Workers	1,197,876 (92%)	110,721 (8%)
Value of Manufacturing	$1,794,417,000 (92%)	$155,532,000 (8%)
Railroad Mileage	21,846 (71%)	8,947 (29%)
Improved Farm Acreage	105,831,000 (65%)	56,832,000 (35%)

1. How many states were in the Union? ＿＿ the Confederacy? ＿＿

2. About how many million people lived in Union states? ＿＿＿＿＿
   in Confederate states? ＿＿＿＿＿

3. In which areas did the Union have an advantage of about 11 to 1?

4. How would an advantage in industry help a region fight a war?

5. Which side had an advantage in miles of railroad track?

6. How would better transportation help a region during a war?

Occupations with Largest Growth, 1990–2005
(numbers in thousands)

Occupation	Employment 1990	2005	Change in Employment Percent
Salespersons, retail	3,619	4,506	24
Registered nurses	1,727	2,494	44
Cashiers	2,633	3,318	26
General office clerks	2,737	3,407	24
Truck drivers	2,362	2,979	26
Managers/executives	3,086	3,684	19
Janitors/housekeepers	3,007	3,562	18
Nursing aides	1,274	1,826	43
Food counter workers	1,607	2,158	34
Waiters/waitresses	1,747	2,196	26

Use the table at the left to answer questions 7–9.

7. America's population is shifting from having a large segment of young people to a large segment of older people. What information in the table supports this?

8. What occupation is expected to have the highest employment by 2005?

9. What is the job outlook for people without a college education?

Working with Line Graphs

Use information on the graph below to answer the questions that follow.

1. What was the percent change in the GNP (gross national product, sometimes called the gross domestic product) of the United States for the year 1989?

_____

2. Which country showed the least change in GNP from 1981 to 1982?

_____

3. Which country showed the greatest fluctuation, or change, in its GNP? Explain your answer.

_____

_____

Economic Growth
Gross Domestic Product Measured in Percent Change

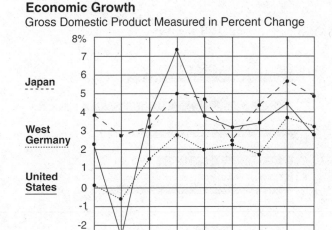

4. In your own words, compare the economic growth of West Germany with that of Japan for the years shown.

_____

5. All three countries experienced overall economic growth between 1981 and 1989. Support that statement with evidence from the graph.

_____

Use information from the table at the left to make a line graph. Plot a point for each year on the graph; then connect the points with a line.

Unemployment Rate in the United States, 1980–1991

Year	%	Year	%
1980	7.1	1986	7.0
1981	7.6	1987	6.2
1982	9.7	1988	5.5
1983	9.6	1989	5.3
1984	7.5	1990	5.5
1985	7.2	1991	6.7

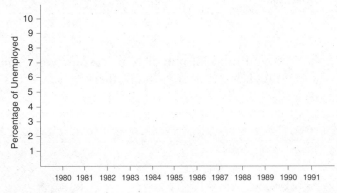

6. Summarize the information on the graph in your own words.

_____

Working with Bar Graphs

Use the information in the bar graph to answer questions 1–3.

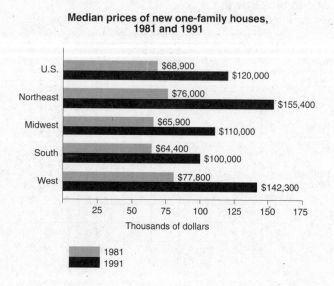

Median prices of new one-family houses, 1981 and 1991

U.S. $68,900 / $120,000
Northeast $76,000 / $155,400
Midwest $65,900 / $110,000
South $64,400 / $100,000
West $77,800 / $142,300

Thousands of dollars

1981
1991

1. Which region saw the greatest increase in the cost of single-family housing in the last decade?

_____

2. In which region did a house remain least expensive from 1981 to 1991?

_____

3. Which region was closest to the national average in both 1981 and 1991?

_____

Use the information in this table to complete the bar graph. Make a bar for each figure.

World's Major Consumers of Primary Energy, 1990

Country	Amount of Energy Consumed (in Quadrillion Btu)
United States	81.17
China	28.85
Japan	18.18
Canada	10.79
United Kingdom	9.13
Netherlands	3.39

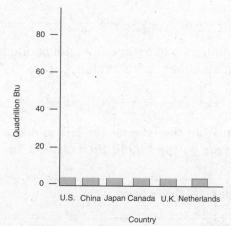

4. Can you think of one or two reasons why some countries consume so much more energy than others?

_____

_____

Working with Pie Graphs

Use the information from these pie graphs to answer the questions that follow.

How the federal government spends its money

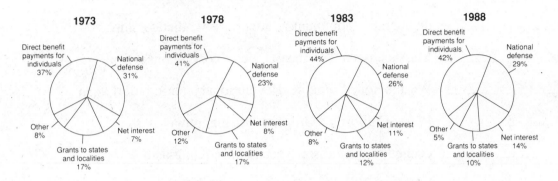

1. Which area consistently receives the largest percentage of the federal budget?

_____

2. Describe what has happened to the percentage of the federal budget given back to state and local governments.

_____

3. During which year can you infer that the country was at war? Why?

_____

4. How can you tell that the national debt has probably increased over the years?

_____

Use the table at the left to complete the pie graph below. Finish the lines dividing up the circle and label the appropriate sections of the pie with their percentages.

Where the Federal Government Gets Its Money

Source	Percentage
Individual income taxes	45
Social Security taxes and contributions	38
Corporate income taxes	8
Excise taxes	4
Other	5

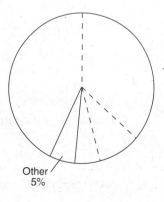

Other
5%

General and Specific Concepts

Each group of words below has one general term and three specific
terms that belong to that general group. Write the name of the general
group on the line. The first one is done as an example.

1. <u>political party</u>   Republican, Democratic, political party, Libertarian

2. _____ democratic, communist, government, dictatorship

3. _____ Massachusetts, Northeast, New York, Connecticut

4. _____ Washington, Franklin, Revolutionary period, Jefferson

5. _____ West, California, Oregon, Washington

6. _____ economy, capitalism, socialism, communism

7. _____ Midwest, Illinois, Wisconsin, Indiana

8. _____ mediterranean, climate, polar, tropical

9. _____ executive, legislative, judicial, government branch

10. _____ corn, wheat, rice, crops

11. _____ hunger, need, thirst, shelter

12. _____ South Carolina, Southeast, Florida, Georgia

13. _____ rain forest, desert, grassland, vegetation

14. _____ peers, groups, families, societies

15. _____ time, decade, century, era

16. _____ river, ocean, body of water, lake

17. _____ country, colony, territory, political region

18. _____ Mississippi, Alabama, South, Tennessee

19. _____ mountain, plain, hill, landform

20. _____ Civil War, Lincoln, Grant, Lee

21. _____ president, government official, premier, prime minister

22. _____ goods, shoes, furniture, automobiles

23. _____ corporation, partnership, sole proprietorship, business

Classifying

Below are the levels of government and some of the functions each level carries out. Many people hold government jobs. Read the lists of functions and then the job descriptions that follow. Decide if each job would be with the federal government, a state government, or a local government.

Federal	State	Local
Federal tax collection	State tax collection	Public safety
Coining of money	Supervision of schools	Administration of schools
Postal service	Public works	Mass transit
Regulation of	Health and welfare programs	Water supply
interstate trade	Courts for state and local laws	Waste disposal
Courts for federal laws	Motor vehicle registration	Libraries
National defense	Licensing of occupations	Museums

1. If you enlist as a soldier in the Army, for which level of government will you be an employee?

2. If you are a firefighter, for which level of government do you work?

3. If you are a clerk in a traffic court, for which level of government do you work?

4. If you test people for their driver's licenses, of which level of government are you an employee?

5. If you are a garbage collector, your company was contracted by which level of government?

6. If you are a construction worker helping repair a major highway, which level of government hired your company to do the work?

7. If you proofread paper money to make sure it was printed correctly, you are an employee of which level of government?

8. If you are a bus driver and your route takes you from the downtown area to the airport and back, for which level of government do you work?

Using Context Clues

As you read each item below, try to figure out the meaning of the bold word. Write its meaning on the line. You can read the *whole* item before you decide on the meaning of the word.

1. An increasing number of interest groups are "cause" or **"ideological"** organizations, often referred to as "single-issue" groups. While they resemble special-interest groups in the narrowness of their concerns, they resemble public-interest groups in that they often are fighting for their vision of what is good for society.

Ideological means _____

2. In 1987, the Supreme Court upheld the 1984 Bail Reform Act. This law permits the **pretrial detention** without bail of criminal suspects who federal courts find threaten the safety of the community. The law was seen as a response to the high number of crimes committed by people free on bail while awaiting trial.

Pretrial detention means _____

3. Everyone at some time or another breaks the written or unwritten laws of society. While some forms of **deviance** are tolerated, other, more serious acts of deviance—such as drug abuse or violent behavior—can result in loss of friends or job, even in imprisonment.

Deviance means _____

4. _____

Eastern Hemisphere Population Densities

Continent	Average Number of People per Square Mile
Asia	168
Europe	173
Africa	45

Densities means _____

5. Hurricanes and tornadoes are common, often destructive windstorms. People of South and Southeast Asia plan their farming activities around the pattern of the more friendly **monsoons,** which blow from one direction for part of the year and from another direction for the other part.

Monsoons are _____

6. Jean Piaget explored the environmental nature of intellectual growth in infants and children. In Piaget's view, the child from age two to seven is intensely **egocentric** in his or her thinking. He or she has no sense of objectivity or others' point of view.

Egocentric means _____

Causes and Effects

Read this article about Prohibition and its effects.

The Eighteenth Amendment, forbidding the manufacture, sale, or transportation of alcoholic beverages, became the law of the land in January of 1920. So began prohibition. The "noble experiment," as Herbert Hoover called it, lasted more than ten years. Alcoholic consumption declined, and so did arrests due to drunkenness and deaths due to alcoholism. At the same time, the business in illegal liquor boomed. Organized crime, and the violence that followed it, moved in to profit from what was a general rebellion against prohibition. Between 1920 and 1928, 135 people were killed by law enforcement officials enforcing prohibition, and 55 officials were also killed. By the end of the 1920s, it was clear that most people did not believe in or support prohibition. Polls taken in 1926 showed that only 19 percent of Americans favored the Eighteenth Amendment. Finally, on December 5, 1933, the Twenty-first Amendment was ratified, repealing the Eighteenth.

Now complete this chart with the effects of Prohibition discussed in the article. The first effect is given as an example.

Effects	Secondary Effects
1. alcoholic consumption down	
2. _____	
3. _____	
4. _____ →	violence (190 killed)
5. anti-prohibition feelings →	_____

Read this article about the causes of the American Revolution.

From the beginning, American society was different from that of the mother country because, despite a fairly rigid class structure, nobility had less importance in America and land ownership was open to many. But it was economic and political differences that caused the final break. From 1765 to 1776, the British government imposed taxes and attempted to control the American economy. The political power of colonial assemblies was reduced. . . . Colonists organized protests that led to armed conflict and the Declaration of Independence.

Complete this chart with causes of the Revolution.

Social differences:	6. _____	7. _____
Economic differences:	8. _____	9. _____
Political differences:	10. _____	

Point of View

Below are two opinions about the best form of government. Read them carefully to understand each point of view. Then answer the questions that follow.

"All communities divide themselves into the few and the many. The first are the rich and wellborn, the other the mass of the people. . . . The people are turbulent and changing; they seldom judge or determine right. Give therefore to the first class a distinct, permanent share in the government. They will check the unsteadiness of the second, and as they cannot receive any advantage by a change, they therefore will ever maintain good government."

Alexander Hamilton (1755–1804)
American political leader
First Secretary of the Treasury

"Men by their constitutions are naturally divided into two parties: (1) Those who fear and distrust the people, and wish to draw all powers from them into the hands of the higher classes. (2) Those who identify themselves with the people, have confidence in them, cherish and consider them as the most honest and safe, although not the most wise depository of the public interests. In every country these two parties exist; and in every one where they are free to think, speak, and write, they will declare themselves."

Thomas Jefferson (1743–1826)
Third President of the U.S.
Writer of the Declaration of Independence

1. In your own words, summarize what Hamilton said.

_____

_____

2. In your own words, summarize what Jefferson said.

_____

_____

3. Which man had a more democratic view of government? Explain your answer.

_____

4. Which man would be more likely to support programs that helped wealthy businesspersons? Explain your answer.

_____

Assessing Data

Read each selection below and then answer the questions.

In a famous series of experiments, Harry F. Harlow took baby monkeys and placed them in cages with what he called "surrogate mothers"—a wire doll-like object with a bottle and nipple from which the monkey could get milk, and a second doll-like object made of soft sponge rubber and terry cloth.

The baby monkeys showed a strong tendency to hug and cuddle with the terry cloth mother. This was true even when they were feeding from the wire mother. It was especially true when a new and strange object was put into the cage. Obviously, the soft touch of the terry cloth mother was satisfying a strong need in the baby for a sense of closeness and physical safety.

1. What is the conclusion about need that the author draws from Harlow's experiments?

_____

2. What two pieces of evidence does the author cite that help support that conclusion?

_____

Americans place a high value on romance. We react negatively to the idea of arranged marriage, but it seems that the free choice we value so highly is not completely free. Studies show that most of us tend to marry people very much like ourselves in looks, attitudes, and values. Whom we marry is influenced to a large degree by group norms or group pressure. In those societies in which marriages are still arranged, it is thought that older people can make better choices than their children can. If love does not exist between the two at the time of marriage, it is believed they will come to love each other in time. These beliefs appear to be true. Studies show little difference between the success and happiness experienced in freely chosen marriages and that achieved in arranged marriages.

3. What conclusion does the author draw about Americans' conception that we have free choice in selecting a spouse?

_____

4. What evidence does the author bring up to prove that point?

_____

5. What conclusion does the author draw about the beliefs behind arranged marriages?

_____

6. What evidence is cited to support that conclusion?

_____

Drawing Conclusions

Read each item and then answer its questions.

In the 1992 presidential election, Bill Clinton had only a narrow 5 percent lead over his main opponent, then President George Bush. Clinton received 43 percent of the popular vote, while Bush received 38 percent. Still, Clinton's victory was termed a landslide because of the electoral college vote. Clinton carried 32 states and the District of Columbia, giving him 370 electoral votes (*all* electoral votes from a state go to the person who carried the state). Bush carried only 18 states with 168 electoral votes.

1. What relationship can you infer between the popular vote and the electoral vote? Explain your answer.

2. From the graph at the right, what can you infer about the kind of climate and land around Phoenix? Explain your answer.

Annual Precipitation in Phoenix, Arizona

Eight researchers had themselves committed to different mental institutions. Once in the hospitals, they began behaving normally. While real patients often realized the researchers were normal, the doctors and staff never did. Once labeled as psychotic, their behavior, no matter how normal, was interpreted as abnormal.

3. What conclusion can you draw about the way people view and, therefore, treat other people? Explain your answer.

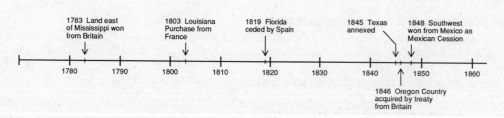

1783 Land east of Mississippi won from Britain
1803 Louisiana Purchase from France
1819 Florida ceded by Spain
1845 Texas annexed
1848 Southwest won from Mexico as Mexican Cession
1846 Oregon Country acquired by treaty from Britain

4. What can you infer about the attitude of the United States toward acquiring land? Explain your answer.

Facts and Opinions

Read this article about robots and then mark each statement that follows it as a fact or an opinion.

Smart industries are turning to robots. Industrial robots were first used in 1961 in auto assembly plants. As the cost of human labor rises and the price of robots drops, more factories are showing an interest in robots. Robots are especially attractive because they can increase production. Production is the single most important factor a businessperson needs to consider. Factories using industrial robots have upped their output by impressive percentages. Of course, robots never ask for a raise or more benefits. They are always at work on time. But they can contribute to unemployment by doing the jobs people currently do.

Now write *fact* or *opinion* before each statement.

1. _____ Smart industries are turning to robots.

2. _____ Industrial robots were first used in 1961.

3. _____ The cost of human labor is rising.

4. _____ The price of robots is dropping.

5. _____ More factories are showing an interest in robots.

6. _____ Robots can increase production.

7. _____ Production is the most important business consideration.

8. _____ Factories using industrial robots have increased their output.

9. _____ The percentage increase in output is impressive.

10. _____ Robots never ask for raises or more benefits.

11. _____ Robots are always at work on time.

12. _____ Robots can contribute to unemployment.

Explain in your own words why the statements that you marked facts are facts.

_____

_____

Working with Diagrams

Use the diagram at the right to answer questions 1–4.

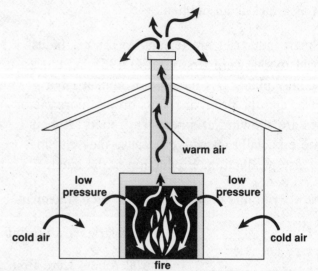

1. What happens to most of the warm air heated by the fire?

_____

2. What happens to the air pressure around the fireplace?

_____

3. What happens to the cold air outside at the base of the house?

_____

_____

4. Judging from this diagram, do you think a fireplace is a good way to heat a room? Why or why not?

_____

_____

Use the diagram below to answer questions 5–8.

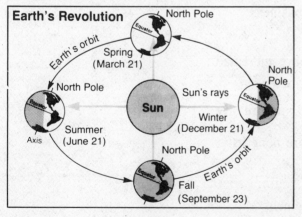

5. Write the season that is beginning in the Northern Hemisphere on each date.

   March 21 _____   June 21 _____

   Sept. 23 _____   Dec. 21 _____

6. The season in the Southern Hemisphere is opposite the season in the Northern Hemisphere. Write the season that is beginning in the Southern Hemisphere on each date.

   March 21 _____   June 21 _____

   Sept. 23 _____   Dec. 21 _____

7. What would happen to the seasons if the earth's axis were not tilted?

_____

_____

8. What would happen to the seasons if the earth did not revolve around the sun?

_____

Working with Tables and Charts

Use the information in the chart below to answer the questions that
follow.

Vitamin B Complex

Vitamin	Food Sources	Recommended Diet Allowance	
		Men	Women
B$_1$ (Thiamine)	Pork; organ meats; legumes; vegetables	1.2–1.4 mg	1.0–1.1 mg
B$_2$ (Riboflavin)	Meat; milk products; eggs; vegetables	1.4–1.7 mg	1.2–1.3 mg
B$_6$ (Pyridoxine)	Yeast; nuts; liver; vegetables; fish; rice	2.0–2.2 mg	2.0 mg
B$_{12}$ (Cobalamin)	Meat; milk products; eggs; fish	3 mcg	3 mcg
Folic acid	Yeast; wheat germ; liver; vegetables	400 mcg	400 mcg
Pantothenic acid	Egg yolk; meat; nuts; whole-grain cereals	4–7 mg*	4–7 mg*
Niacin	Milk; meats; cereals; legumes	16–19 mg**	13–14 mg**
Biotin	Eggs; liver; yeast	100–200 mcg*	100–200 mcg*

*Estimated recommended diet allowance
**Niacin equivalents

1. In your own words, what information is the chart giving?

2. How many individual vitamins make up the vitamin B complex?

3. What foods are a good source of B$_{12}$?

4. What vitamins will vegetables supply?

5. How many milligrams (mg) of niacin a day should a man take in?

Use the table below to answer questions 6 and 7.

lake	surface area (sq. miles)	average depth (feet)	volume (cubic miles)	replacement time (years)
Erie	9,900	60	113	3
Ontario	7,300	280	390	8
Huron	23,000	190	850	25
Michigan	22,000	280	1,200	70
Superior	32,000	485	2,900	180

6. How much water does Lake Erie hold?

7. Which lake is smallest in surface area but second in depth?

Working with Line Graphs

Use the graph at the left to answer questions 1–5.

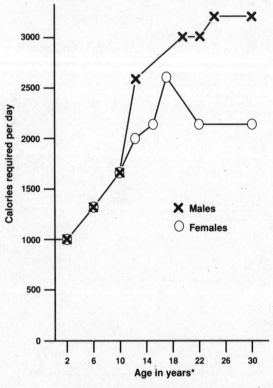

*Values given for any age may vary somewhat
depending on how active a person is

1. About how many calories does a two-year-old boy need daily?

_____

a two-year-old girl?

_____

2. At what age do the caloric needs of males and females begin to differ?

_____

3. How many calories does a man at age 22 need each day?

_____

4. At what age does a woman's required caloric intake hit a plateau?

_____

5. Why would both females and males have an increasing need for calories until age 18?

_____

_____

Use the chart at the left to make your own line graph. Plot the points for birds and then connect them with a solid line. Plot the points for mammals and connect them with a dotted line. Plot the points for reptiles and connect them with circles.

Survival in Captivity

Age in years	Percent Remaining Alive		
	Birds	*Mammals*	*Reptiles*
20	50	43	39
30	19	10	28
40	3	7	9

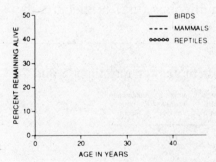

Working with Bar Graphs

Use the graph below to answer the questions that follow.

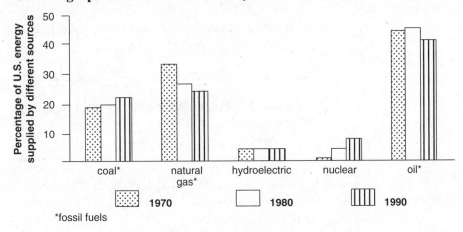

1970   1980   1990

*fossil fuels

1. Which source has consistently supplied the largest percentage of energy?

_____

2. Which source increased the most between 1970 and 1990?

_____

3. Which source supplied the smallest amount of energy in 1990?

_____

4a. What kinds of fuels are coal, gas, and oil?

_____

b. About what percentage of energy did these three fuels together supply in 1990?

_____

Use the information from the table at the left to make your own bar graph at the right. Make a bar for each figure in the table.

Speed of Sound in Various Materials

Material	Speed (ft/sec)
Air (68°F)	1,130
Water (59°F)	4,760
Brick	11,970
Oak	12,630
Aluminum	16,730
Steel	17,060
Granite	19,690

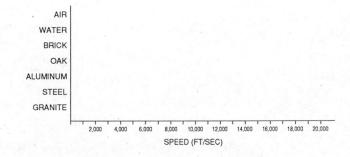

Working with Pie Graphs

Use the pie graph on the left to answer questions 1-2.

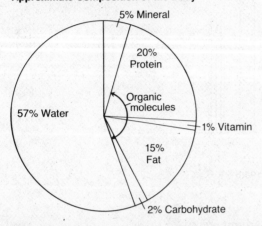

Approximate Composition of the Body

1. What substance makes up more than half of the human body?

_____

2a. What substances are made of organic molecules?

_____

b. What percentage of the body do these organic substances make up?

_____

Use the information in the table at the left to complete the pie graph at the right. Label each section with the appropriate element and percentage. Then answer the questions that follow.

Elements in the Earth's Crust

Element	Percentage
Oxygen	46
Silicon	28
Aluminum	8
Iron	6
Magnesium	4
Others	8

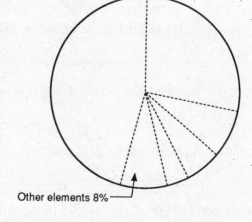

Other elements 8%

3. What element accounts for almost half the earth's crust?

_____

4. What element accounts for between one-fourth and one-third?

_____

General and Specific Concepts

Each group of items has one general term and three specific terms that belong to that general group. Write the name of the general group on the line. The first one is done as an example.

1. <u>atomic particle</u>   proton, neutron, electron, atomic particle

2. _____   mammal, human, bear, elephant

3. _____   oak tree, rosebush, algae, plant

4. _____   heart, lung, organ, brain

5. _____   natural gas, petroleum, coal, fuel

6. _____   digestive system, circulatory system, nervous system, body system

7. _____   tide, current, wave, ocean movement

8. _____   vertebrate, trout, gorilla, horse

9. _____   Venus, Earth, Mars, planet

10. _____   rain, precipitation, sleet, snow

11. _____   screw, lever, pulley, tool

12. _____   motion, acceleration, rotation, revolution

13. _____   tea, solution, antifreeze, carbonated water

14. _____   fossil fuel, wind, sun, energy resource

15. _____   parrot, eagle, bird, pigeon

16. _____   nylon, polyester, rayon, synthetic

17. _____   television, electronic device, computer, tape recorder

18. _____   beetle, wasp, insect, cockroach

19. _____   genetic trait, hair texture, eye color, sex

20. _____   solid, gas, matter, liquid

21. _____   oxygen, carbon, element, hydrogen

22. _____   hair, body covering, scale, feather

23. _____   planet, star, asteroid, heavenly body

Classifying

Read the description of Isaac Newton's three laws of motion. Then read the examples of motion and classify each as following the first, second, or third law.

First Law: A moving object will keep going in the same direction and at the same speed unless a force acts on it. An object at rest will remain still unless a force acts on it.

Second Law: An object will change speed and direction when a force acts on it. The greater the force, the greater the change in speed. The heavier the object, the greater the force needed to change its motion. The direction of the object's motion will be the same as the direction in which the force is moving.

Third Law: For every action, there is an equal and opposite reaction.

1. The side of an ice rink is the force that stops a hockey puck when the puck slides into it. This example follows which of Newton's laws?

_____

2. As a car moves forward, the air it meets is forced to flow toward the back of the car. This example follows which of Newton's laws?

_____

3. A spacecraft that escapes the earth's atmosphere will keep moving in the same direction and at the same speed because there is no air resistance or gravity to slow it. This example follows which of Newton's laws?

_____

4. You need to push twice as hard to move a shopping cart with twenty pounds of food in it as one with ten pounds. This example follows which of Newton's laws?

_____

5. A pile of leaves remains still on a calm, windless fall day. This example follows which of Newton's laws?

_____

6. A man doing push-ups lifts himself up by pushing down on the floor. This example follows which of Newton's laws?

_____

Using Context Clues

As you read each item below, try to determine the meaning of the bold word. Then write the meaning on the line that follows. You can read the *whole* item before you decide.

1. Dioxin is not the name of one chemical but of a family of chemicals. Each of the 75 members of the family has the same basic three-ring structure of benzene and oxygen. The **toxicity** of a particular dioxin is determined by the position and amount of chlorine that is attached to its outer edge. The dioxin TCDD has four chlorine atoms and is the most poisonous chemical ever made by humans. Other dioxins have six or more chlorine atoms and are less toxic than TCDD.

   Toxicity is _____

2. Spanish moss is one of the most common and eye-catching plants in the South. Many people believe it actually kills the plants it lives on. However, Spanish moss is not **parasitic**. It makes its own food and does not harm the plant on which it grows.

   Parasitic means _____

3. ▬

   Major Seismic Activity, 1970–1992

Site of Earthquake	Year	Site of Earthquake	Year	Site of Earthquake	Year
China	1970	China	1976	Ecuador	1987
Peru	1970	Indonesia	1977	Armenia	1988
United States	1971	Iran	1978	United States	1989
Nicaragua	1972	Algeria	1980	Romania	1990
Pakistan	1974	Japan	1983	Philippines	1990
Turkey	1975	Chile	1985	Costa Rica; Panama	1991
Guatemala	1976	Mexico	1985	United States	1992

   Seismic refers to _____

4. Interferon is a naturally **synthesized** substance that fights viruses. As such, it may one day help fight cancer. The problem is that cells in mammals such as humans make only the smallest amounts of interferon. To synthesize more—for research and perhaps eventually for medical use—scientists have identified the actual genes that contain the instructions for manufacturing interferon and have transferred this genetic material to other cells, which have become "interferon factories."

   Synthesize means _____

Applying Scientific Information

Study the diagram at the right. Then answer the questions.

1. Summarize the meaning of the diagram in your own words.

   _____

   _____

   _____

   _____

2. Suppose a snake eats the frog. How much of the 100 calories that was originally absorbed by the petunia will the snake receive?

   _____

3. Based on what the diagram tells you, which food could people eat to make the most efficient use of the sun's energy—lettuce or beef?

   _____

4. More than half the world goes to bed hungry. Millions of square miles of land are now devoted to pastureland or to crops used to feed beef cattle and hogs. How could the information in the diagram be used to help solve the hunger problem?

   _____

   _____

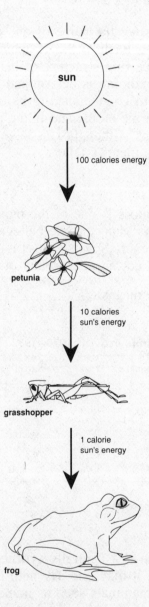

Causes and Effects

Read the article below about the greenhouse effect. Then fill in the chart that follows.

The greenhouse effect has been in the evening news lately. Scientists argue whether this dramatic altering of the environment is now a reality, but they do not argue about the cause if such a phenomenon does eventually occur or about the possible secondary effects the greenhouse effect would have.

Beginning in the late 1700s, with the rise of industrialization, humans found more and more uses for fossil fuels. The burning of oil, gas, or coal releases gases, among them carbon dioxide. In the last 200 years, with widespread burning of these fuels, an increasing amount of carbon dioxide has been released into the air. The gas has accumulated in the earth's atmosphere.

At some point, much of the solar heat that now reflects off the earth and back into space will be blocked by the carbon dioxide, in the way the roof of a greenhouse for plants allows solar light and heat in but not as much of the heat out. Indeed, this trapping of heat near the earth and the increase in global temperature that would result are what is meant by "the greenhouse effect."

What would be the effects of this greenhouse the size of the earth? A temperature increase of just 2–3°F worldwide could lead to melting of the polar ice caps. A rise in sea level would result. What are now coastal cities and lands would be under water. Dry desert areas would increase in size as climates became warmer and the warm atmosphere could retain more moisture. Available farmland would therefore shrink. Countless species of animals and plants, if not destroyed, would be altered as natural selection favored those which could adapt to warmer, drier weather.

Even if the claims that the greenhouse effect now exists prove premature, many scientists believe that such a situation is likely if our excessive use of fossil fuels continues.

Now complete this chart with the causes and effects mentioned in the article.

Burning of fossil fuels over 200 years
↓
Release of carbon dioxide
↓

1. _____
↓

GREENHOUSE EFFECT:	Carbon dioxide traps heat; global temperature increases

↓   ↓   ↓

2. _____ Desert areas spread **5.** _____
↓   ↓

Rise in sea level **4.** _____
↓

3. _____

Analogies

Read each scientific description below. Then choose the common, everyday object that is most similar to it. Circle the letter of your answer. On the line that follows, explain *why* the two are similar.

1. The rotation of the earth on its axis is most like the
   a. flight of a bird
   b. spinning of a top
   c. circling of a plane overhead

   _____

2. The human circulatory system is made up of relatively large arteries and veins that branch out into smaller and smaller blood vessels. The circulatory system is most like a system of
   a. rivers and streams
   b. individual tubes
   c. interstate highways

   _____

3. Sound waves travel out from their source in increasing circles. The action of sound waves is most like water waves
   a. rippling out from the spot where a stone dropped
   b. moving onto a sandy beach
   c. bubbling in a hot whirlpool bath

   _____

4. In nuclear fission a high-speed atomic particle is shot at the nucleus of an atom, splitting it into its particles and sending them in all directions. This action is most like
   a. shooting a basketball through a hoop
   b. breaking a group of billiard balls at the start of a game
   c. hitting a baseball into the stands

   _____

5. Electricity moves through the wires in a closed circuit. The movement of electricity is most like
   a. wind blowing through a window
   b. a car moving on the road
   c. water flowing through pipes

   _____

Facts and Opinions

Read the following article about fire research.

Scientists are always looking for better ways to prevent the tremendous loss of life and property due to fire each year. One problem is that many fire codes were developed before today's synthetic materials—and the poisonous fumes they emit when burning—were even heard of. Another problem is the seemingly unstoppable habit of smoking when in bed or when tired to the point of falling asleep.

Each year about 12,000 people die in fires, or from the burns or smoke inhalation suffered during the fire. Of those 12,000, about 2,300 deaths can be attributed to carelessly dropped cigarettes. Many fire researchers, therefore, urge the development of a "fire-safe" cigarette. Like a cigar, such a cigarette would stay lit only if smoked. The cigarette would extinguish itself if untouched.

According to U.S. Congressman Joseph Moakley of Massachusetts, "There are hundreds and hundreds of children lying in burn hospitals today who don't know what a cigarette is, but they're there as a result of a carelessly discarded cigarette." Yet the tobacco industry has fought congressional attempts to require that fire-safe cigarettes be produced. According to the director of the Burn Council, the tobacco companies "enjoy having the cigarettes left unattended burn up. It is, I think, the ideal in planned obsolescence . . . to put out a product that will consume itself whether you're using it or not."

Now write *fact* or *opinion* before each statement below.

1. _____ Many fire codes were developed before modern synthetic materials were even heard of.

2. _____ Some synthetic materials produce poisonous gases when they burn.

3. _____ It's impossible to stop people from smoking in bed.

4. _____ Each year about 12,000 die as a result of fires.

5. _____ About 2,300 die because a cigarette dropped and continued to burn.

6. _____ A cigar stays lit only if someone is smoking it.

7. _____ "There are hundreds and hundreds of children lying in burn hospitals . . . as a result of a carelessly discarded cigarette."

8. _____ Tobacco companies "enjoy having the cigarettes left unattended burn up."

Assessing Data

Read each item below. Then answer the questions about conclusions and supporting data.

1. One spring morning in New Hampshire in the early 1980s, a state fish and wildlife worker was busy stocking streams and lakes with trout for that summer's fishers. As he released a batch into one pond, an astonishing thing happened. The young fish tried to swim back to shore. To the man, the trout writhed and squirmed the way a fish on land does as it desperately gasps for oxygen. Later, tests revealed a high acid content in the pond. Acid rain, it seems, had made the pond unfit for fish.

   a. What conclusion did the author reach about the pond?

   _____

   b. What two pieces of evidence did the author include to support that conclusion?

   _____

   _____

2. Plants became quite different from green algae when they became adapted to living on land. Land offered plants many advantages, such as abundant sunlight and space. But living on land also had disadvantages. Plants were in danger of drying out on land. Water was not immediately available as it was to algae that lived in water. But plants adapted to a land environment. Their roots can reach water below ground, and a waxy coating on their leaves helps prevent water loss. Stiff cell walls support plants, enabling them to grow upright toward the sun. Also, a layer around the reproductive structures protects the spores and gametes from drying out. These adaptations helped plants to become very successful.

   a. What conclusion does the author draw about plants' ability to adapt?

   _____

   b. What four pieces of evidence does the author include to support that conclusion?

   _____

   _____

   _____

   _____

Drawing Conclusions

Use the information in each item to draw your own conclusion.

1. Archaeologists have found the fossil remains of shellfish at high altitudes in the Andes Mountains of South America. What does the presence of such fossils suggest about that location?

_____

2. What can you conclude about the effect of cold temperatures on insects?

_____

_____

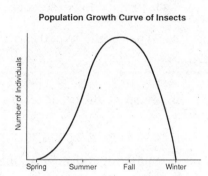

Population Growth Curve of Insects

3. When gas is heated to very high temperatures, its structure changes. The intense heat causes the gas atoms to split into negatively and positively charged particles. This gas of very hot charged particles is plasma. Plasmas exist in only a few places on earth. One place is inside a neon or fluorescent light bulb. Electricity provides the heat in these bulbs. In space, plasmas are very common.
What must be true about certain areas of outer space for plasmas to exist there?

_____

4. When a woman turned her microwave oven on, the microwave, dishwasher, television set, and lights all went out. She immediately turned the oven off and went to check the circuit breakers. One was off, and as she turned it on, all the other electrical appliances came on.
What can you conclude was the reason the power went off?

_____

5. __
The Planets' Orbits and Periods of Revolution

Planet	Length of Orbit Compared to Earth's	Period of Revolution
Earth	1.0	1.0 year
Mercury	0.4	0.2 year (88 days)
Venus	0.7	0.7 year (243 days)

What conclusion can you draw about the speed of Mercury's orbit compared to Earth's?

_____

Testing Hypotheses

Read each situation described below. Pay attention to the hypothesis stated. Think how the hypothesis could be tested.

1. For years many people have complained about feeling depressed during the winter months but happy or at least content during summer. Researchers now believe that the limited amount of sunlight in the winter may be the cause of the depression. They call such low feelings "seasonal affective disorder," or SAD.

   a. What is the hypothesis concerning SAD?

   _____

   b. What could be done to test whether the hypothesis is true?

   _____

2. A man bought a new trouble flashlight for his truck and inserted a 6-volt battery he had had at home. The flashlight did not work. The man felt the cause was most likely that the battery was dead.

   a. What is the man's hypothesis?

   _____

   b. What could he do to test his hypothesis?

   _____

3. A woman planted tomatoes in an 18-inch planter on her balcony in the city but was disappointed when the plants yielded little. When she dug the plants up in the fall, she saw that the roots of each were short and confined. She concluded that she must have planted the tomatoes too close together.

   a. What was the woman's hypothesis?

   _____

   b. What could she do next summer to test her hypothesis?

   _____

Thinking About the Nonfiction You've Read

Answer these questions about the nonfiction selection you've just read.

1. In your own words, summarize the author's main idea.

_____

_____

_____

2. Give one or two details that the author used to support that main idea.

_____

_____

3. Are there any figures of speech, descriptions, or other uses of
   words that you found interesting? If so, write them here.

_____

_____

4. Are there any words you don't know? If so, try to determine their
   meanings from the context and write the meanings here. Then
   check the definitions in a dictionary.

_____

_____

_____

5. Did you learn anything interesting from this selection? If so,
   explain what it was.

_____

_____

_____

6. Did you enjoy reading this nonfiction selection? Why or why not?

_____

_____

Thinking About the Commentary You've Read

Answer these questions about the piece of commentary you've just read.

1. In your own words, summarize the author's main idea.

_____

_____

_____

2. Give one or two details that the author used to support that main idea.

_____

_____

3. Are there any figures of speech, descriptions, or other uses of words that you found interesting? If so, write them here.

_____

_____

4. Are there any words you don't know? If so, try to determine their meanings from the context and write the meanings here. Then check the definitions in a dictionary.

_____

_____

_____

5. How did the author feel about the subject? Describe the tone here. Try to give some examples from the commentary.

_____

_____

_____

6. Do you disagree with any idea the author had? If so, explain why.

_____

_____

7. Did you enjoy reading this commentary? Why or why not?

_____

_____

Thinking About the Story You've Read

Answer these questions about the story you've just read.

1. In your own words, summarize what happened in the story selection.

    _____

    _____

2a. Name the characters in the story. Describe how you imagine each character looks.

    _____

    _____

 b. Tell what kind of person each character seems to be. Use details from the story to explain your answer.

    _____

    _____

3. Can you tell what the setting of the story is? If so, write it here. Explain how you know.

    _____

4. Are there any figures of speech, descriptions, or other uses of words that you found interesting? If so, write them here.

    _____

    _____

5. Are there any words you don't know? If so, try to determine their meanings from the context and write the meanings here. Then check the definitions in a dictionary.

    _____

    _____

6. What is the mood of the story? Explain your answer.

    _____

    _____

7. Did you enjoy reading this story? Why or why not?

    _____

Thinking About the Drama You've Read

Answer these questions about the drama selection you've just read.

1. In your own words, summarize what happened in the drama selection.

_____

_____

_____

2a. Name the characters in the drama. Describe how you imagine each character looks.

_____

_____

_____

b. Tell what kind of person each character seems to be. Use details from the drama to explain your answer.

_____

_____

_____

3. Can you tell what the setting of the selection is? If so, write it here. Explain how you know.

_____

4. Are there any words you don't know? If so, try to determine their meanings from the context and write the meanings here. Then check the definitions in a dictionary.

_____

_____

_____

5. What is the mood of the selection? Explain your answer.

_____

6. Did you enjoy reading this drama selection? Why or why not?

_____

_____

Thinking About the Poem You've Read

Answer these questions about the poem you've just read.

1. In your own words, summarize the meaning of the poem.

_____

_____

2a. What is the title of the poem?

_____

  b. Does the title help you understand what the poem is about? If so, how?

_____

_____

3. Are there any figures of speech, descriptions, or other uses of words that you found interesting? If so, write them here.

_____

_____

4. Are there any words you don't know? If so, try to determine their meanings from the context and write the meanings here. Then check the definitions in a dictionary.

_____

_____

5. How did the poem make you feel? Describe the mood of the poem here.

_____

6. Can you apply anything you learned in the poem to your own life? If so, explain what.

_____

_____

_____

7. Did you enjoy reading this poem? Why or why not?

_____

_____

Getting the Main Idea

As you read each selection below, try to understand the author's main idea.

When Gracie had a migraine, she would tie a damp bandana as tightly as possible around her forehead and lie down in a dark, absolutely quiet room. But if she had a show to do, she worked. No matter what happened, she worked. Once, in vaudeville, for example, we were playing in Oakland and after our last show we were in a cab going back across the bridge to San Francisco. Gracie was asleep, her head resting against my shoulder. Suddenly the cab stopped short and she went flying forward, smashing her face against the partition and breaking her nose. We rushed to St. Mary's Hospital where they stopped the bleeding and bandaged her nose. In those days the best painkiller was ice; it wasn't addictive and it was particularly effective if you poured some whiskey over it. Gracie didn't miss a single performance. She was in pain and could barely speak, but she did three shows the next day. In fact, the cab company refused to pay any damages, claiming we didn't lose anything because Gracie had worked the next day.

1. In your own words, what is the main idea of the selection above?

_____

_____

War is always attractive to young men who know nothing about it, but we had also been seduced into uniform by Kennedy's challenge to "ask what you can do for your country" and by the missionary idealism he had awakened in us. America seemed omnipotent then: the country could still claim it had never lost a war, and we believed we were ordained to play cop to the Communists' robber and spread our own political faith around the world. Like the French soldiers of the late eighteenth century, we saw ourselves as the champions of "a cause that was destined to triumph." So, when we marched into the rice paddies on that damp March afternoon, we carried, along with our packs and rifles, the implicit convictions that the Viet Cong would be quickly beaten and that we were doing something altogether noble and good. We kept the packs and rifles; the convictions, we lost.

2. In your own words, summarize the main idea of the selection above.

_____

_____

Inferences

Read the following selection from a short story.

Trembling, weak with emotion, her eyes on the silent figure, Mrs. Smith hurried up to the fence. . . . The oldest boy ran a little ahead. He will never forget that figure, that face. It will always remain as something epic, that return of the private. He fixed his eyes on the pale face covered with a ragged bear.

"Who *are* you, sir?" asked the wife, or, rather, started to ask, for he turned, stood a moment, and then cried:

"Emma!"

"Edward!"

The children stood in a curious row to see their mother kiss this bearded, strange man, the elder girl sobbing sympathetically with her mother. Illness had left the soldier partly deaf, and this added to the strangeness of his manner.

But the youngest child stood away, even after the girl had recognized her father and kissed him. The man turned then to the baby, and said in a curiously unpaternal tone:

"Come here, my little man; don't you know me?" But the baby backed away under the fence and stood peering at him critically.

"My little man!" What meaning in those words! This baby seemed like some other woman's child, and not the infant he had left in his wife's arms. The war had come between him and his baby—he was only a strange man to him. . . .

"And this is Tom," the private said, drawing the oldest boy to him. "*He'll* come and see me. *He* knows his poor old pap when he comes home from the war."

The mother heard the pain and reproach in his voice and hastened to apologize.

1. Where does this scene in the story take place? How do you know?

_____

2. What is the man's relationship to the others in the scene? How do you know?

_____

3. Where has the man been? How do you know?

_____

4. How does the baby feel about the man? How do you know?

_____

5. How does the man feel about the baby's reaction? How do you know?

_____

Basic Arithmetic Facts

See how quickly you can do these problems. Write your starting time below and then your finishing time. If you get any problems wrong, your teacher can give you a new sheet to practice again. Try to work the problems in 3 minutes because that is how long a GED grad takes.

Starting time: _____ Finishing time: _____ Solving time: _____

A. 5 +2	8 +0	3 +3	6 +1	0 +7	1 +3	4 +4	5 +9	7 +9	2 +0
B. 6 +0	7 +7	9 +8	0 +9	1 +1	4 +3	3 +5	6 +6	0 +0	2 +4
C. 9 +9	3 +2	8 +7	8 +1	6 +2	1 +5	0 +1	5 +5	1 +8	7 +2
D. 6 +3	0 +6	7 +1	4 +7	3 +8	4 +5	2 +8	9 +1	0 +8	1 +6
E. 4 +0	8 +3	1 +4	3 +7	5 +4	6 +5	3 +0	8 +5	9 +4	0 +2
F. 7 +4	2 +2	8 +4	6 +8	4 +1	1 +9	3 +6	9 +7	4 +6	3 +9
G. 9 +5	5 +0	2 +1	0 +4	8 +6	5 +7	6 +9	1 +2	9 +3	2 +6
H. 5 +1	1 +7	6 +4	8 +2	4 +9	7 +0	0 +3	7 +6	2 +3	1 +0
I. 9 +0	3 +4	7 +3	5 +6	4 +2	2 +9	0 +5	8 +8	7 +5	9 +2
J. 3 +1	7 +8	9 +6	2 +7	5 +3	4 +8	6 +7	5 +8	8 +9	2 +5

Basic Subtraction Facts

See how quickly you can do these problems. Write your starting time below and then your finishing time. If you get any problems wrong, your teacher can give you a new sheet to practice again. Try to work the problems in 3 minutes because that is how long a GED grad takes.

Starting time: _____ Finishing time: _____ Solving time: _____

A. $5-4$ $7-3$ $2-1$ $17-8$ $14-6$ $3-0$ $9-7$ $6-5$ $5-1$ $8-8$

B. $15-9$ $12-6$ $8-4$ $3-2$ $11-5$ $2-2$ $7-5$ $4-3$ $14-7$ $18-9$

C. $10-7$ $6-3$ $9-1$ $13-7$ $8-1$ $13-9$ $11-2$ $9-9$ $12-5$ $11-7$

D. $8-0$ $10-4$ $13-4$ $8-3$ $6-2$ $1-0$ $3-3$ $6-4$ $9-3$ $12-8$

E. $9-2$ $5-3$ $11-9$ $7-0$ $9-6$ $15-8$ $17-9$ $4-1$ $10-3$ $6-6$

F. $10-1$ $7-4$ $1-1$ $6-0$ $12-4$ $14-9$ $5-2$ $9-4$ $4-2$ $16-8$

G. $7-2$ $11-4$ $13-8$ $9-8$ $4-4$ $15-7$ $7-6$ $4-0$ $10-5$ $2-0$

H. $11-3$ $8-5$ $5-0$ $7-7$ $14-5$ $10-6$ $8-7$ $13-6$ $10-9$ $6-1$

I. $11-6$ $7-1$ $16-7$ $12-7$ $5-5$ $8-2$ $11-8$ $10-2$ $3-1$ $10-8$

J. $9-0$ $12-3$ $8-6$ $9-5$ $13-5$ $15-6$ $14-8$ $12-9$ $0-0$ $16-9$

Basic Multiplication Facts

See how quickly you can do these problems. Write your starting time below and then your finishing time. If you get any problems wrong, your teacher can give you a new sheet to practice again. Try to work the problems in 3 minutes because that is how long a GED grad takes.

Starting time: _____ Finishing time: _____ Solving time: _____

A.
$$\begin{array}{r} 2 \\ \times 2 \\ \hline \end{array} \quad \begin{array}{r} 5 \\ \times 4 \\ \hline \end{array} \quad \begin{array}{r} 8 \\ \times 1 \\ \hline \end{array} \quad \begin{array}{r} 3 \\ \times 7 \\ \hline \end{array} \quad \begin{array}{r} 0 \\ \times 4 \\ \hline \end{array} \quad \begin{array}{r} 6 \\ \times 6 \\ \hline \end{array} \quad \begin{array}{r} 3 \\ \times 9 \\ \hline \end{array} \quad \begin{array}{r} 9 \\ \times 2 \\ \hline \end{array} \quad \begin{array}{r} 7 \\ \times 4 \\ \hline \end{array} \quad \begin{array}{r} 1 \\ \times 1 \\ \hline \end{array}$$

B.
$$\begin{array}{r} 4 \\ \times 3 \\ \hline \end{array} \quad \begin{array}{r} 2 \\ \times 6 \\ \hline \end{array} \quad \begin{array}{r} 7 \\ \times 7 \\ \hline \end{array} \quad \begin{array}{r} 5 \\ \times 1 \\ \hline \end{array} \quad \begin{array}{r} 9 \\ \times 0 \\ \hline \end{array} \quad \begin{array}{r} 1 \\ \times 3 \\ \hline \end{array} \quad \begin{array}{r} 3 \\ \times 8 \\ \hline \end{array} \quad \begin{array}{r} 5 \\ \times 2 \\ \hline \end{array} \quad \begin{array}{r} 8 \\ \times 2 \\ \hline \end{array} \quad \begin{array}{r} 0 \\ \times 6 \\ \hline \end{array}$$

C.
$$\begin{array}{r} 7 \\ \times 2 \\ \hline \end{array} \quad \begin{array}{r} 9 \\ \times 5 \\ \hline \end{array} \quad \begin{array}{r} 3 \\ \times 4 \\ \hline \end{array} \quad \begin{array}{r} 1 \\ \times 2 \\ \hline \end{array} \quad \begin{array}{r} 7 \\ \times 0 \\ \hline \end{array} \quad \begin{array}{r} 8 \\ \times 6 \\ \hline \end{array} \quad \begin{array}{r} 4 \\ \times 7 \\ \hline \end{array} \quad \begin{array}{r} 2 \\ \times 3 \\ \hline \end{array} \quad \begin{array}{r} 3 \\ \times 1 \\ \hline \end{array} \quad \begin{array}{r} 0 \\ \times 0 \\ \hline \end{array}$$

D.
$$\begin{array}{r} 8 \\ \times 4 \\ \hline \end{array} \quad \begin{array}{r} 1 \\ \times 7 \\ \hline \end{array} \quad \begin{array}{r} 6 \\ \times 2 \\ \hline \end{array} \quad \begin{array}{r} 4 \\ \times 5 \\ \hline \end{array} \quad \begin{array}{r} 3 \\ \times 6 \\ \hline \end{array} \quad \begin{array}{r} 9 \\ \times 8 \\ \hline \end{array} \quad \begin{array}{r} 2 \\ \times 5 \\ \hline \end{array} \quad \begin{array}{r} 6 \\ \times 3 \\ \hline \end{array} \quad \begin{array}{r} 5 \\ \times 9 \\ \hline \end{array} \quad \begin{array}{r} 7 \\ \times 8 \\ \hline \end{array}$$

E.
$$\begin{array}{r} 0 \\ \times 2 \\ \hline \end{array} \quad \begin{array}{r} 6 \\ \times 1 \\ \hline \end{array} \quad \begin{array}{r} 2 \\ \times 9 \\ \hline \end{array} \quad \begin{array}{r} 4 \\ \times 6 \\ \hline \end{array} \quad \begin{array}{r} 9 \\ \times 4 \\ \hline \end{array} \quad \begin{array}{r} 7 \\ \times 5 \\ \hline \end{array} \quad \begin{array}{r} 5 \\ \times 5 \\ \hline \end{array} \quad \begin{array}{r} 1 \\ \times 8 \\ \hline \end{array} \quad \begin{array}{r} 7 \\ \times 6 \\ \hline \end{array} \quad \begin{array}{r} 4 \\ \times 0 \\ \hline \end{array}$$

F.
$$\begin{array}{r} 8 \\ \times 3 \\ \hline \end{array} \quad \begin{array}{r} 1 \\ \times 5 \\ \hline \end{array} \quad \begin{array}{r} 6 \\ \times 4 \\ \hline \end{array} \quad \begin{array}{r} 0 \\ \times 5 \\ \hline \end{array} \quad \begin{array}{r} 9 \\ \times 3 \\ \hline \end{array} \quad \begin{array}{r} 5 \\ \times 7 \\ \hline \end{array} \quad \begin{array}{r} 4 \\ \times 2 \\ \hline \end{array} \quad \begin{array}{r} 7 \\ \times 1 \\ \hline \end{array} \quad \begin{array}{r} 2 \\ \times 7 \\ \hline \end{array} \quad \begin{array}{r} 6 \\ \times 8 \\ \hline \end{array}$$

G.
$$\begin{array}{r} 9 \\ \times 6 \\ \hline \end{array} \quad \begin{array}{r} 4 \\ \times 4 \\ \hline \end{array} \quad \begin{array}{r} 0 \\ \times 3 \\ \hline \end{array} \quad \begin{array}{r} 1 \\ \times 9 \\ \hline \end{array} \quad \begin{array}{r} 6 \\ \times 7 \\ \hline \end{array} \quad \begin{array}{r} 4 \\ \times 1 \\ \hline \end{array} \quad \begin{array}{r} 2 \\ \times 8 \\ \hline \end{array} \quad \begin{array}{r} 3 \\ \times 3 \\ \hline \end{array} \quad \begin{array}{r} 8 \\ \times 5 \\ \hline \end{array} \quad \begin{array}{r} 1 \\ \times 0 \\ \hline \end{array}$$

H.
$$\begin{array}{r} 3 \\ \times 0 \\ \hline \end{array} \quad \begin{array}{r} 5 \\ \times 3 \\ \hline \end{array} \quad \begin{array}{r} 1 \\ \times 4 \\ \hline \end{array} \quad \begin{array}{r} 7 \\ \times 3 \\ \hline \end{array} \quad \begin{array}{r} 8 \\ \times 8 \\ \hline \end{array} \quad \begin{array}{r} 5 \\ \times 6 \\ \hline \end{array} \quad \begin{array}{r} 6 \\ \times 0 \\ \hline \end{array} \quad \begin{array}{r} 2 \\ \times 1 \\ \hline \end{array} \quad \begin{array}{r} 0 \\ \times 7 \\ \hline \end{array} \quad \begin{array}{r} 9 \\ \times 9 \\ \hline \end{array}$$

I.
$$\begin{array}{r} 5 \\ \times 8 \\ \hline \end{array} \quad \begin{array}{r} 0 \\ \times 9 \\ \hline \end{array} \quad \begin{array}{r} 8 \\ \times 7 \\ \hline \end{array} \quad \begin{array}{r} 9 \\ \times 1 \\ \hline \end{array} \quad \begin{array}{r} 2 \\ \times 0 \\ \hline \end{array} \quad \begin{array}{r} 0 \\ \times 8 \\ \hline \end{array} \quad \begin{array}{r} 4 \\ \times 8 \\ \hline \end{array} \quad \begin{array}{r} 7 \\ \times 9 \\ \hline \end{array} \quad \begin{array}{r} 6 \\ \times 5 \\ \hline \end{array} \quad \begin{array}{r} 1 \\ \times 6 \\ \hline \end{array}$$

J.
$$\begin{array}{r} 9 \\ \times 7 \\ \hline \end{array} \quad \begin{array}{r} 5 \\ \times 0 \\ \hline \end{array} \quad \begin{array}{r} 4 \\ \times 9 \\ \hline \end{array} \quad \begin{array}{r} 8 \\ \times 9 \\ \hline \end{array} \quad \begin{array}{r} 0 \\ \times 1 \\ \hline \end{array} \quad \begin{array}{r} 2 \\ \times 4 \\ \hline \end{array} \quad \begin{array}{r} 3 \\ \times 5 \\ \hline \end{array} \quad \begin{array}{r} 8 \\ \times 0 \\ \hline \end{array} \quad \begin{array}{r} 3 \\ \times 2 \\ \hline \end{array} \quad \begin{array}{r} 6 \\ \times 9 \\ \hline \end{array}$$

Basic Division Facts

See how quickly you can do these problems. Write your starting time below and then your finishing time. If you get any problems wrong, your teacher can give you a new sheet to practice again. Try to work the problems in 3 minutes because that is how long a GED grad takes.

Starting time: _____ Finishing time: _____ Solving time: _____

A. $6\overline{)12}$ $5\overline{)20}$ $1\overline{)4}$ $2\overline{)8}$ $9\overline{)9}$ $3\overline{)15}$ $8\overline{)16}$

B. $9\overline{)36}$ $2\overline{)14}$ $3\overline{)3}$ $7\overline{)0}$ $4\overline{)8}$ $6\overline{)36}$ $9\overline{)27}$

C. $7\overline{)42}$ $5\overline{)25}$ $2\overline{)4}$ $1\overline{)1}$ $3\overline{)9}$ $9\overline{)45}$ $3\overline{)27}$

D. $6\overline{)24}$ $2\overline{)10}$ $1\overline{)3}$ $2\overline{)6}$ $5\overline{)0}$ $4\overline{)32}$ $7\overline{)21}$

E. $5\overline{)40}$ $7\overline{)56}$ $4\overline{)4}$ $8\overline{)0}$ $1\overline{)2}$ $9\overline{)72}$ $4\overline{)20}$

F. $6\overline{)42}$ $3\overline{)18}$ $1\overline{)0}$ $1\overline{)8}$ $7\overline{)7}$ $8\overline{)40}$ $9\overline{)63}$

G. $7\overline{)14}$ $4\overline{)24}$ $5\overline{)5}$ $2\overline{)0}$ $1\overline{)5}$ $9\overline{)81}$ $3\overline{)21}$

H. $5\overline{)10}$ $3\overline{)24}$ $6\overline{)0}$ $3\overline{)6}$ $6\overline{)6}$ $7\overline{)49}$ $2\overline{)12}$

I. $9\overline{)18}$ $8\overline{)64}$ $2\overline{)16}$ $8\overline{)32}$ $4\overline{)16}$ $5\overline{)45}$ $6\overline{)30}$

J. $6\overline{)18}$ $3\overline{)12}$ $4\overline{)28}$ $9\overline{)54}$ $8\overline{)72}$ $6\overline{)48}$ $4\overline{)36}$

K. $7\overline{)35}$ $4\overline{)0}$ $1\overline{)6}$ $5\overline{)35}$ $8\overline{)8}$ $4\overline{)12}$ $8\overline{)24}$

L. $3\overline{)0}$ $1\overline{)9}$ $8\overline{)56}$ $1\overline{)7}$ $2\overline{)18}$ $8\overline{)48}$ $9\overline{)0}$

M. $2\overline{)2}$ $7\overline{)49}$ $5\overline{)15}$ $7\overline{)28}$ $5\overline{)30}$ $6\overline{)54}$

Adding and Subtracting Whole Numbers

Try to do these addition problems in 4 minutes.

Starting time: _____ Finishing time: _____ Solving time: _____

1a. 12 + 56	**b.** 72 + 19	**c.** 63 + 27	**d.** 55 + 45	**e.** 83 + 59	**f.** 156 + 65	**g.** 210 + 44

2a. 512 +79   **b.** 290 +584   **c.** 671 +619   **d.** 185 +866   **e.** 906 +294   **f.** 1,338 +2,491   **g.** 5,445 +5,786

3a. 22 70 + 35   **b.** 54 35 + 62   **c.** 80 32 + 48   **d.** 47 69 + 42   **e.** 11 99 + 25   **f.** 56 67 + 81   **g.** 16 39 + 23

4a. 124 431 +420   **b.** 212 330 +549   **c.** 526 109 +721   **d.** 666 305 +503   **e.** 724 562 +574   **f.** 812 843 + 857   **g.** 142 968 + 535

Try to do these subtraction problems in 5 minutes.

Starting time: _____ Finishing time: _____ Solving time: _____

5a. 56 − 12   **b.** 20 − 13   **c.** 35 − 18   **d.** 72 − 28   **e.** 90 − 45   **f.** 44 − 23

6a. 562 − 90   **b.** 403 − 15   **c.** 676 − 28   **d.** 931 − 55   **e.** 522 − 74   **f.** 610 − 75

7a. 212 − 188   **b.** 230 − 215   **c.** 925 − 587   **d.** 705 − 598   **e.** 349 − 169   **f.** 300 − 165

8a. 5,281 − 290   **b.** 4,090 − 362   **c.** 8,005 − 412   **d.** 6,972 − 888   **e.** 1,112 − 650   **f.** 4,000 − 965

9a. 2,525 −1,606   **b.** 6,098 −5,759   **c.** 3,210 −2,155   **d.** 3,205 −1,836   **e.** 9,640 −7,777   **f.** 4,006 −1,583

Multiplying and Dividing Whole Numbers

Try to do these multiplication problems in 4 minutes.

Starting time: _____ Finishing time: _____ Solving time: _____

1a. $\begin{array}{r} 15 \\ \times\ 4 \\ \hline \end{array}$	**b.** $\begin{array}{r} 22 \\ \times\ 3 \\ \hline \end{array}$	**c.** $\begin{array}{r} 54 \\ \times\ 5 \\ \hline \end{array}$	**d.** $\begin{array}{r} 35 \\ \times\ 5 \\ \hline \end{array}$	**e.** $\begin{array}{r} 76 \\ \times\ 8 \\ \hline \end{array}$	**f.** $\begin{array}{r} 46 \\ \times\ 7 \\ \hline \end{array}$	**g.** $\begin{array}{r} 89 \\ \times\ 9 \\ \hline \end{array}$
2a. $\begin{array}{r} 12 \\ \times\ 24 \\ \hline \end{array}$	**b.** $\begin{array}{r} 25 \\ \times\ 12 \\ \hline \end{array}$	**c.** $\begin{array}{r} 50 \\ \times\ 35 \\ \hline \end{array}$	**d.** $\begin{array}{r} 83 \\ \times\ 17 \\ \hline \end{array}$	**e.** $\begin{array}{r} 26 \\ \times\ 52 \\ \hline \end{array}$	**f.** $\begin{array}{r} 272 \\ \times\ 55 \\ \hline \end{array}$	**g.** $\begin{array}{r} 163 \\ \times\ 20 \\ \hline \end{array}$
3a. $\begin{array}{r} 125 \\ \times\ 16 \\ \hline \end{array}$	**b.** $\begin{array}{r} 423 \\ \times\ 31 \\ \hline \end{array}$	**c.** $\begin{array}{r} 564 \\ \times\ 45 \\ \hline \end{array}$	**d.** $\begin{array}{r} 1{,}906 \\ \times\ 64 \\ \hline \end{array}$	**e.** $\begin{array}{r} 2{,}575 \\ \times\ 20 \\ \hline \end{array}$	**f.** $\begin{array}{r} 3{,}333 \\ \times\ 36 \\ \hline \end{array}$	

Try to do these division problems in 6 minutes.

Starting time: _____ Finishing time: _____ Solving time: _____

4a. $5\overline{)725}$ **b.** $6\overline{)198}$ **c.** $3\overline{)288}$ **d.** $9\overline{)261}$ **e.** $8\overline{)675}$ **f.** $5\overline{)1{,}026}$

5a. $12\overline{)180}$ **b.** $24\overline{)576}$ **c.** $14\overline{)308}$ **d.** $35\overline{)630}$ **e.** $52\overline{)1{,}248}$

6a. $28\overline{)7{,}280}$ **b.** $35\overline{)7{,}420}$ **c.** $24\overline{)1{,}120}$ **d.** $55\overline{)1{,}375}$ **e.** $18\overline{)7{,}292}$

Adding and Subtracting Decimals

Try to do these addition problems in 3 minutes.

Starting time: _____ Finishing time: _____ Solving time: _____

1a. 1.2 + 0.5	**b.** 2.4 + 1.5	**c.** 3.9 + 0.4	**d.** 5.5 + 1.5	**e.** 7.5 + 6.6
2a. 12.59 + 5.12	**b.** 25.06 +10.75	**c.** 33.48 + 0.08	**d.** 20.05 65.55 +10.75	**e.** 38.69 58.69 +48.69
3a. 1.312 +5.008	**b.** 5.572 +9.004	**c.** 0.989 +0.852	**d.** 2.555 +2.755	**e.** 6.333 +3.798
4a. 19.99 + 0.5	**b.** 60.2 + 3.57	**c.** 35.02 39.6 +31.05	**d.** 5.2 10.98 + 0.5	**e.** 2.73 3.004 +8.5

Try to do these subtraction problems in 4 minutes.

Starting time: _____ Finishing time: _____ Solving time: _____

5a. 5.7 − 0.8	**b.** 4.2 − 1.5	**c.** 9.3 − 2.4	**d.** 5.5 − 4.6	**e.** 6.0 − 1.5
6a. 12.12 − 5.59	**b.** 5.05 − 3.65	**c.** 10.50 − 7.68	**d.** 10.08 − 1.99	**e.** 4.24 − 0.39
7a. 0.989 −0.852	**b.** 7.775 −1.085	**c.** 6.008 − 6.002	**d.** 8.080 −5.564	**e.** 4.203 −1.309
8a. 10.5 − 3.75	**b.** 6.08 − 5.9	**c.** 10.12 − 8.125	**d.** 9.005 −4.05	**e.** 3 − 1.05

Multiplying and Dividing Decimals

Try to do these multiplication problems in 6 minutes.

Starting time: _____ Finishing time: _____ Solving time: _____

1a. $\begin{array}{r} 25 \\ \times\ 0.5 \\ \hline \end{array}$	**b.** $\begin{array}{r} 16 \\ \times\ 0.4 \\ \hline \end{array}$	**c.** $\begin{array}{r} 12 \\ \times\ 0.3 \\ \hline \end{array}$	**d.** $\begin{array}{r} 28 \\ \times\ 1.6 \\ \hline \end{array}$	**e.** $\begin{array}{r} 30 \\ \times\ 2.5 \\ \hline \end{array}$	**f.** $\begin{array}{r} 55 \\ \times\ 3.3 \\ \hline \end{array}$
2a. $\begin{array}{r} 6.2 \\ \times\ 3 \\ \hline \end{array}$	**b.** $\begin{array}{r} 10.6 \\ \times\ 8 \\ \hline \end{array}$	**c.** $\begin{array}{r} 90.9 \\ \times\ 2 \\ \hline \end{array}$	**d.** $\begin{array}{r} 44.5 \\ \times\ 90 \\ \hline \end{array}$	**e.** $\begin{array}{r} 33.3 \\ \times\ 30 \\ \hline \end{array}$	**f.** $\begin{array}{r} 63.7 \\ \times\ 15 \\ \hline \end{array}$
3a. $\begin{array}{r} 10.2 \\ \times\ 2.5 \\ \hline \end{array}$	**b.** $\begin{array}{r} 7.7 \\ \times\ 7.7 \\ \hline \end{array}$	**c.** $\begin{array}{r} 22.1 \\ \times\ 5.3 \\ \hline \end{array}$	**d.** $\begin{array}{r} 68.6 \\ \times\ 4.4 \\ \hline \end{array}$	**e.** $\begin{array}{r} 59.9 \\ \times\ 1.0 \\ \hline \end{array}$	**f.** $\begin{array}{r} 15.5 \\ \times\ 3.5 \\ \hline \end{array}$
4a. $\begin{array}{r} 19.98 \\ \times\ 3 \\ \hline \end{array}$	**b.** $\begin{array}{r} 24 \\ \times\ 4.42 \\ \hline \end{array}$	**c.** $\begin{array}{r} 37.5 \\ \times\ 2.15 \\ \hline \end{array}$	**d.** $\begin{array}{r} 60.65 \\ \times\ 3.2 \\ \hline \end{array}$	**e.** $\begin{array}{r} 100.50 \\ \times\ 7 \\ \hline \end{array}$	**f.** $\begin{array}{r} 32.72 \\ \times\ 2.84 \\ \hline \end{array}$

Try to do these division problems in 3 minutes.

Starting time: _____ Finishing time: _____ Solving time: _____

5a. $2\overline{)7.2}$ **b.** $6\overline{)3.60}$ **c.** $5\overline{)25.55}$ **d.** $10\overline{)50.5}$ **e.** $7\overline{)0.49}$

6a. $1.5\overline{)60}$ **b.** $2.2\overline{)88}$ **c.** $0.9\overline{)81}$ **d.** $0.05\overline{)100}$ **e.** $1.2\overline{)6}$

7a. $8\overline{)1.64}$ **b.** $4.2\overline{)21}$ **c.** $1.8\overline{)0.054}$ **d.** $0.8\overline{)64.8}$ **e.** $3.3\overline{)9.9}$

8a. $0.9\overline{)0.81}$ **b.** $0.15\overline{)3.0}$ **c.** $2.8\overline{)0.56}$ **d.** $0.25\overline{)0.505}$

Multiplying and Dividing with Multiples of 10

Try to do these multiplication problems in 2 minutes.

Starting time: _____ Finishing time: _____ Solving time: _____

1a. 30 $\times$ 7	**b.** 20 $\times$ 6	**c.** 50 $\times$ 5	**d.** 150 $\times$ 2	**e.** 300 $\times$ 8	**f.** 450 $\times$ 8	**g.** 500 $\times$ 9
2a. 12 $\times$ 50	**b.** 61 $\times$ 20	**c.** 36 $\times$ 30	**d.** 99 $\times$ 10	**e.** 35 $\times$ 20	**f.** 54 $\times$ 40	**g.** 82 $\times$ 80
3a. 10 $\times$ 10	**b.** 20 $\times$ 30	**c.** 50 $\times$ 20	**d.** 40 $\times$ 40	**e.** 40 $\times$ 80	**f.** 700 $\times$ 20	**g.** 900 $\times$ 30
4a. 400 $\times$ 20	**b.** 500 $\times$ 50	**c.** 350 $\times$ 20	**d.** 660 $\times$ 50	**e.** 250 $\times$ 30	**f.** 740 $\times$ 20	**g.** 800 $\times$ 40

Try to do these division problems in 2 minutes.

Starting time: _____ Finishing time: _____ Solving time: _____

5a. $5\overline{)200}$ **b.** $9\overline{)1,800}$ **c.** $3\overline{)9,300}$ **d.** $40\overline{)1,600}$ **e.** $50\overline{)250}$

6a. $10\overline{)350}$ **b.** $10\overline{)240}$ **c.** $100\overline{)3,300}$ **d.** $100\overline{)6,800}$ **e.** $10\overline{)15,000}$

7a. $100\overline{)5,000}$ **b.** $15\overline{)3,000}$ **c.** $12\overline{)3,600}$ **d.** $20\overline{)1,000}$ **e.** $100\overline{)750}$

Try to do these multiplication problems in 2 minutes.

Starting time: _____ Finishing time: _____ Solving time: _____

8a. $550 \times 0.1 =$ _____ **b.** $10 \times 0.1 =$ _____ **c.** $230 \times 0.001 =$ _____

9a. $3 \times 0.01 =$ _____ **b.** $5.6 \times 100 =$ _____ **c.** $0.25 \times 1,000 =$ _____

10a. $1.75 \times 1,000 =$ _____ **b.** $6.56 \times 10 =$ _____ **c.** $3.33 \times 100 =$ _____

11a. $72 \times 0.1 =$ _____ **b.** $4.29 \times 1,000 =$ _____ **c.** $0.5 \times 0.001 =$ _____

Adding and Subtracting Fractions

Try to do these addition problems in 4 minutes.

Starting time: _____ Finishing time: _____ Solving time: _____

1a. $\frac{1}{5} + \frac{2}{5} =$ **b.** $\frac{1}{2} + \frac{1}{2} =$ **c.** $\frac{2}{7} + \frac{3}{7} =$ **d.** $5 + \frac{2}{3} =$ **e.** $4 + 1\frac{3}{4} =$

2a. $2\frac{1}{2} + \frac{1}{2} =$ **b.** $\frac{1}{6} + 5\frac{1}{6} =$ **c.** $1\frac{3}{8} + 1\frac{3}{8} =$ **d.** $\frac{1}{12} + \frac{7}{12} =$ **e.** $7 + 2\frac{3}{10} =$

3a. $\frac{1}{4} + \frac{1}{2} =$ **b.** $\frac{2}{3} + \frac{1}{2} =$ **c.** $\frac{3}{5} + \frac{3}{10} =$ **d.** $\frac{5}{12} + \frac{3}{4} =$ **e.** $\frac{5}{6} + \frac{3}{4} =$

4a. $1\frac{1}{2} + \frac{3}{4} =$ **b.** $2\frac{4}{5} + \frac{1}{10} =$ **c.** $6\frac{1}{3} + 1\frac{3}{4} =$ **d.** $\frac{9}{10} + \frac{9}{20} =$ **e.** $2\frac{1}{2} + 3\frac{1}{3} =$

Try to do these subtraction problems in 6 minutes.

Starting time: _____ Finishing time: _____ Solving time: _____

5a. $\frac{4}{5} - \frac{2}{5} =$ **b.** $\frac{2}{3} - \frac{1}{3} =$ **c.** $\frac{5}{7} - \frac{2}{7} =$ **d.** $1\frac{9}{10} - \frac{3}{10} =$ **e.** $5\frac{5}{6} - 2\frac{1}{6} =$

6a. $4 - \frac{1}{2} =$ **b.** $3 - 1\frac{1}{3} =$ **c.** $10 - 5\frac{2}{5} =$ **d.** $8 - \frac{15}{16} =$ **e.** $7 - 3\frac{1}{4} =$

7a. $\frac{3}{4} - \frac{1}{2} =$ **b.** $\frac{5}{6} - \frac{2}{3} =$ **c.** $\frac{9}{10} - \frac{1}{5} =$ **d.** $\frac{11}{12} - \frac{2}{3} =$ **e.** $\frac{5}{6} - \frac{1}{4} =$

8a. $5\frac{5}{6} - \frac{1}{3} =$ **b.** $4\frac{2}{3} - 1\frac{1}{2} =$ **c.** $1\frac{2}{5} - \frac{9}{10} =$ **d.** $6\frac{1}{2} - 5\frac{3}{4} =$ **e.** $6\frac{1}{5} - 3\frac{2}{3} =$

Multiplying and Dividing Fractions

Try to do these multiplication problems in 6 minutes.

Starting time: _____ Finishing time: _____ Solving time: _____

1a. $\frac{1}{2} \times \frac{1}{3} =$ **b.** $\frac{2}{3} \times \frac{3}{4} =$ **c.** $\frac{1}{4} \times \frac{1}{3} =$ **d.** $\frac{5}{8} \times \frac{1}{2} =$ **e.** $\frac{1}{12} \times \frac{1}{2} =$

2a. $5 \times \frac{1}{2} =$ **b.** $\frac{3}{4} \times 4 =$ **c.** $10 \times \frac{1}{2} =$ **d.** $\frac{11}{12} \times 12 =$ **e.** $\frac{2}{3} \times 8 =$

3a. $3\frac{1}{3} \times \frac{1}{2} =$ **b.** $2\frac{5}{7} \times 7 =$ **c.** $\frac{3}{4} \times 5\frac{5}{6} =$ **d.** $5 \times 1\frac{9}{10} =$ **e.** $10\frac{1}{2} \times 4 =$

4a. $1\frac{1}{2} \times 5\frac{1}{2} =$ **b.** $4\frac{2}{3} \times 3\frac{6}{7} =$ **c.** $3\frac{3}{8} \times 2\frac{8}{9} =$ **d.** $1\frac{1}{3} \times 1\frac{1}{12} =$ **e.** $1\frac{1}{8} \times 1\frac{1}{3} =$

Try to do these division problems in 6 minutes.

Starting time: _____ Finishing time: _____ Solving time: _____

5a. $\frac{1}{2} \div \frac{1}{3} =$ **b.** $\frac{1}{3} \div \frac{1}{2} =$ **c.** $\frac{1}{4} \div \frac{1}{2} =$ **d.** $\frac{5}{8} \div \frac{1}{8} =$ **e.** $\frac{4}{9} \div \frac{2}{3} =$

6a. $5 \div \frac{1}{3} =$ **b.** $\frac{1}{3} \div 5 =$ **c.** $4 \div \frac{2}{9} =$ **d.** $\frac{2}{9} \div 4 =$ **e.** $10 \div \frac{1}{2} =$

7a. $4\frac{1}{2} \div 5 =$ **b.** $5 \div 4\frac{1}{2} =$ **c.** $1\frac{2}{3} \div 6 =$ **d.** $6 \div 1\frac{2}{3} =$ **e.** $5\frac{1}{4} \div \frac{3}{4} =$

8a. $3\frac{2}{3} \div 2\frac{2}{3} =$ **b.** $10\frac{1}{2} \div 1\frac{1}{8} =$ **c.** $6\frac{1}{4} \div \frac{5}{8} =$ **d.** $7\frac{1}{2} \div 1\frac{2}{3} =$ **e.** $1\frac{5}{6} \div 3\frac{1}{3} =$

Rounding Numbers

1. **Round these numbers to the nearest ten.**

   a.   24 _____   c.   55 _____   e.   138 _____
   b.   62 _____   d.   89 _____   f.   267 _____

2. **Round these numbers to the nearest hundred.**

   a.   110 _____   c.   612 _____   e.   999 _____
   b.   585 _____   d.   750 _____   f.   1,219 _____

3. **Round these numbers to the nearest thousand.**

   a. 1,892 _____   c. 3,101 _____   e. 14,301 _____
   b. 7,871 _____   d. 6,500 _____   f. 21,920 _____

4. **Round these numbers to the nearest ten thousand.**

   a. 11,950 _____   c. 39,000 _____   e. 110,500 _____
   b. 63,856 _____   d. 22,400 _____   f. 529,612 _____

5. Tim Newman's car has 62,192 miles on it. How much is that, rounded to the nearest 1,000 miles?

   _____

6. The Mendozas pay $379 a month rent. How much is that, to the nearest $10?

   _____

7. Jackie Moses's new job will pay her $258 a week after deductions. How much is that, to the nearest $10?

   _____

8. Mike and Marie Kristan bought a new couch for $499. How much is that, rounded to the nearest $10?

   _____

9. The paid attendance at the ballpark was 28,152. Round this to the nearest 10,000.

   _____

10. Last year Judy Derva paid $2,182 in federal income tax. What is that, rounded to the nearest $100?

   _____

Estimating Answers

Estimate the answer to each word problem. First round the numbers you need. Then add, subtract, multiply, or divide.

1. The winning candidate for county sheriff got about 828,000 votes. The losing candidate got about 580,000 votes. About how many people voted in the election?

   _____

2. Mr. Wright takes home $264 pay each week. He pays $59 to rent his room each week. About how much money does he have left after paying his rent?

   _____

3. D. J. Jones spent $19.95 on an oil change for his car and $58.95 for a tune-up. About how much was the total bill?

   _____

4. Mitchell Wood drives 19 miles round trip to work each day. He works 5 days a week. About how many miles does he drive to and from work each week?

   _____

5. Mitchell gets 2 weeks' vacation each year. About how many miles does Mitchell drive to and from work each year?

   _____

6. Vicki Lemek must bake cookies for her son's class. There are 18 children in the class. Vicki makes a batch of 41 cookies. About how many cookies will each child get?

   _____

7. At a discount furniture store Jackson Silvers paid $49 for a kitchen table, $29 for two chairs, and $310 for a couch. About how much did he pay in all?

   _____

8. Emma Puhl had $3,289 withheld in income tax last year. She will get a refund of $112. About how much income tax did Emma owe for the year?

   _____

9. A sale advertised dresses for $29.95. About how much would 3 dresses cost?

   _____

Visualizing Word Problems: A

Read each word problem. Decide which diagram best shows the situation described in the problem. Circle the letter of that diagram. You don't have to solve the problems.

1. Larry Kohl runs 2.5 miles every day. How many miles does he run each week?

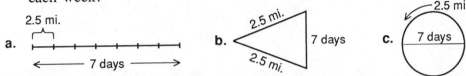

2. Shauna Gayle's gross pay each week is $250.00. Of that amount, $37.50 is withheld for federal income tax and $17.50 for Social Security. How much does Ms. Gayle take home each week?

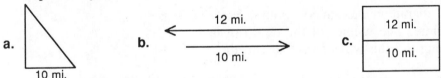

3. A salesman left his company and drove 10 miles west to stop at a customer's. Then he drove 12½ miles north to stop at a second customer's. From there he could get on the expressway and drive directly back to his company. How many miles did he drive on the expressway?

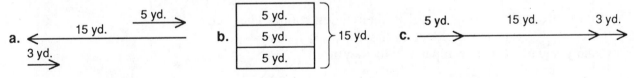

4. A running back ran for 5 yards on one play. The quarterback lost 15 yards on the next play. On the third play the running back ran for 3 yards. How many net yards did the team have so far?

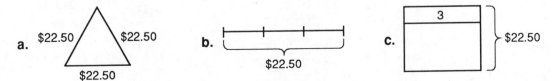

5. Three women went out to lunch and decided to split the bill evenly. If the total bill, including tip, was $22.50, how much did each woman pay?

Visualizing Word Problems: B

Read each word problem carefully. Then draw a diagram that shows the situation described in the problem. You don't have to solve the problems. Remember: There is more than one good way to picture a problem.

1. Wade Willis makes monthly car payments of $189.50 each. How much has he paid in one year for his car?

2. A dinner bill at a restaurant was $24.90. The tax was $0.75, and the tip was $3.75. How much was paid in all?

3. Jill Vavra works from 9 to 5. She gets 1 hour for lunch, a 15-minute break in the morning, and a 15-minute break in the afternoon. How many hours does she actually work each day?

4. An older man finished a local marathon race in 8½ hours. His son finished the race in half that time. The winner of the race finished in half the son's time. How long did the winner take to run the race?

5. The Elliots are wallpapering a wall in their living room. The wall is 20 feet by 10 feet, and the door in the wall is 4 feet by 9 feet. How many square feet of wallpaper will they need?

Choosing the Numbers You Need

Read each word problem carefully. Then write the information you need to solve the problem and the numbers you need to work with. You don't have to solve the problems. The first one is done as an example.

1. Douglas took Lana to the movies. The tickets cost $6.50 apiece. He bought 2 boxes of popcorn and 2 cups of soda pop for a total of $5.50. How much did the evening cost Douglas?

   cost of each ticket—$6.50

   how many tickets—2

   how much for food—$5.50

2. At a company 95 people are plant workers, 18 are office workers, and 7 are managers. What percentage of the company's employees are office workers?

3. A car dealer is offering incentives to buy: either a $500 rebate or 5% off. The Vargases want to buy a new car worth $10,499 and trade in their old car for $900. Which incentive should they take?

4. Two summers ago the company softball team won 10 of 12 games. Last summer the team won 7 of 12. This summer the team won 4 of 12. What is the average number of games the team has won in each season?

5. Mrs. Orsini is making a double batch of lasagna for a large family party. Her recipe calls for ⅜ pound of ground lean pork. The recipe feeds 12 people. How much pork will Mrs. Orsini need?

Deciding Which Operation to Use

Read each word problem carefully. Then decide which operation or operations you must use to solve it. Write the operations on the lines below the problems. You don't have to solve the problems.

1. Red delicious apples cost $0.98 a pound. How much will 2.5 pounds cost?

_____

2. Mimi Yops has a checking balance of $512.30. She writes checks for $30.00, $16.15, and $92.40. Then she deposits her paycheck of $412.66. What is her current balance?

_____

3. Jack Traynor bought a flashlight for $9.95 and batteries for $3.29. Sales tax is 6%. How much will Mr. Traynor pay in all?

_____

4. Gas costs $1.149 a gallon. How many gallons will $10.00 buy?

_____

5. On Friday Dave Janek bowled 160 and 175. On Saturday night he bowled 195, 163, and 177. What was his bowling average for those 5 games?

_____

6. An appliance saleswoman makes a salary of $100 a week. She makes 30% commission on what she sells. One week she sold $1,283 worth of appliances. How much did she earn that week altogether?

_____

7. The Kovachs are buying carpeting for 2 rooms. The living room is 15 feet by 12 feet, and the dining room is 12 feet by 9 feet. How many square feet of carpeting will they need to buy?

_____

8. On December 1 Dan weighed 189. On January 1 he weighed 195. Scientists estimate that 3,500 unused calories add 1 pound to a person's weight. How many calories did Dan eat in December that he did not burn up?

_____

Choosing the Right Setup

Read each word problem carefully. Select the correct way to solve the problem. Circle the letter of the setup you pick. You don't have to solve the problems.

1. The Phillips's car insurance went up 5% this year. They had been paying $526 a year. What will their insurance cost now?
   a. 526×0.05
   b. $\frac{526 \times 5}{12}$
   c. $(526 \times 0.05) + 526$

2. Marty Lieber wants to buy doughnuts for the 22 persons who work in his office. If he wants everyone to be able to have at least 2 doughnuts, how many dozen should he buy?
   a. $\frac{22 \times 2}{12}$
   b. 22×2
   c. $(22 + 12)2$

3. A store advertised 2 heads of lettuce for 89¢. How much would 3 heads of lettuce cost?
   a. $(89 \times 2) + 3$
   b. $\frac{89 \times 3}{2}$
   c. $\frac{89 \times 2}{3}$

4. Larissa gives massages at the health club. Her rates are as follows:
   $$\begin{array}{ll} \$25 & 30 \text{ minutes} \\ \$35 & 45 \text{ minutes} \\ \$45 & 60 \text{ minutes} \end{array}$$
   One day she gave 1 60-minute massage, 2 45-minute massages, and 2 30-minute massages. How much did she make that day?
   a. $45(60) + 35(45)2 + 25(30)2$
   b. $60 + 2(45) + 2(30)$
   c. $45 + 2(35) + 2(25)$

5. At the end of the day a store clerk had 5 pennies, 10 nickels, 20 dimes, and 14 quarters left in his change drawer. How much total change did he write on his balance sheet?
   a. $5(0.01) + 10(0.05) + 20(0.10) + 14(0.25)$
   b. $(5 + 10 + 20 + 14) \times (0.01 + 0.05 + 0.10 + 0.25)$
   c. $(5 \times 10 \times 20 \times 14) + (0.01 \times 0.05 \times 0.10 \times 0.25)$

6. The IRS allows a deduction of $0.28 per business mile driven. Fred drove his business car 22.5 miles on Monday, 30.0 miles on Wednesday, and 10.9 miles on Friday. How much will he be able to deduct for that week?
   a. $\frac{22.5 + 30.0 + 10.9}{0.28}$
   b. $(22.5 + 30.0 + 10.9)0.28$
   c. $(0.28 + 22.5)(30.0 + 10.9)$

Setting Up a Word Problem

Read each word problem carefully. Then write an expression that shows a way to set up the problem. You don't have to solve the problems.

1. A woman won $1,000 in a church raffle. She kept $200 for herself and then evenly divided the rest among her 5 sons. How much money did each son get?

_____

2. A phone call outside Steve Sand's local calling area costs 12¢ for the first minute and 4¢ for each minute after that. How much would a 20-minute call cost?

_____

3. A factory worker makes $9.00 an hour and time and a half for overtime. If he works 40 hours during the week and 5 hours overtime on Saturday, how much will he earn that week?

_____

4. Mary Wong will get a 5% raise this year. Her current salary is $18,500. How much will her annual salary be after her raise?

_____

5. Mr. Armas wants to limit his cholesterol intake to 300 mg a day. He has already eaten the following:

pork chop	100 mg
cheese	100 mg
butter pats	30 mg

How many more mg of cholesterol can he have today?

_____

6. A hardware store is advertising a special: 2 gallons of house paint for $18.99. How much would 5 gallons cost?

_____

7. Tania Wells charges $12 for a haircut and $40 for a permanent in her home. One Saturday she cut 5 persons' hair and gave 2 permanents. How much did she earn that day?

_____

Percent Problems

Read each word problem carefully. Then circle the letter of the grid that shows how to set up the problem. You don't have to solve the problems.

1. Of the approximately 500,000 people who voted for mayor in a city, 55% voted for the Democrat, 42% voted for the Republican, and 3% voted for an independent candidate. About how many votes did the winner get?

a.
part	percent
55	
whole	
500,000	100

b.
part	percent
	55
whole	
500,000	100

c.
part	percent
45	
whole	
55	100

2. The Smoliks have an account with a balance of $1,050. If they earn $52.50 in interest on that balance, what percent interest does the account earn?

a.
part	percent
52.50	
whole	
1,050	100

b.
part	percent
52.50	1,050
whole	
	100

c.
part	percent
	52.50
whole	
1,050	100

3. A store advertised 20% off VCRs. If the sale price was $39 off the original price, what does the VCR normally sell for?

a.
part	percent
20	39
whole	
	100

b.
part	percent
	20
whole	
39	100

c.
part	percent
39	20
whole	
	100

Read each word problem carefully. Then place the numbers you need to work with in the correct places in the equation and grid. You don't have to solve the problems.

4. Mr. Gaida paid $24 for a winter coat for his son. If the coat had been marked 40% off, what was its original price?

100% − 40% = _____

part	percent
whole	
	100

5. Today Peggy Charles makes $21,630 as an administrative aide. Last year she was making $21,000 at the same job. What was the percent increase of the raise she got?

21,630 − _____ = _____

change	percent
original	
	100

Answers

Writing Skills

Combining Sentences
(page 44)

A. Sample paragraph:

Many actors and extras in early Western movies were real cowboys. They had worked on ranches and in Wild West shows. They came to California because they had heard they could earn five dollars a day and a box lunch for riding and roping in the movies. Hoot Gibson was one of these cowboys. He had grown up in Nebraska, punching cattle and competing in rodeos. Gibson was a reckless stuntman who became a Western movie star.

B. Sample paragraph:

Today, people plant irises in flower gardens. Many years ago, people in Europe ate iris roots because they believed the roots cured many illnesses. People also chewed the roots to mask bad breath. They gave pieces of iris root to babies to teethe on. A certain kind of iris root, called orrisroot, is used today in perfumes, powders, and medicines.

Independent and Dependent Thoughts
(page 45)

Before the automobile was available**,** many people rode bicycles. Now, adults are riding bicycles again **because** they are concerned about physical fitness. The many bicycle types can be confusing**, but** you can find the one that is best for you. **When** you choose a bicycle**,** you should think about how you want to use the bicycle.

If you want a sturdy bicycle for errands and short trips**,** you will be happiest with a one-speed or a three-speed bike. However, some people want to take long rides up and down hills**, so** they need a touring or racing bike. These bikes have ten or more speeds**, and** they are lighter in weight.

The city bicycle is another type. **Although** it has many gears like a touring bicycle, it is sturdy like a three-speed bike. The all-terrain bicycle is even sturdier than the city bicycle. **Whether** you ride it on or off the pavement**,** it will perform well. Its many gears give it power **even when** it is going up steep slopes and through soft sandy areas.

Subject-Verb Agreement
(page 46)

A.
1. is
2. wears
3. travel
4. are
5. doesn't
6. runs
7. compete
8. receives
9. were
10. has

B. 1–2. Answers will vary. In each sentence *does* should be used correctly in the verb.

C. 1–2. Answers will vary. In each sentence *doesn't* should be used correctly in the verb.

Subject-Verb Agreement
(page 47)

A. When people **decide** to paint a room, they want to get started right away. However, there **are** good reasons to do some preparation first. Grease on a kitchen wall **keeps** paint from sticking well. Washing the walls **gets** rid of any dust or grease. Wiping with a mop **helps** clean the ceiling. New paint also **doesn't** hold well

to a shiny surface, like enamel. If the enamel is roughed up with sandpaper, new paint jobs **hold** better. Floor wax on the baseboards also **stops** paint from sticking. Wax remover **takes** it off. Professional painters **remove** the rust from radiators and pipes with sandpaper or steel wool. A careful painter then **puts** on metal primer. The painter should make sure each of these areas **is** dry before starting to paint.

B. 1–2. Answers will vary. In each sentence *get* should be used correctly as the verb.

C. 1–2. Answers will vary. In each sentence *gets* should be used correctly as the verb.

Verb Forms
(page 48)

A. Stevie Wonder **showed** his musical talent early in life. At 9 years of age, he played the piano, drum, and harmonica. Stevie had never **seen** the instruments he played; he had been blind since birth. His hearing, though, was very sensitive. If a coin was dropped, he **knew** what it was by the sound it made. His sensitivity to musical pitch and rhythm helped him sing and play like a much older performer.

Ronnie White, a singer with the Miracles, **saw** Stevie do a concert for his friends. Ronnie quickly **got** Stevie an audition with Berry Gordy, the president of Motown Records. Gordy immediately **gave** Stevie a five-year recording contract. At age 10, Stevie was a professional singer, but he was also still a kid. He kept on doing the things he had always **done.** The new recording artist still **ran** around the neighborhood with his friends and rode a bicycle while his brother steered. He got by on a weekly allowance of $2.50. During this period, he **did** concerts mostly on weekends. His remarkable talent continued to develop. By the time he was 12, he had **become** a star.

B. 1–2. Answers will vary. In each sentence *saw* should be used correctly in the verb.

C. 1–2. Answers will vary. In each sentence *seen* should be used correctly in the verb.

Verb Forms
(page 49)

A. *On the Waterfront* is a movie classic that first **came** out in 1954. Frank Sinatra had **gone** out for the leading role, but the director **gave** it to Marlon Brando. Brando played Terry Malloy, a longshoreman who also **did** errands for the head of the local longshoremen's union. The movie is about corruption and violence. Terry is an ex-boxer who **threw** an important fight and ruined his career in the ring. He knows that the union boss that he works for now has **stolen** money from the union. Recently, Terry **brought** a friend, Joey, to a rooftop meeting, which resulted in Joey's death. Before long, Terry has **fallen** in love with Joey's sister, Edie. He has **chosen** to risk his life in the fight for an honest union. However, he feels that if Edie **knew** the things he had **done,** she would hate him. A suspenseful story and powerful performances make *On the Waterfront* a movie that still **appeals** to audiences today.

B. 1–2. Answers will vary. In each sentence *did* should be used correctly in the verb.

C. 1–2. Answers will vary. In each sentence *done* should be used correctly in the verb.

Spelling Plurals
(page 50)

abilities	bargains
aches	bushes
aisles	companies
analyses	deeds
answers	dollars

emergencies	potatoes
entrances	rhythms
guesses	roles
halves	rolls
heroes	sandwiches
judgments	sighs
libraries	sites
loaves	souls
morals	speeches
neighbors	titles
nickels	tongues
nieces	veins
pears	views
policemen	weeks

Plurals and Possessive Nouns
(page 51)

A. A **person's** right to vote is an important right. Most U.S. **citizens** aged 18 or older can vote if they are registered. **Persons** who have been convicted of certain crimes lose their right to vote. A few other groups of people do not have voting rights.

Voters must go to the correct polling place. A **voter's** polling location depends on where the voter lives. Each state is divided into **counties** or **wards.** These are further divided into **precincts.** Voters must go to the polling place in the precinct where they live. Election **officials** check each name against the **precinct's** registration list.

U.S. **citizens** vote by secret ballot. A secret **ballot's** advantage is that voters don't have to worry about what **others** will think of their vote. Voters go into a curtained booth to mark their **ballots.**

B. 1–2. Answers will vary. In each sentence *company's* should be used correctly.

C. 1–2. Answers will vary. In each sentence *companies* should be used correctly.

Possessive Pronouns and Contractions
(page 52)

A.
1. you're
2. it's
3. your; your
4. their
5. they're; their
6. it's
7. you're
8. it's
9. they're
10. its
11. its
12. who's
13. Whose

B. 1–2. Answers will vary. In each sentence *it's* should be used correctly.

C. 1–2. Answers will vary. In each sentence *its* should be used correctly.

Punctuation
(page 53)

I recently saw one of your products at a friend's house. It was called the Sleeper, and it plugged into an electrical outlet. By moving the dial, you could get the sound of rain, a waterfall, or waves on a beach. My friend said it masked the sounds of street traffic; therefore, it helped him get to sleep and stay asleep. He bought it about three years ago from *Lindley's,* a mail-order catalog. Do you still make the Sleeper? If you do, let me know how I can get one. Please answer as soon as possible. I would like to give it as a gift.

Capitalization
(page 54)

I enjoyed **A**lbert **W**inslow's article on opportunities in the state of **O**hio. However, I would like to point out a few errors that I noticed. First of all, **C**leveland is the largest city in the state, but it is not the capital, nor is it the location of **O**hio **U**niversity. Also, the shoreline along **L**ake **E**rie is mostly rocky as he describes it, but there are some sandy beaches. His discussion of **C**incinnati's **R**iver **F**estival should have mentioned that it takes place in **A**ugust. His section on **O**hio's history stated that **G**eneral **A**nthony **W**ayne built **F**ort **G**oodwill. The correct name of the fort was **F**ort **R**ecovery. Finally, his list of **U.S.** leaders born in **O**hio left out **P**resident **U**lysses **S.** **G**rant. I was glad **M**r. **W**inslow liked **O**hio, but I think next time he should try to keep his facts straight.

Organizing Ideas
(page 55)

A. Sample paragraph:
  Regular exercise has many benefits. First of all, the person who exercises regularly has a good time. He or she has the fun of taking part in a sport or other activity and being with friends. People who exercise regularly also usually find that they have more energy and feel more relaxed. In addition, they tone up their muscles and burn off fat when they exercise, so they look better.
B. Sample map:

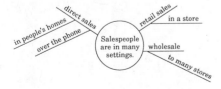

Writing Topic Sentences
(page 56)

Sample topic sentences:
A. Everyone dreams every night.
B. Wild animals don't make good pets.
C. Atlanta is a growing city.

Transitions
(page 57)

Following a budget helps people keep from running out of money. **In addition,** a budget helps people spend their money for the things they need or want most. **For instance,** a person on a budget may eat a brown-bag lunch at work in order to buy a cassette tape. There are three major steps in budgeting.
  First, estimate your income. If your only income is a regular salary, this step is easy. **However,** you may have a job whose hours vary, or you may sometimes get extra money from a side job. **In that case,** choose a past period of time to help you estimate your future income.
  Next, estimate your expenses. On one hand, you will have certain fixed expenses, such as rent or mortgage and a car payment. **On the other hand,** you will have expenses that vary, depending partly on your choices. These expenses include clothing, food, and entertainment.
  Finally, write down what you actually spend. This helps you adjust your budget. **For example,** you may find you are able to spend less for clothes than you have allowed. **As a result,** you may be able to increase your allowance for entertainment.

Irrelevant Details
(page 58)

These sentences should be crossed out:

A. Some people also win money in sweepstakes.
B. Neither do birds.
  Some people are also very frightened of snakes and spiders.
C. Many people enjoy sports activities.
  Some people are more easygoing than others.

Social Studies

Working with a U.S. Map—Regions
(page 59)

1a. Minnesota, Wisconsin, Illinois, Michigan, Indiana, Ohio
  b. North Dakota, South Dakota, Nebraska, Kansas, Iowa, Missouri
  c. Some states gained population while others lost.
2a. Any five states: California, Arizona, New Mexico, Texas, Louisiana, Mississippi, Alabama, Georgia, Florida
  b. With the exception of Louisiana, all of the sun belt states gained population in the last decade.
3. The North Central states
4. Any three states: Montana, Wyoming, Colorado, Idaho, Utah, Nevada
5. Alaska and Hawaii

Working with a U.S. Map—States
(page 60)

1a. the Democrats
  b. Any six states: Texas, Oklahoma, Kansas, Nebraska, Wyoming, Colorado, New Mexico, Nevada, Idaho, Oregon
2a. the Republicans

b. Any five states: South Dakota, Minnesota, Iowa, Wisconsin, Illinois, Michigan, Ohio

3. Fifteen states did not hold gubernatorial races in 1990. Some of these states had Republican governors in office.

Working with a World Map
(page 61)

1. The areas are in southern Europe, the Middle East, southern and eastern Asia, and northern and central Africa.

2. eastern Asia

3. Some groups moved west into the area that is now France. Others moved into central Asia.

4. At the time shown by the map, North America was about half covered by ice.

5. The fact that migration occurred through large expanses where ice is shown supports the fact that at some point ice retreated from at least a part of the area.

Working with Tables
(page 62)

1. 23; 11

2. 22 million; 9 million

3. in industrial workers and value of manufacturing

4. An advantage in industry would help because the region would be able to manufacture weapons and uniforms.

5. the Union

6. Better transportation would help a region move soldiers and supplies more quickly.

7. The greatest projected increases, in terms of percentages, are in health fields. More workers are needed in these fields for an older population.

8. salespersons, with 4,506,000 jobs

9. Many of the top ten growth jobs do *not* require a college education, so the outlook is good.

Working with Line Graphs
(page 63)

1. almost 3 percent

2. West Germany

3. the United States. The graph shows more fluctuations up and down as well as greater extremes of fluctuation than the other two countries.

4. The ups and downs of Japan's and West Germany's economies were very similar, with highs and lows occurring at roughly the same time (except in 1985 through 1987). The main difference was that Japan always had a higher rate of economic growth than West Germany.

5. The rate of growth for each country was lower in 1981 than in 1989. For the U.S. it was 2.3 percent in 1981 and 2.8 percent in 1989. For West Germany it was 0.2 percent in 1981 and 3.3 percent in 1989. For Japan it was 3.9 percent in 1981 and 4.9 percent in 1989.

6.

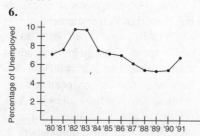

Sample summary: The unemployment rate has remained below 10 percent since 1980. It was highest in 1982 to 1983 and lowest in 1989, but it seems to be rising again.

Working with Bar Graphs
(page 64)

1. the Northeast (more than 50 percent)

2. the South

3. the Midwest

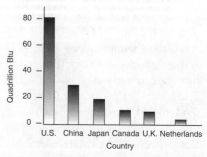

4. Energy consumption is related to the population of a country, its level of industrialization, and its standard of living.

Working with Pie Graphs
(page 65)

1. direct benefit payments for individuals

2. After a stable period in the 1970s, the percentage given back to states and local governments steadily decreased in the 1980s.

3. The country was at war in 1973, when the percentage given to national defense was highest.

4. because the percentage given to paying interest has steadily increased over the years

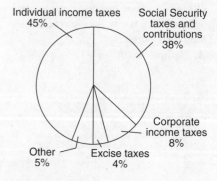

General and Specific Concepts
(page 66)

1. Answer given as example.
2. government   3. Northeast
4. Revolutionary period
5. West   6. economy
7. Midwest   8. climate
9. government branch   10. crops
11. need   12. Southeast
13. vegetation   14. groups
15. time   16. body of water
17. political region   18. South
19. landform   20. Civil War
21. government official
22. goods   23. business

Classifying
(page 67)

1. federal   2. local   3. state
4. state   5. local   6. state
7. federal   8. local

Using Context Clues
(page 68)

1. having to do with a strong belief in a cause
2. holding someone in jail before their trial
3. breaking a written or an unwritten law of society
4. the average number of people living in certain areas
5. seasonal winds
6. centered on oneself with no sense of others' viewpoints

Causes and Effects
(page 69)

1. Answer given as example.
2. arrests due to drunkenness down
3. deaths due to alcoholism down
4. organized crime into business of illegal liquor

5. repeal of Prohibition
6. nobility of less importance
7. land ownership open to many
8. British-imposed taxes
9. attempts to control American economy
10. power of colonial assemblies reduced

Point of View
(page 70)

1. Sample summary: The upper class should be given more political power than the lower class because they are naturally better able to govern.
2. Sample summary: Some people will always try to give power to the upper class because they wrongly do not respect and trust the majority of the people to govern themselves.
3. Jefferson, because he believed all the people should have an equal voice in government
4. Hamilton, because he supported the wealthy upper class over the majority of the people

Assessing Data
(page 71)

1. that babies have a need for closeness and safety, or physical attachment, with someone
2. that a baby monkey would hug the terry cloth mother even when feeding from the wire mother, and that the baby would especially hug the terry cloth mother when a strange object was placed in the cage.
3. that Americans are mistaken in thinking their choice is entirely free
4. studies that show we tend to marry people very much like ourselves, showing that we are subject to group norms
5. that the beliefs are likely true
6. studies that show little difference between freely chosen and arranged marriages in success and happiness

Drawing Conclusions
(page 72)

1. The popular vote is the actual number of people who voted for a candidate. No matter how small the winner's lead in a given state, that person gets all the electoral votes from that state. Therefore, electoral votes do not reflect the true popularity of a candidate.
2. Phoenix must be in a desert because of the extremely low level of precipitation.
3. People tend to see others behave the way they have been led to believe they will behave.
4. The United States was quite willing to acquire land in any way it could.

Facts and Opinions
(page 73)

1. opinion   2. fact   3. fact
4. fact   5. fact   6. fact
7. opinion   8. fact   9. opinion
10. fact   11. fact   12. fact
Each fact can be proved by research or by observing the situation.

Science

Working with Diagrams
(page 74)

1. The warm air goes up the chimney.
2. The air pressure lowers.
3. The cold air is pulled into the house because of the difference in air pressure.
4. A fireplace is not a good way to heat a room because it actually pulls cold air in from the outside, heats it, and then sends it up the chimney.
5. March 21: spring; June 21: summer; Sept. 23: fall; Dec. 21: winter
6. March 21: fall; June 21: winter; Sept. 23: spring; Dec. 21: summer

7. If the earth's axis were not tilted, there would be no change in seasons because a particular spot on earth would never tilt toward or away from the sun.
8. If the earth didn't revolve around the sun, there would be no change in seasons because a particular spot on earth would always be tilted toward or away from the sun.

Working with Tables and Charts
(page 75)

1. The chart is listing the vitamins that make up the vitamin B complex, the kinds of food that supply each, and the recommended diet allowance for both men and women.
2. eight   **3.** meat, milk products, eggs, and fish   **4.** B_1, B_2, B_6, and folic acid   **5.** 16–19
6. 113 cu mi   **7.** Lake Ontario

Working with Line Graphs
(page 76)

1. 1,000; 1,000
2. age 10   **3.** 3,000   **4.** age 22
5. because they are growing

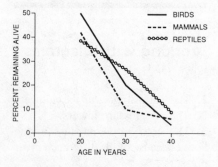

Working with Bar Graphs
(page 77)

1. oil   **2.** nuclear energy

3. hydroelectric   **4a.** fossil
b. between 85 and 90 percent

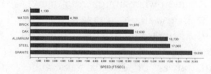

Working with Pie Graphs
(page 78)

1. water   **2a.** proteins, vitamins, fats, carbohydrates   **b.** 38 percent

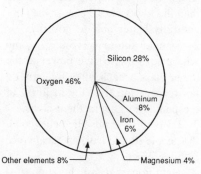

3. oxygen   **4.** silicon

General and Specific Concepts
(page 79)

1. Answer given as example.
2. mammal   **3.** plant
4. organ   **5.** fuel
6. body system
7. ocean movement   **8.** vertebrate
9. planet   **10.** precipitation
11. tool   **12.** motion
13. solution   **14.** energy resource
15. bird   **16.** synthetic
17. electronic device   **18.** insect
19. genetic trait   **20.** matter
21. element   **22.** body covering
23. heavenly body

Classifying
(page 80)

1. first   **2.** third   **3.** first
4. second   **5.** first   **6.** third

Using Context Clues
(page 81)

1. Toxicity is the ability to poison.
2. Parasitic means living and feeding off another living organism, thereby harming it.
3. Seismic refers to earthquakes.
4. Synthesize means to make, manufacture, or produce.

Applying Scientific Information
(page 82)

1. The diagram is showing the transfer of energy in food.
2. 1/10 of 1 calorie
3. lettuce
4. More people could be fed if land was planted with crops that humans could eat.

Causes and Effects
(page 83)

1. Carbon dioxide accumulates in atmosphere.
2. Polar ice caps melt some.
3. Coastal areas flooded.
4. Less farmland available.
5. Animal and plant species become extinct or adapt.

Analogies
(page 84)

1. b; because the earth spins around on its axis the way a top spins around
2. a; because small blood vessels flow into increasingly larger vessels the way small streams flow into increasingly larger rivers
3. a; because sound waves move out in a circular pattern, not linearly as waves hitting a beach or randomly as waves in a whirlpool bath

4. b; because the nucleus of the atom breaks up and its particles scatter the way the triangle of billiard balls breaks up and the balls scatter in all directions

5. c; because both electricity and water are flowing through a closed system of wires or pipes

Facts and Opinions
(page 85)

1. fact   2. fact   3. opinion
4. fact   5. fact   6. fact
7. fact   8. opinion

Assessing Data
(page 86)

1a. Acid rain had made the pond unfit for fish.
 b. The fish tried to swim back to shore and appeared to be gasping for oxygen; tests revealed a high acid content in the pond.
2a. Plants have adapted to land very successfully.
 b. Their roots can reach water below ground; a waxy coating helps prevent water loss; cell walls enable plants to grow toward the sun; a layer protects the reproductive structures.

Drawing Conclusions
(page 87)

1. The land was probably below sea level at one point and was raised up as the mountains formed.
2. Insects cannot live in cold temperatures.
3. There must be areas in outer space that are extremely hot in order for plasmas to form naturally.
4. Too much power was running through the circuit when the microwave oven was turned on.
5. Mercury's orbit must be generally faster than the earth's because its distance is almost half that of the earth's

yet it completes it in one-fifth the time.

Testing Hypotheses
(page 88)

1a. SAD is due to the limited amount of sunlight people receive during the winter.
 b. Sample test: Expose people to bright light for several hours a day in the winter to see if they feel better.
2a. The battery was dead.
 b. Sample tests: Either check the battery on a battery tester, or try another battery to see if it works.
3a. She planted the tomato plants too close together.
 b. Sample test: Get a larger planter or plant fewer plants so that she can allow more space between the plants to see if they grow better.

Interpreting Literature and the Arts

Getting the Main Idea
(page 94)

1. Gracie would never miss a performance.
2. The young men who went to fight in Vietnam lost the idealism that originally made them volunteer.

Inferences
(page 95)

1. It takes place at the home of the man; because the narrator refers to the man's "return" and to a "fence"

and the soldier refers to coming "home."
2. He is husband and father to them; the woman is called the "wife" and she kisses him; he is called the girl's father and knows the children's names; he calls himself their "poor old pap" and expects the baby to respond.
3. He has been fighting in a war; he is called a "soldier" and a "private"; he thinks about "the war" coming between him and his child; he refers to himself as coming "home from the war."
4. The baby does not recognize him and is suspicious and afraid of him; the child holds back from him, hiding behind the fence, and he looks at the man "critically."
5. The man is hurt and angry about the baby's reaction; he feels separate from the baby and contrasts this child's reaction to the oldest boy's; the wife hears "pain and reproach" in his voice and wants to explain.

Mathematics

Basic Arithmetic Facts
(page 96)

A. 7, 8, 6, 7, 7, 4, 8, 14, 16, 2
B. 6, 14, 17, 9, 2, 7, 8, 12, 0, 6
C. 18, 5, 15, 9, 8, 6, 1, 10, 9, 9
D. 9, 6, 8, 11, 11, 9, 10, 10, 8, 7
E. 4, 11, 5, 10, 9, 11, 3, 13, 13, 2
F. 11, 4, 12, 14, 5, 10, 9, 16, 10, 12
G. 14, 5, 3, 4, 14, 12, 15, 3, 12, 8
H. 6, 8, 10, 10, 13, 7, 3, 13, 5, 1
I. 9, 7, 10, 11, 6, 11, 5, 16, 12, 11
J. 4, 15, 15, 9, 8, 12, 13, 13, 17, 7

Basic Subtraction Facts
(page 97)

A. 1, 4, 1, 9, 8, 3, 2, 1, 4, 0
B. 6, 6, 4, 1, 6, 0, 2, 1, 7, 9

C. 3, 3, 8, 6, 7, 4, 9, 0, 7, 4
D. 8, 6, 9, 5, 4, 1, 0, 2, 6, 4
E. 7, 2, 2, 7, 3, 7, 8, 3, 7, 0
F. 9, 3, 0, 6, 8, 5, 3, 5, 2, 8
G. 5, 7, 5, 1, 0, 8, 1, 4, 5, 2
H. 8, 3, 5, 0, 9, 4, 1, 7, 1, 5
I. 5, 6, 9, 5, 0, 6, 3, 8, 2, 2
J. 9, 9, 2, 4, 8, 9, 6, 3, 0, 7

Basic Multiplication Facts
(page 98)

A. 4, 20, 8, 21, 0, 36, 27, 18, 28, 1
B. 12, 12, 49, 5, 0, 3, 24, 10, 16, 0
C. 14, 45, 12, 2, 0, 48, 28, 6, 3, 0
D. 32, 7, 12, 20, 18, 72, 10, 18, 45, 56
E. 0, 6, 18, 24, 36, 35, 25, 8, 42, 0
F. 24, 5, 24, 0, 27, 35, 8, 7, 14, 48
G. 54, 16, 0, 9, 42, 4, 16, 9, 40, 0
H. 0, 15, 4, 21, 64, 30, 0, 2, 0, 81
I. 40, 0, 56, 9, 0, 0, 32, 63, 30, 6
J. 63, 0, 36, 72, 0, 8, 15, 0, 6, 54

Basic Division Facts
(page 99)

A. 2, 4, 4, 4, 1, 5, 2
B. 4, 7, 1, 0, 2, 6, 3
C. 6, 5, 2, 1, 3, 5, 9
D. 4, 5, 3, 3, 0, 8, 3
E. 8, 8, 1, 0, 2, 8, 5
F. 7, 6, 0, 8, 1, 5, 7
G. 2, 6, 1, 0, 5, 9, 7
H. 2, 8, 0, 2, 1, 7, 6
I. 2, 8, 8, 4, 4, 9, 5
J. 3, 4, 7, 6, 9, 8, 9
K. 5, 0, 6, 7, 1, 3, 3
L. 0, 9, 7, 7, 9, 6, 0
M. 1, 7, 3, 4, 6, 9

Adding and Subtracting Whole Numbers
(page 100)

1a. 68   **b.** 91   **c.** 90
d. 100   **e.** 142   **f.** 221
g. 254
2a. 591   **b.** 874   **c.** 1,290
d. 1,051   **e.** 1,200   **f.** 3,829
g. 11,231

3a. 127   **b.** 151   **c.** 160
d. 158   **e.** 135   **f.** 204
g. 78
4a. 975   **b.** 1,091   **c.** 1,356
d. 1,474   **e.** 1,860   **f.** 2,512
g. 1,645
5a. 44   **b.** 7   **c.** 17   **d.** 44
e. 45   **f.** 21
6a. 472   **b.** 388   **c.** 648
d. 876   **e.** 448   **f.** 535
7a. 24   **b.** 15   **c.** 338
d. 107   **e.** 180   **f.** 135
8a. 4,991   **b.** 3,728   **c.** 7,593
d. 6,084   **e.** 462   **f.** 3,035
9a. 919   **b.** 339   **c.** 1,055
d. 1,369   **e.** 1,863   **f.** 2,423

Multiplying and Dividing Whole Numbers
(page 101)

1a. 60   **b.** 66   **c.** 270
d. 175   **e.** 608   **f.** 322
g. 801
2a. 288   **b.** 300   **c.** 1,750
d. 1,411   **e.** 1,352   **f.** 14,960
g. 3,260
3a. 2,000   **b.** 13,113
c. 25,380   **d.** 121,984
e. 51,500   **f.** 119,988
4a. 145   **b.** 33   **c.** 96
d. 29   **e.** 84 r3   **f.** 205 r1
5a. 15   **b.** 24   **c.** 22   **d.** 18
e. 24
6a. 260   **b.** 212   **c.** 46 r16
d. 25   **e.** 405 r2

Adding and Subtracting Decimals
(page 102)

1a. 1.7   **b.** 3.9   **c.** 4.3
d. 7.0   **e.** 14.1
2a. 17.71   **b.** 35.81   **c.** 33.56
d. 96.35   **e.** 146.07
3a. 6.320   **b.** 14.576
c. 1.841   **d.** 5.310   **e.** 10.131
4a. 20.49   **b.** 63.77
c. 105.67   **d.** 16.68

e. 14.234
5a. 4.9   **b.** 2.7   **c.** 6.9
d. 0.9   **e.** 4.5
6a. 6.53   **b.** 1.40   **c.** 2.82
d. 8.09   **e.** 3.85
7a. 0.137   **b.** 6.690   **c.** 0.006
d. 2.516   **e.** 2.894
8a. 6.75   **b.** 0.18   **c.** 1.995
d. 4.955   **e.** 1.95

Multiplying and Dividing Decimals
(page 103)

1a. 12.5   **b.** 6.4   **c.** 3.6
d. 44.8   **e.** 75.0   **f.** 181.5
2a. 18.6   **b.** 84.8   **c.** 181.8
d. 4,005.0   **e.** 999.0   **f.** 955.5
3a. 25.50   **b.** 59.29
c. 117.13   **d.** 301.84
e. 59.90   **f.** 54.25
4a. 59.94   **b.** 106.08
c. 80.625   **d.** 194.080
e. 703.50   **f.** 92.9248
5a. 3.6   **b.** 0.60   **c.** 5.11
d. 5.05   **e.** 0.07
6a. 40   **b.** 40   **c.** 90
d. 2,000   **e.** 5
7a. 0.205   **b.** 5   **c.** 0.03
d. 81   **e.** 3
8a. 0.9   **b.** 20   **c.** 0.2
d. 2.02

Multiplying and Dividing with Multiples of 10
(page 104)

1a. 210   **b.** 120   **c.** 250
d. 300   **e.** 2,400   **f.** 3,600
g. 4,500
2a. 600   **b.** 1,220   **c.** 1,080
d. 990   **e.** 700   **f.** 2,160
g. 6,560
3a. 100   **b.** 600   **c.** 1,000
d. 1,600   **e.** 3,200   **f.** 14,000
g. 27,000
4a. 8,000   **b.** 25,000
c. 7,000   **d.** 33,000   **e.** 7,500
f. 14,800   **g.** 32,000

5a. 40   **b.** 200   **c.** 3,100
d. 40   **e.** 5
6a. 35   **b.** 24   **c.** 33
d. 68   **e.** 1,500
7a. 50   **b.** 200   **c.** 300
d. 50   **e.** 7.5
8a. 55.0   **b.** 1.0   **c.** 0.230
9a. 0.03   **b.** 560   **c.** 250
10a. 1,750   **b.** 65.6   **c.** 333
11a. 7.2   **b.** 4,290   **c.** 0.0005

Adding and Subtracting Fractions
(page 105)

1a. $\frac{3}{5}$ **b.** 1   **c.** $\frac{5}{7}$ **d.** $5\frac{2}{3}$
e. $5\frac{3}{4}$
2a. 3   **b.** $5\frac{1}{3}$ **c.** $2\frac{3}{4}$ **d.** $\frac{2}{3}$
e. $9\frac{3}{10}$
3a. $\frac{3}{4}$ **b.** $1\frac{1}{6}$ **c.** $\frac{9}{10}$ **d.** $1\frac{1}{6}$
e. $1\frac{7}{12}$
4a. $2\frac{1}{4}$ **b.** $2\frac{9}{10}$ **c.** $8\frac{1}{12}$
d. $1\frac{7}{20}$ **e.** $5\frac{5}{6}$
5a. $\frac{2}{5}$ **b.** $\frac{1}{3}$ **c.** $\frac{3}{7}$ **d.** $1\frac{3}{5}$
e. $3\frac{2}{3}$
6a. $3\frac{1}{2}$ **b.** $1\frac{2}{3}$ **c.** $4\frac{3}{5}$
d. $7\frac{1}{16}$ **e.** $3\frac{3}{4}$
7a. $\frac{1}{4}$ **b.** $\frac{1}{6}$ **c.** $\frac{7}{10}$ **d.** $\frac{1}{4}$
e. $\frac{7}{12}$
8a. $5\frac{1}{2}$ **b.** $3\frac{1}{6}$ **c.** $\frac{1}{2}$ **d.** $\frac{3}{4}$
e. $2\frac{8}{15}$

Multiplying and Dividing Fractions
(page 106)

1a. $\frac{1}{6}$ **b.** $\frac{1}{2}$ **c.** $\frac{1}{12}$ **d.** $\frac{5}{16}$
e. $\frac{1}{24}$
2a. $2\frac{1}{2}$ **b.** 3   **c.** 5   **d.** 11
e. $5\frac{1}{3}$
3a. $1\frac{2}{3}$ **b.** 19   **c.** $4\frac{3}{8}$
d. $9\frac{1}{2}$ **e.** 42

4a. $8\frac{1}{4}$ **b.** 18   **c.** $9\frac{3}{4}$
d. $1\frac{4}{9}$ **e.** $1\frac{1}{2}$
5a. $1\frac{1}{2}$ **b.** $\frac{2}{3}$ **c.** $\frac{1}{2}$ **d.** 5
e. $\frac{2}{3}$
6a. 15   **b.** $\frac{1}{15}$ **c.** 18
d. $\frac{1}{18}$ **e.** 20
7a. $\frac{9}{10}$ **b.** $1\frac{1}{9}$ **c.** $\frac{5}{18}$ **d.** $3\frac{3}{5}$
e. 7
8a. $1\frac{3}{8}$ **b.** $9\frac{1}{3}$ **c.** 10
d. $4\frac{1}{2}$ **e.** $\frac{11}{20}$

Rounding Numbers
(page 107)

1a. 20   **b.** 60   **c.** 60   **d.** 90
e. 140   **f.** 270
2a. 100   **b.** 600   **c.** 600
d. 800   **e.** 1,000   **f.** 1,200
3a. 2,000   **b.** 8,000   **c.** 3,000
d. 7,000   **e.** 14,000
f. 22,000
4a. 10,000   **b.** 60,000
c. 40,000   **d.** 20,000
e. 110,000   **f.** 530,000
5. 62,000   **6.** $380
7. $260   **8.** $500
9. 30,000
10. $2,200

Estimating Answers
(page 108)

1. 1,400,000   **2.** $200   **3.** $80
4. 100   **5.** 5,000   **6.** 2
7. $400   **8.** $3,200   **9.** $90

Visualizing Word Problems
(page 109)

1. a   **2.** c   **3.** a   **4.** a   **5.** b

Visualizing Word Problems
(page 110)

Sample diagrams follow.

1.
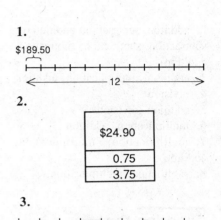

2.
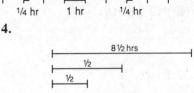

3.
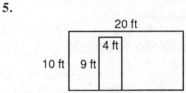

4.

5.

Choosing the Numbers You Need
(page 111)

1. Answer given as example.
2. total number of employees—95, 18, 7
 number of office workers—18
3. cost of new car—$10,499
 value of rebate—$500
 value of percent off—5% of 10,499
4. total number of wins—10, 7, 4
 number of seasons—3
5. amount of pork for one batch—3/8 pound
 number of batches—2 (double)

Deciding Which Operation to Use
(page 112)

1. multiplication

2. addition, subtraction, addition (or subtraction, subtraction, subtraction, addition)

3. addition, multiplication, addition

4. division

5. addition, division

6. multiplication, addition

7. multiplication, multiplication, addition

8. subtraction, multiplication

Choosing the Right Set-up
(page 113)

1. c **2.** a **3.** b **4.** c
5. a **6.** b

Setting Up a Word Problem
(page 114)

1. $\dfrac{1,000 - 200}{5}$

2. $1(12¢) + (20 - 1)(4¢)$

3. $40(\$9) + 5(1\frac{1}{2})(\$9)$

4. $\$18,500 + (0.05 \times \$18,500)$

5. $300 - 100 - 100 - 30$ or
$300 - (100 + 100 + 30)$

6. $\dfrac{\$18.99}{2} \times 5$

7. $5(\$12) + 2(\$40)$

Percent Problems
(page 115)

1. b **2.** a **3.** c
4. $100\% - 40\% = 60\%$

part	percent
24	60
whole	
	100

5. $21,630 - 21,000 = 630$

change	percent
630	
original	
21,000	100

GED Practice Test Charts

GED Writing Skills Practice Test Form AA

Skill	Practice Test Items	Corresponding Glencoe Pages
Sentence structure		
Fragment	7, 23	*P: 157–58 **S: 29–36
Coordination	3, 12	P: 158–59 S: 63–67
Subordination	6, 15	P: 166–67 S: 71–79
Parallelism	4, 19, 21	P: 190 S: 55–62
Usage		
Subject-verb agreement		
Noun-verb pairs	18, 20	P: 171 S: 180–83
Interrupting phrases	1, 16	P: 175 S: 184–87
Verb tense	22, 25	P: 162 S: 164–69
Mechanics		
Capitalization	14	P: 179 S: 205–9, 269–70
Punctuation (comma usage)		
Between items in series	13, 17, 24	P: 191 S: 59–62
After introductory dependent clauses	2, 5	P: 166–67 S: 71–75
Spelling	9, 10, 26	P: 160, 180, 189 S: 162–63, 203–4, 209–10
Items with no correction necessary	8, 11, 27	

*P = Passing the GED
**S = Springboard for Passing the GED Writing Skills Test

GED Writing Skills Practice Test Form BB

Skill	Practice Test Items	Corresponding Glencoe Pages
Sentence structure		
Fragment	9	*P: 157–58 **S: 29–36
Run-on	6	P: 158 S: 89–93
Comma splice	11	P: 159 S: 94–97
Coordination	8	P: 158–59 S: 67–71
Subordination	2, 18	P: 166–67 S: 71–79
Clarity	10, 24	P: 187 S: 40–44, 147–49
Usage		
Subject-verb agreement		
Interrupting phrase	20, 22	P: 175 S: 184–87
Verb tense	3, 12, 13, 17, 19, 26	P: 162 S: 164–69
Pronouns		
Pronoun shift	5	P: 186 S: 194–95
Agreement w/antecedent	4	P: 184 S: 194–95
Mechanics		
Capitalization	1, 14	P: 164, 176, 179, 192 S: 205–9, 269–70
Punctuation (comma usage)		
After introductory dependent clause	7	P: 166–67 S: 71–75
Spelling	15, 21, 23, 25	P: 160, 189 S: 162–63, 209–10
Items with no correction necessary	16, 27	

*P = Passing the GED
**S = Springboard for Passing the GED Writing Skills Test

GED Writing Skills Practice Test Form DD

Skill	Practice Test Items	Corresponding Glencoe Pages
Sentence structure		
Run-on	3	*P: 158 / **S: 89–93
Coordination	24	P: 158–59 / S: 67–71
Subordination	4, 14, 16, 26	P: 166–67 / S: 71–79
Parallelism	5	P: 190 / S: 55–62
Usage		
Subject-verb agreement		
Noun-verb pairs	22, 27	P: 171 / S: 180–83
Verb tense	1, 2, 8, 9, 13, 21	P: 162 / S: 164–69
Agreement w/antecedent	7	P: 184 / S: 194–95
Mechanics		
Punctuation (comma usage)		
Between items in series	25	P: 191 / S: 59–62
After introductory dependent clause	18, 19	P: 166–67 / S: 71–75
Spelling	6, 12, 15, 20	P: 160, 189 / S: 162–63, 209–10
Items with no correction necessary	10, 11, 17, 23	

*P = Passing the GED
**S = Springboard for Passing the GED Writing Skills Test

GED Writing Skills Practice Test Form CC

Skill	Practice Test Items	Corresponding Glencoe Pages
Sentence structure		
Fragment	26	*P: 157–58 / **S: 29–36
Run-on	7, 12, 23	P: 158 / S: 89–93
Subordination	5, 16	P: 166–67 / S: 71–79
Comma Splice	14	P: 159 / S: 94–97
Clarity	15	P: 187 / S: 40–44, 147–49
Usage		
Subject-verb agreement		
Noun-verb pairs	18, 21, 24	P: 171 / S: 180–83
Interrupting phrases	1	P: 175 / S: 184–87
Verb tense	3, 4, 6, 11, 17	P: 162 / S: 164–69
Mechanics		
Capitalization	19	P: 179 / S: 205–9, 269–70
Punctuation (comma usage)		
After introductory dependent clauses	22	P: 166–67 / S: 71–75
Spelling	8, 13, 25	P: 160, 180, 189 / S: 162–63, 203–4, 209–10

Items with no correction necessary | 2, 9, 10, 27

*P = Passing the GED
**S = Springboard for Passing the GED Writing Skills Test

GED Social Studies Practice Test Form BB

Skill	Practice Test Items	Corresponding Glencoe Pages
Comprehension		
Restating information	1, 28	*P: 251 **S: 40–42, 128–30
Summarizing	7, 20	P: 86, 250 S: 54–58, 133–36
Identifying implications	3, 4, 9, 10, 30	P: 74–75 S: 96–98
Application		
Applying information	5, 15, 19, 25, 26, 27, 29	P: 79–80, 92, 102, 258 S: 174–77
Classifying	12, 13	P: 258–59 S: 81–83
Analysis		
Recognizing assumptions	2, 17	P: 259 S: 66–70, 185–87, 218–19
Identifying cause-effect relationships	6, 8, 14, 22, 23, 31, 32	P: 90, 97, 259 S: 96–98, 145–48, 229–31
Analyzing analogous relationships	21	P: 95 S: 50–51, 62–63
Evaluation		
Assessing data/drawing conclusions	11, 16, 18, 24	P: 78–79, 91, 99, 101, 250 S: 89–91, 100–3, 190–93, 212–14

*P = Passing the GED
**S = Springboard for Passing the GED Social Studies Test

GED Social Studies Practice Test Form AA

Skill	Practice Test Items	Corresponding Glencoe Pages
Comprehension		
Restating information	29	*P: 251 **S: 40–42, 128–30
Summarizing	9, 15, 22	S: 86, 250 S: 54–58, 133–36
Identifying implications	5, 13	P: 74–75 S: 96–98, 133–36
Application		
Applying information	1, 2, 10, 16, 17, 18, 21, 24, 28	P: 79–80, 92, 102, 258 S: 174–77
Classifying	7, 8	S: 258–59 S: 81–83
Analysis		
Distinguishing fact, opinion, hypothesis	4, 25	P: 259–60 S: 105–9, 154–55, 180–81
Recognizing assumptions	6, 31	P: 259 S: 66–67
Identifying conclusions	19, 30	P: 91, 101, 259 S: 87–88
Identifying cause-effect relationships	11, 14, 23, 26	P: 90, 97, 259 S: 96–98, 145–48, 229–31
Analyzing analogous relationships	32	P: 95 S: 50–51, 62–63
Evaluation		
Assessing data/drawing conclusions	12, 20, 27	P: 78–79, 91, 99, 101, 250. S: 89–91, 100–3, 190–93, 212–14
Recognizing role of values	3	P: 260 S: 159–61, 195–97, 244–45

*P = Passing the GED
**S = Springboard for Passing the GED Social Studies Test

GED Social Studies Practice Test Form DD

Skill	Practice Test Items	Corresponding Glencoe Pages
Comprehension		
Restating information	1, 8, 11, 16, 18, 19, 21, 32	*P: 251 **S: 40–42, 128–30
Summarizing	3, 26	P: 86, 250 S: 54–58, 133–36
Identifying implications	31	P: 74–75 S: 96–98, 133–36
Application		
Applying information	2, 4, 14, 15, 17	P: 79–80, 92, 102, 258 S: 174–77
Classifying	27, 28, 29, 30	P: 258–59 S: 81–83
Analysis		
Distinguishing fact, opinion, hypothesis	7, 12, 20	P: 259–60 S: 105–9, 154–55, 180–81
Identifying cause-effect relationships	9	P: 90, 97 259 S: 96–98, 145–48, 229–31
Identifying conclusions	5, 6	P: 91, 101, 259 S: 87–88
Evaluation		
Assessing data/drawing conclusions	10, 23, 24, 25	P: 78–79, 91, 99, 101, 250 S: 89–91, 100–3, 190–93, 212–14
Recognizing role of values	13, 22	P: 260 S: 159–61, 195–97, 244–45

*P = *Passing the GED*
**S = *Springboard for Passing the GED Social Studies Test*

GED Social Studies Practice Test Form CC

Skill	Practice Test Items	Corresponding Glencoe Pages
Comprehension		
Restating information	1, 4, 9, 10, 19, 21, 23, 24, 25, 28	*P: 251 **S: 40–42, 128–30
Summarizing	12	P: 86, 250 S: 54–58, 133–36
Application		
Applying information	2, 3, 5, 6, 13, 14, 15, 16, 20	P: 79–80, 92, 102, 258 S: 174–77
Analysis		
Distinguishing fact, opinion, hypothesis	18	P: 259–60 S: 105–9, 154–55, 180–81
Identifying conclusions	27	P: 91, 101, 259 S: 87–88
Identifying cause-effect relationships	7, 8, 22, 26, 29, 31	P: 90, 97, 259 S: 96–98, 145–48, 229–31
Evaluation		
Assessing data/drawing conclusions	11, 17, 32	P: 78–79, 91, 99, 101, 250 S: 89–91, 100–3, 190–93, 212–14
Recognizing role of values	30	P: 260 S: 159–61, 195–97, 244–45

*P = *Passing the GED*
**S = *Springboard for Passing the GED Social Studies Test*

GED Science Practice Test
Form AA

Skill	Practice Test Items	Corresponding Glencoe Pages
Comprehension		
Restating information	1, 9, 12, 24, 25	*P: 332–34 **S: 39–41, 117–19
Summarizing	11	P: 331–32 S: 52–55, 123–25
Identifying implications	10	P: 74–75 S: 134–36
Application		
Applying information	6, 18, 19, 20, 22, 27, 28	P: 79–80, 92, 102, 336–37 S: 166–68
Classifying	13, 14, 15, 16	P: 345 S: 67–69
Analysis		
Identifying cause-effect relationships	7, 8, 17, 23, 29, 30, 32, 33	P: 90, 97, 337–38 S: 61–63, 134–36, 208–10
Analyzing analogous relationships	21	P: 95 S: 59–60, 166–68
Evaluation		
Assessing data	5, 31	P: 78–79, 91, 99, 101, 339 S: 94–97, 182–85, 218–19
Recognizing role of values	2, 3, 4, 26	S: 152–54, 189–91

*P = Passing the GED
**S = Springboard for Passing the GED Science Test

GED Science Practice Test
Form BB

Skill	Practice Test Items	Corresponding Glencoe Pages
Comprehension		
Restating information	3, 15, 26, 27	*P: 332–34 **S: 39–41, 117–19
Identifying implications	4, 10	P: 74–75 S: 134–36
Application		
Applying information	13, 16, 17, 20, 23, 25	P: 79–80, 92, 102, 336–37 S: 166–68
Classifying	6, 7, 8, 14, 28, 29, 30, 32	P: 345 S: 67–69
Predicting outcomes	21, 24	P: 92, 336–37 S: 203–5
Analysis		
Distinguishing fact, opinion, hypothesis	11	P: 330 S: 83–85, 171–73
Identifying cause-effect relationships	2, 5, 18, 19	P: 90, 97, 337–38 S: 61–63, 134–36, 208–10
Evaluation		
Assessing data/drawing conclusions	9, 12, 31, 33	P: 78–79, 91, 99, 101, 339 S: 75–78, 94–97, 128–30, 182–85, 218–19
Judging course of action	1, 22	P: 339 S: 75–78, 128–30

*P = Passing the GED
**S = Springboard for Passing the GED Science Test

GED Science Practice Test Form DD

Skill	Practice Test Items	Corresponding Glencoe Pages
Comprehension		
Restating information	1, 2, 3, 19, 20, 22, 24, 27, 28	*P: 332–34, **S: 39–41, 117–19
Summarizing	10	P: 331–32, S: 52–55, 123–25
Application		
Applying information	6, 7, 8, 9, 17, 25, 26, 29, 32	P: 79–80, 92, 102, 336–37, S: 166–68
Classifying	12, 13, 14, 15, 16	P: 345, S: 67–69
Predicting outcomes	18	P: 92, 336–37, S: 203–5
Analysis		
Identifying cause-effect relationships	4, 11, 31	P: 90, 97, 337–38, S: 61–63, 134–36, 208–10
Evaluation		
Assessing data/drawing conclusions	5, 21, 23, 30, 33	P: 78–79, 91, 99, 101, 339, S: 75–78, 94–97, 128–30, 182–85, 218–19

*P = *Passing the GED*
**S = *Springboard for Passing the GED Science Test*

GED Science Practice Test Form CC

Skill	Practice Test Items	Corresponding Glencoe Pages
Comprehension		
Restating information	1, 2, 4, 5, 9, 15, 16, 23, 29	*P: 332–34, **S: 39–41, 117–19
Application		
Applying information	3, 8, 10, 11, 17, 24, 25, 26, 28, 30, 31	P: 79–80, 92, 102, 336–37, S: 166–68
Classifying	13, 27	P: 345, S: 67–69
Predicting outcomes	7, 32	P: 92, 336–37, S: 203–5
Analysis		
Identifying cause-effect relationships	6 12, 14, 21, 33	P: 90, 97, 337–38, S: 61–63, 134–36, 208–10
Evaluation		
Assessing data/drawing conclusions	18, 19, 20, 22	P: 78–79, 91, 99, 101, 339, S: 94–97, 182–85, 218–19

*P = *Passing the GED*
**S = *Springboard for Passing the GED Science Test*

GED Interpreting Literature and the Arts Practice Test Form AA

Skill/Genre	Practice Test Items	Corresponding Glencoe Pages
Literal Comprehension		
Restating ideas		
Commentary	1	*P: 99
		**S: 92–95
Classical Drama	6, 9	P: 119
		S: 178–81
Popular Nonfiction	10	P: 90
		S: 51–54
Classical Fiction	16, 17, 19	P: 106
		S: 123–26
Inferential Comprehension		
Understanding implications		
Commentary	3, 4	P: 99, 101
		S: 100–2
Popular Poetry	21, 22	P: 126
		S: 46–47
Inferring about characters		
Classical Drama	7, 8	P: 121
		S: 189–91
Classical Fiction	18, 20	P: 108
		S: 133–41
Application		
Applying ideas	15	P: 92
		S: 107–9
Analysis		
Examining style/purpose		
Commentary	2	P: 105
		S: 92–95, 110–13
Popular Nonfiction	11, 13, 14	P: 93
		S: 61–65
Examining assumptions		
Commentary	5	P: 99, 101
		S: 89–91
Examining tone		
Popular Nonfiction	12	P: 103–4
		S: 103–6

*P = Passing the GED
**S = Springboard for Passing the GED Test of Interpreting Literature and the Arts

GED Interpreting Literature and the Arts Practice Test Form BB

Skill/Genre	Practice Test Items	Corresponding Glencoe Pages
Literal Comprehension		
Restating ideas		
Popular Poetry	6, 7, 10	*P: 125, 126, 128
		**S: 206–9, 212–15
Classical Nonfiction	12, 14	P: 90, 107–16
		S: 51–54, 130–32
Commentary	20	P: 99
		S: 92–95, 96–99
Summarizing		
Popular Poetry	8	P: 125, 126
		S: 206–9
Commentary	22	P: 98, 99
		S: 92–95
Inferential Comprehension		
Understanding implications		
Commentary	17, 18, 21	P: 101
		S: 100–2
Understanding consequences		
Popular Poetry	9	P: 90, 126–29
		S: 51–54, 206–9
Classical Nonfiction	13, 15, 16	P: 90
		S: 51–54
Inferring about characters		
Classical Drama	5	P: 121
		S: 185–91
Application		
Applying ideas	1, 2, 4	P: 123
		S: 150–52
Analysis		
Examining style/purpose		
Classical Drama	3	P: 105
		S: 189–91
Examining mood	11	P: 115
		S: 156–59
Examining use of detail		
Commentary	19	P: 99
		S: 92–95

*P = Passing the GED
**S = Springboard for Passing the GED Test of Interpreting Literature and the Arts

GED Interpreting Literature and the Arts Practice Test Form DD

Skill/Genre	Practice Test Items	Corresponding Glencoe Pages
Literal Comprehension		
Restating ideas		
Classical Drama	2, 3, 4	*P: 119 **S: 178–81
Classical Fiction	9, 11	P: 106 S: 123–26
Commentary	13	P: 99 S: 92–95, 96–99
Summarizing		
Popular Poetry	19	P: 125, 126 S: 206–9
Commentary		P: 98,99 S: 92–95
Inferential Comprehension		
Understanding implications		
Commentary	14, 15	P: 101 S: 100–2
Inferring the main idea		
Classical Fiction	8, 12	P: 110 S: 142–45
Classical Nonfiction		P: 90 S: 51–54
Inferring about characters		
Classical Drama	1, 5, 6, 7	P: 121 S: 185–91
Application		
Applying ideas	10, 20	P: 123 S: 150–52
Analysis		
Examining style/purpose		
Commentary	16	P: 105 S: 110–113
Examining poetic devices		
Classical poetry	21, 22	P: 131 S: 220–22
Examining use of detail		
Commentary	17, 18	P: 99 S: 92–95

*P = Passing the GED
**S = Springboard for Passing the GED Test of Interpreting Literature and the Arts

GED Interpreting Literature and the Arts Practice Test Form CC

Skill/Genre	Practice Test Items	Corresponding Glencoe Pages
Literal Comprehension		
Restating ideas		
Commentary	14, 15	*P: 99 **S: 92–95
Classical Drama	19	P: 119 S: 178–81
Popular Nonfiction	11	P: 90 S: 51–54
Classical Fiction	1, 2, 3	P: 106 S: 123–26
Summarizing		
Popular Poetry	8, 9	P: 125, 126 S: 206–9
Inferential Comprehension		
Understanding vocabulary		
Popular Nonfiction	10	P: 87–88 S: 39–45
Inferring about characters		
Classical Drama	20, 21	P: 121 S: 189–91
Classical Fiction	5, 7	P: 108 S: 133–41
Application		
Applying ideas	4, 13, 17	P: 92 S: 107–9
Analysis		
Examining style/purpose		
Commentary	18	P: 105 S: 92–95, 110–13
Popular Nonfiction	12	P: 93 S: 61–65
Classical Drama	22	P: 117–24 S: 189–91
Examining assumptions		
Commentary	16	P: 99, 101 S: 89–91
Examining mood	6	P: 115 S: 156–59

*P = Passing the GED
**S = Springboard for Passing the GED Test of Interpreting Literature and the Arts

GED Mathematics Practice Test Form AA

Computation Skill	Practice Test Items	Corresponding Glencoe Pages
Basic Arithmetic		
Division of fractions	5	P: 444-45 **S: 89-91
Percents	3, 8, 18	P: 447-53 S: 97-108
Measurement		
Square measure (area)	4	P: 501 S: 177-79, 235-38
Cubic measure (volume)	13, 28	P: 514-15 S: 267-70
Data analysis		
Graphs	12, 15	P: 454-59 S: 115-23
Means (averages)	11	P: 462 S: 124-25
Number Relationships		
Comparing/ordering data	16, 19	P: 473 S: 146-47
Scientific notation	25	P: 476 S: 152-55
Geometry		
Triangles	20, 22, 24, 27	P: 502-8 S: 239-55
Circles	23	P: 510-12 S: 255-59
Algebra		
Proportions	1, 9	P: 466-67 S: 130-33
Numerical expressions	2, 7, 26	P: 524-25 S: 300-6
Equations		
Evaluating/setting up	10, 14	P: 530, 534 S: 310-14, 318-20
With two unknowns	6, 17	P: 537 S: 323-26
Inequalities	21	P: 536 S: 320-23

*P = *Passing the GED*
**S = *Springboard for Passing the GED Mathematics Test*

GED Mathematics Practice Test Form BB

Computation Skill	Practice Test Items	Corresponding Glencoe Pages
Basic Arithmetic		
Division, whole numbers	3, 5, 9	*P: 420-21, 430 **S: 39-45, 65-67
Multiplication, fractions	1	P: 442-43 S: 85-89
Percents	4, 15, 19	P: 447-53 S: 97-108
Insufficient data	6	P: 412 S: 67-69
Data Analysis		
Graphs	10	P: 454-59 S: 115-23
Means (averages)	20	P: 462 S: 124-25
Probability	25	P: 465 S: 134-36
Number Relationships		
Number lines	2	P: 468 S: 137-38
Square roots	8	P: 475 S: 150-51
Scientific notation	17	P: 476 S: 152-55
Measurement		
Cubic measure (volume)	13	P: 514-15 S: 179-81, 266-67
Geometry		
Triangles	7, 11, 14, 27	P: 502-8 S: 239-55
Algebra		
Proportions	16	P: 466-67 S: 130-33
Numerical expressions	12	P: 524-25 S: 300-6
Algebraic expressions	26	P: 528-29 S: 308-10
Equations		
Evaluating/setting up	22, 23, 28	P: 530, 534 S: 310-14, 318-20
With two unknowns	18, 24	P: 537 S: 323-26
Slope on coordinate grid	21	P: 516-17, 538 S: 271-74, 340-43

*P = *Passing the GED*
**S = *Springboard for Passing the GED Mathematics Test*

GED Mathematics Practice Test Form CC

Computation Skill	Practice Test Items	Corresponding Glencoe Pages
Basic Arithmetic		
Subtraction of whole numbers	4	*P: 414–15 / **S: 26–32
Multiplication of whole numbers	11	P: 417–19 / S: 33–38
Division of decimals	9	P: 430–33 / S: 61–66
Addition of fractions	3	P: 436 / S: 76–80
Multiplication of fractions	1	P: 442–43 / S: 85–89
Division of fractions	13	P: 444–45 / S: 89–91
Percents	5, 17, 20, 23	P: 447–53 / S: 97–108
Measurement		
Linear measure (perimeter)	22, 26	P: 490 / S: 174–76
Square measure (area)	6	P: 501 / S: 177–79, 235–38
Data Analysis		
Graphs	15, 16	P: 454–59 / S: 115–23
Probability	28	P: 465 / S: 134
Number Relationships		
Comparing/ordering data	8	P: 473 / S: 146–47
Geometry		
Plane geometry	12	P: 494–98 / S: 222–29
Triangles	19, 24	P: 502–8 / S: 239–55
Circles	14	P: 510–12 / S: 255–59
Algebra		
Numerical expressions	7, 18, 27	P: 524–25 / S: 300–6
Equations		
Evaluating/setting up	2	P: 530, 534 / S: 310–14, 318–20
With two unknowns	10	P: 537 / S: 323–26
Inequalities	21	P: 536 / S: 320–23
Slope on coordinate grid	25	P: 516–17, 538 / S: 271–74, 340–43

GED Mathematics Practice Test Form DD

Computation Skill	Practice Test Items	Corresponding Glencoe Pages
Basic Arithmetic		
Division, whole numbers	12	*P: 420–21, 430 / **S: 39–45, 65–67
Multiplication, decimals	7	P: 428–29 / S: 57–60
Rounding, decimals	9	P: 424 / S: 53
Percents	5, 6, 15, 27	P: 447–53 / S: 97–108
Measurement		
Cubic measure (volume)	19, 25	P: 514–15 / S: 267–70
Data Analysis		
Graphs	1, 13	P: 454–59 / S: 115–23
Means (averages)	4	P: 462 / S: 124–25
Probability	22	P: 465 / S: 134–36
Geometry		
Triangles	21, 24, 28	P: 502–8 / S: 239–55
Algebra		
Proportions	11, 14, 26	P: 466–67 / S: 130–33
Numerical expressions	2, 8, 10, 16, 18, 20, 23	P: 524–25 / S: 300–6
Algebraic expressions	17	P: 528–29 / S: 308–10
Equations		
Evaluating/setting up	3	P: 530, 534 / S: 310–14, 318–20

*P = *Passing the GED*
**S = *Springboard for Passing the GED Mathematics Test*

(continued)

Performance Charts

Use with the practice test items in the white columns of *Passing the GED*. As you complete a column of items, check your answers in the book. Then on this page, circle the number of each item you answered incorrectly.

Interpreting Literature

Nonfiction (pages 83–97)
1 2 3 4 5 6 7 8 9 10 11 12 13
14 15 16 17 18 19 20 21 22 23 24
25 26 27 28 29

Commentary (pages 98–105)
1 2 3 4 5 6 7 8 9 10 11 12 13
14 15

Fiction (pages 106–16)
1 2 3 4 5 6 7 8 9 10 11 12 13
14 15 16 17 18 19 20 21 22 23 24

Drama (pages 117–24)
1 2 3 4 5 6 7 8 9 10 11 12 13

Poetry (pages 125–32)
1 2 3 4 5 6 7 8 9 10 11 12 13
14 15 16 17

Use with the practice test items in the white columns of *Passing the GED*. As you complete a column of items, check your answers in the book. Then on this page, circle the number of each item you answered incorrectly.

Writing Skills

Writing Sentences (pages 157–96)

1	2	3	4	5	6	7	8	9	10	11	12	13
14	15	16	17	18	19	20	21	22	23	24		
25	26	27	28	29	30	31	32	33	34	35		
36	37	38	39	40	41	42	43	44	45	46		
47	48	49	50	51	52	53	54	55	56	57		
58	59	60	61	62	63	64	65	66	67	68		
69	70	71	72	73	74	75	76	77	78	79		
80	81	82	83	84	85	86	87	88	89	90		
91	92	93	94	95	96	97	98	99	100	101		

Writing Essays (pages 204–15)

Each time you write an essay about a topic in the white column, show your teacher the topic, and ask him or her to read your essay.

Use with the practice test items in the white columns of *Passing the GED*. As you complete a column of items, check your answers in the book. Then on this page, circle the number of each item you answered incorrectly.

Social Studies

Geography (pages 261–68)
1   2   3   4   5   6   7   8   9   10   11   12   13
14   15   16   17   18   19   20

Behavioral Sciences (pages 269–77)
1   2   3   4   5   6   7   8   9   10   11   12   13
14   15   16   17   18   19   20   21

Economics (pages 278–87)
1   2   3   4   5   6   7   8   9   10   11   12   13
14   15   16   17   18   19   20   21   22

Political Science (pages 288–97)
1   2   3   4   5   6   7   8   9   10   11   12   13
14   15   16   17   18   19   20   21   22   23   24
25

U.S. History (pages 298–311)
1   2   3   4   5   6   7   8   9   10   11   12   13
14   15   16   17   18   19   20   21   22   23   24
25   26   27   28   29   30   31   32   33   34

Use with the practice test items in the white columns of *Passing the GED*. As you complete a column of items, check your answers in the book. Then on this page, circle the number of each item you answered incorrectly.

Science

Biology (pages 340–59)

1   2   3   4   5   6   7   8   9   10   11   12   13
14   15   16   17   18   19   20   21   22   23   24
25   26   27   28   29   30   31   32   33   34   35
36   37   38   39   40

Earth Science (pages 360–70)

1   2   3   4   5   6   7   8   9   10   11   12   13
14   15   16   17   18   19   20   21   22   23

Chemistry (pages 371–78)

1   2   3   4   5   6   7   8   9   10   11   12   13
14   15   16   17   18   19

Physics (pages 379–86)

1   2   3   4   5   6   7   8   9   10   11   12   13
14   15   16   17   18   19   20   21   22   23   24
25

Use with the practice test items in the white columns of *Passing the GED*. As you complete a column of items, check your answers in the book. Then on this page, circle the number of each item you answered incorrectly.

Mathematics

Whole Numbers (pages 413–22)
1 2 3 4 5 6 7 8 9 10 11 12 13
14 15 16 17 18 19 20 21 22 23 24
25

Decimals (pages 423–33)
1 2 3 4 5 6 7 8 9 10 11 12 13
14 15 16 17 18 19 20 21 22 23 24
25 26 27 28 29 30 31 32 33 34 35
36 37 38 39 40 41 42 43 44 45 46

Fractions (pages 434–46)
1 2 3 4 5 6 7 8 9 10 11 12 13
14 15 16 17 18 19 20 21 22 23 24
25 26 27 28 29 30 31 32 33 34 35
36 37 38 39 40 41 42 43 44 45 46
47 48 49 50 51

Percents (pages 447–53)
1 2 3 4 5 6 7 8 9 10 11 12 13
14 15 16 17 18 19 20 21 22 23

Data Analysis (pages 454–67)
1 2 3 4 5 6 7 8 9 10 11 12 13
14 15 16 17 18 19 20 21 22 23 24
25 26 27 28 29 30 31 32 33 34 35
36 37 38 39 40 41 42 43 44 45 46
47 48 49 50 51 52 53 54 55

Number Relationships (pages 468–77)
1 2 3 4 5 6 7 8 9 10 11 12 13
14 15 16 17 18 19 20 21 22 23 24
25 26 27 28 29 30 31 32 33 34

Measurement (pages 478–90)
1 2 3 4 5 6 7 8 9 10 11 12 13
14 15 16 17 18 19 20 21 22 23 24
25 26 27 28 29 30 31 32 33 34 35
36 37 38 39 40 41 42 43 44 45 46

Arithmetic Review (pages 491–492)
47 48 49 50 51 52 53 54

Geometry (pages 493–521)
1 2 3 4 5 6 7 8 9 10 11 12 13
14 15 16 17 18 19 20 21 22 23 24
25 26 27 28 29 30 31 32 33 34 35
36 37 38 39 40 41 42 43 44 45 46
47 48 49 50 51 52 53 54 55 56 57
58 59 60 61 62 63 64 65 66 67 68
69 70 71 72 73 74 75 76 77 78 79
80 81 82 83 84 85 86 87 88 89 90
91 92 93 94 95 96 97 98 99 100 101
102 103 104 105 106 107 108 109 110
111 112 113 114 115 116 117 118

Algebra (pages 522–544)
1 2 3 4 5 6 7 8 9 10 11 12 13
14 15 16 17 18 19 20 21 22 23 24
25 26 27 28 29 30 31 32 33 34 35
36 37 38 39 40 41 42 43 44 45 46
47 48 49 50 51 52 53 54 55 56 57
58 59 60 61 62 63 64 65 66 67 68
69 70 71 72 73 74 75 76 77 78 79
80 81 82 83 84 85 86 87 88 89 90
91 92 93 94 95 96 97 98 99 100 101
102 103 104 105 106 107

Pretest Answer Sheets

Writing Skills Pretest, Part I
Name: _____

1. ① ② ③ ④ ⑤   7. ① ② ③ ④ ⑤   13. ① ② ③ ④ ⑤   19. ① ② ③ ④ ⑤   25. ① ② ③ ④ ⑤
2. ① ② ③ ④ ⑤   8. ① ② ③ ④ ⑤   14. ① ② ③ ④ ⑤   20. ① ② ③ ④ ⑤   26. ① ② ③ ④ ⑤
3. ① ② ③ ④ ⑤   9. ① ② ③ ④ ⑤   15. ① ② ③ ④ ⑤   21. ① ② ③ ④ ⑤   27. ① ② ③ ④ ⑤
4. ① ② ③ ④ ⑤   10. ① ② ③ ④ ⑤   16. ① ② ③ ④ ⑤   22. ① ② ③ ④ ⑤   28. ① ② ③ ④ ⑤
5. ① ② ③ ④ ⑤   11. ① ② ③ ④ ⑤   17. ① ② ③ ④ ⑤   23. ① ② ③ ④ ⑤
6. ① ② ③ ④ ⑤   12. ① ② ③ ④ ⑤   18. ① ② ③ ④ ⑤   24. ① ② ③ ④ ⑤

Social Studies Pretest
Name: _____

1. ① ② ③ ④ ⑤   8. ① ② ③ ④ ⑤   15. ① ② ③ ④ ⑤   22. ① ② ③ ④ ⑤   29. ① ② ③ ④ ⑤
2. ① ② ③ ④ ⑤   9. ① ② ③ ④ ⑤   16. ① ② ③ ④ ⑤   23. ① ② ③ ④ ⑤   30. ① ② ③ ④ ⑤
3. ① ② ③ ④ ⑤   10. ① ② ③ ④ ⑤   17. ① ② ③ ④ ⑤   24. ① ② ③ ④ ⑤   31. ① ② ③ ④ ⑤
4. ① ② ③ ④ ⑤   11. ① ② ③ ④ ⑤   18. ① ② ③ ④ ⑤   25. ① ② ③ ④ ⑤   32. ① ② ③ ④ ⑤
5. ① ② ③ ④ ⑤   12. ① ② ③ ④ ⑤   19. ① ② ③ ④ ⑤   26. ① ② ③ ④ ⑤
6. ① ② ③ ④ ⑤   13. ① ② ③ ④ ⑤   20. ① ② ③ ④ ⑤   27. ① ② ③ ④ ⑤
7. ① ② ③ ④ ⑤   14. ① ② ③ ④ ⑤   21. ① ② ③ ④ ⑤   28. ① ② ③ ④ ⑤

Science Pretest
Name: _____

1. ① ② ③ ④ ⑤   8. ① ② ③ ④ ⑤   15. ① ② ③ ④ ⑤   22. ① ② ③ ④ ⑤   29. ① ② ③ ④ ⑤
2. ① ② ③ ④ ⑤   9. ① ② ③ ④ ⑤   16. ① ② ③ ④ ⑤   23. ① ② ③ ④ ⑤   30. ① ② ③ ④ ⑤
3. ① ② ③ ④ ⑤   10. ① ② ③ ④ ⑤   17. ① ② ③ ④ ⑤   24. ① ② ③ ④ ⑤   31. ① ② ③ ④ ⑤
4. ① ② ③ ④ ⑤   11. ① ② ③ ④ ⑤   18. ① ② ③ ④ ⑤   25. ① ② ③ ④ ⑤   32. ① ② ③ ④ ⑤
5. ① ② ③ ④ ⑤   12. ① ② ③ ④ ⑤   19. ① ② ③ ④ ⑤   26. ① ② ③ ④ ⑤   33. ① ② ③ ④ ⑤
6. ① ② ③ ④ ⑤   13. ① ② ③ ④ ⑤   20. ① ② ③ ④ ⑤   27. ① ② ③ ④ ⑤
7. ① ② ③ ④ ⑤   14. ① ② ③ ④ ⑤   21. ① ② ③ ④ ⑤   28. ① ② ③ ④ ⑤

Interpreting Literature and the Arts Pretest
Name: _____

1. ① ② ③ ④ ⑤ 6. ① ② ③ ④ ⑤ 11. ① ② ③ ④ ⑤ 16. ① ② ③ ④ ⑤ 21. ① ② ③ ④ ⑤
2. ① ② ③ ④ ⑤ 7. ① ② ③ ④ ⑤ 12. ① ② ③ ④ ⑤ 17. ① ② ③ ④ ⑤ 22. ① ② ③ ④ ⑤
3. ① ② ③ ④ ⑤ 8. ① ② ③ ④ ⑤ 13. ① ② ③ ④ ⑤ 18. ① ② ③ ④ ⑤
4. ① ② ③ ④ ⑤ 9. ① ② ③ ④ ⑤ 14. ① ② ③ ④ ⑤ 19. ① ② ③ ④ ⑤
5. ① ② ③ ④ ⑤ 10. ① ② ③ ④ ⑤ 15. ① ② ③ ④ ⑤ 20. ① ② ③ ④ ⑤

Mathematics Pretest
Name: _____

1. ① ② ③ ④ ⑤ 7. ① ② ③ ④ ⑤ 13. ① ② ③ ④ ⑤ 19. ① ② ③ ④ ⑤ 25. ① ② ③ ④ ⑤
2. ① ② ③ ④ ⑤ 8. ① ② ③ ④ ⑤ 14. ① ② ③ ④ ⑤ 20. ① ② ③ ④ ⑤ 26. ① ② ③ ④ ⑤
3. ① ② ③ ④ ⑤ 9. ① ② ③ ④ ⑤ 15. ① ② ③ ④ ⑤ 21. ① ② ③ ④ ⑤ 27. ① ② ③ ④ ⑤
4. ① ② ③ ④ ⑤ 10. ① ② ③ ④ ⑤ 16. ① ② ③ ④ ⑤ 22. ① ② ③ ④ ⑤ 28. ① ② ③ ④ ⑤
5. ① ② ③ ④ ⑤ 11. ① ② ③ ④ ⑤ 17. ① ② ③ ④ ⑤ 23. ① ② ③ ④ ⑤
6. ① ② ③ ④ ⑤ 12. ① ② ③ ④ ⑤ 18. ① ② ③ ④ ⑤ 24. ① ② ③ ④ ⑤

Posttest Answer Sheets

Writing Skills Posttest, Part I
Name: _____

1. ① ② ③ ④ ⑤   12. ① ② ③ ④ ⑤   23. ① ② ③ ④ ⑤   34. ① ② ③ ④ ⑤   45. ① ② ③ ④ ⑤

2. ① ② ③ ④ ⑤   13. ① ② ③ ④ ⑤   24. ① ② ③ ④ ⑤   35. ① ② ③ ④ ⑤   46. ① ② ③ ④ ⑤

3. ① ② ③ ④ ⑤   14. ① ② ③ ④ ⑤   25. ① ② ③ ④ ⑤   36. ① ② ③ ④ ⑤   47. ① ② ③ ④ ⑤

4. ① ② ③ ④ ⑤   15. ① ② ③ ④ ⑤   26. ① ② ③ ④ ⑤   37. ① ② ③ ④ ⑤   48. ① ② ③ ④ ⑤

5. ① ② ③ ④ ⑤   16. ① ② ③ ④ ⑤   27. ① ② ③ ④ ⑤   38. ① ② ③ ④ ⑤   49. ① ② ③ ④ ⑤

6. ① ② ③ ④ ⑤   17. ① ② ③ ④ ⑤   28. ① ② ③ ④ ⑤   39. ① ② ③ ④ ⑤   50. ① ② ③ ④ ⑤

7. ① ② ③ ④ ⑤   18. ① ② ③ ④ ⑤   29. ① ② ③ ④ ⑤   40. ① ② ③ ④ ⑤   51. ① ② ③ ④ ⑤

8. ① ② ③ ④ ⑤   19. ① ② ③ ④ ⑤   30. ① ② ③ ④ ⑤   41. ① ② ③ ④ ⑤   52. ① ② ③ ④ ⑤

9. ① ② ③ ④ ⑤   20. ① ② ③ ④ ⑤   31. ① ② ③ ④ ⑤   42. ① ② ③ ④ ⑤   53. ① ② ③ ④ ⑤

10. ① ② ③ ④ ⑤   21. ① ② ③ ④ ⑤   32. ① ② ③ ④ ⑤   43. ① ② ③ ④ ⑤   54. ① ② ③ ④ ⑤

11. ① ② ③ ④ ⑤   22. ① ② ③ ④ ⑤   33. ① ② ③ ④ ⑤   44. ① ② ③ ④ ⑤   55. ① ② ③ ④ ⑤

Social Studies Posttest
Name: _____

1. ① ② ③ ④ ⑤   14. ① ② ③ ④ ⑤   27. ① ② ③ ④ ⑤   40. ① ② ③ ④ ⑤   53. ① ② ③ ④ ⑤

2. ① ② ③ ④ ⑤   15. ① ② ③ ④ ⑤   28. ① ② ③ ④ ⑤   41. ① ② ③ ④ ⑤   54. ① ② ③ ④ ⑤

3. ① ② ③ ④ ⑤   16. ① ② ③ ④ ⑤   29. ① ② ③ ④ ⑤   42. ① ② ③ ④ ⑤   55. ① ② ③ ④ ⑤

4. ① ② ③ ④ ⑤   17. ① ② ③ ④ ⑤   30. ① ② ③ ④ ⑤   43. ① ② ③ ④ ⑤   56. ① ② ③ ④ ⑤

5. ① ② ③ ④ ⑤   18. ① ② ③ ④ ⑤   31. ① ② ③ ④ ⑤   44. ① ② ③ ④ ⑤   57. ① ② ③ ④ ⑤

6. ① ② ③ ④ ⑤   19. ① ② ③ ④ ⑤   32. ① ② ③ ④ ⑤   45. ① ② ③ ④ ⑤   58. ① ② ③ ④ ⑤

7. ① ② ③ ④ ⑤   20. ① ② ③ ④ ⑤   33. ① ② ③ ④ ⑤   46. ① ② ③ ④ ⑤   59. ① ② ③ ④ ⑤

8. ① ② ③ ④ ⑤   21. ① ② ③ ④ ⑤   34. ① ② ③ ④ ⑤   47. ① ② ③ ④ ⑤   60. ① ② ③ ④ ⑤

9. ① ② ③ ④ ⑤   22. ① ② ③ ④ ⑤   35. ① ② ③ ④ ⑤   48. ① ② ③ ④ ⑤   61. ① ② ③ ④ ⑤

10. ① ② ③ ④ ⑤   23. ① ② ③ ④ ⑤   36. ① ② ③ ④ ⑤   49. ① ② ③ ④ ⑤   62. ① ② ③ ④ ⑤

11. ① ② ③ ④ ⑤   24. ① ② ③ ④ ⑤   37. ① ② ③ ④ ⑤   50. ① ② ③ ④ ⑤   63. ① ② ③ ④ ⑤

12. ① ② ③ ④ ⑤   25. ① ② ③ ④ ⑤   38. ① ② ③ ④ ⑤   51. ① ② ③ ④ ⑤   64. ① ② ③ ④ ⑤

13. ① ② ③ ④ ⑤   26. ① ② ③ ④ ⑤   39. ① ② ③ ④ ⑤   52. ① ② ③ ④ ⑤

Science Posttest
Name: _____

1. ① ② ③ ④ ⑤ 15. ① ② ③ ④ ⑤ 29. ① ② ③ ④ ⑤ 43. ① ② ③ ④ ⑤ 57. ① ② ③ ④ ⑤
2. ① ② ③ ④ ⑤ 16. ① ② ③ ④ ⑤ 30. ① ② ③ ④ ⑤ 44. ① ② ③ ④ ⑤ 58. ① ② ③ ④ ⑤
3. ① ② ③ ④ ⑤ 17. ① ② ③ ④ ⑤ 31. ① ② ③ ④ ⑤ 45. ① ② ③ ④ ⑤ 59. ① ② ③ ④ ⑤
4. ① ② ③ ④ ⑤ 18. ① ② ③ ④ ⑤ 32. ① ② ③ ④ ⑤ 46. ① ② ③ ④ ⑤ 60. ① ② ③ ④ ⑤
5. ① ② ③ ④ ⑤ 19. ① ② ③ ④ ⑤ 33. ① ② ③ ④ ⑤ 47. ① ② ③ ④ ⑤ 61. ① ② ③ ④ ⑤
6. ① ② ③ ④ ⑤ 20. ① ② ③ ④ ⑤ 34. ① ② ③ ④ ⑤ 48. ① ② ③ ④ ⑤ 62. ① ② ③ ④ ⑤
7. ① ② ③ ④ ⑤ 21. ① ② ③ ④ ⑤ 35. ① ② ③ ④ ⑤ 49. ① ② ③ ④ ⑤ 63. ① ② ③ ④ ⑤
8. ① ② ③ ④ ⑤ 22. ① ② ③ ④ ⑤ 36. ① ② ③ ④ ⑤ 50. ① ② ③ ④ ⑤ 64. ① ② ③ ④ ⑤
9. ① ② ③ ④ ⑤ 23. ① ② ③ ④ ⑤ 37. ① ② ③ ④ ⑤ 51. ① ② ③ ④ ⑤ 65. ① ② ③ ④ ⑤
10. ① ② ③ ④ ⑤ 24. ① ② ③ ④ ⑤ 38. ① ② ③ ④ ⑤ 52. ① ② ③ ④ ⑤ 66. ① ② ③ ④ ⑤
11. ① ② ③ ④ ⑤ 25. ① ② ③ ④ ⑤ 39. ① ② ③ ④ ⑤ 53. ① ② ③ ④ ⑤
12. ① ② ③ ④ ⑤ 26. ① ② ③ ④ ⑤ 40. ① ② ③ ④ ⑤ 54. ① ② ③ ④ ⑤
13. ① ② ③ ④ ⑤ 27. ① ② ③ ④ ⑤ 41. ① ② ③ ④ ⑤ 55. ① ② ③ ④ ⑤
14. ① ② ③ ④ ⑤ 28. ① ② ③ ④ ⑤ 42. ① ② ③ ④ ⑤ 56. ① ② ③ ④ ⑤

Interpreting Literature and the Arts Posttest
Name: _____

1. ① ② ③ ④ ⑤ 10. ① ② ③ ④ ⑤ 19. ① ② ③ ④ ⑤ 28. ① ② ③ ④ ⑤ 37. ① ② ③ ④ ⑤
2. ① ② ③ ④ ⑤ 11. ① ② ③ ④ ⑤ 20. ① ② ③ ④ ⑤ 29. ① ② ③ ④ ⑤ 38. ① ② ③ ④ ⑤
3. ① ② ③ ④ ⑤ 12. ① ② ③ ④ ⑤ 21. ① ② ③ ④ ⑤ 30. ① ② ③ ④ ⑤ 39. ① ② ③ ④ ⑤
4. ① ② ③ ④ ⑤ 13. ① ② ③ ④ ⑤ 22. ① ② ③ ④ ⑤ 31. ① ② ③ ④ ⑤ 40. ① ② ③ ④ ⑤
5. ① ② ③ ④ ⑤ 14. ① ② ③ ④ ⑤ 23. ① ② ③ ④ ⑤ 32. ① ② ③ ④ ⑤ 41. ① ② ③ ④ ⑤
6. ① ② ③ ④ ⑤ 15. ① ② ③ ④ ⑤ 24. ① ② ③ ④ ⑤ 33. ① ② ③ ④ ⑤ 42. ① ② ③ ④ ⑤
7. ① ② ③ ④ ⑤ 16. ① ② ③ ④ ⑤ 25. ① ② ③ ④ ⑤ 34. ① ② ③ ④ ⑤ 43. ① ② ③ ④ ⑤
8. ① ② ③ ④ ⑤ 17. ① ② ③ ④ ⑤ 26. ① ② ③ ④ ⑤ 35. ① ② ③ ④ ⑤ 44. ① ② ③ ④ ⑤
9. ① ② ③ ④ ⑤ 18. ① ② ③ ④ ⑤ 27. ① ② ③ ④ ⑤ 36. ① ② ③ ④ ⑤ 45. ① ② ③ ④ ⑤

Mathematics Posttest
Name: _____

1. ① ② ③ ④ ⑤ 13. ① ② ③ ④ ⑤ 25. ① ② ③ ④ ⑤ 37. ① ② ③ ④ ⑤ 49. ① ② ③ ④ ⑤

2. ① ② ③ ④ ⑤ 14. ① ② ③ ④ ⑤ 26. ① ② ③ ④ ⑤ 38. ① ② ③ ④ ⑤ 50. ① ② ③ ④ ⑤

3. ① ② ③ ④ ⑤ 15. ① ② ③ ④ ⑤ 27. ① ② ③ ④ ⑤ 39. ① ② ③ ④ ⑤ 51. ① ② ③ ④ ⑤

4. ① ② ③ ④ ⑤ 16. ① ② ③ ④ ⑤ 28. ① ② ③ ④ ⑤ 40. ① ② ③ ④ ⑤ 52. ① ② ③ ④ ⑤

5. ① ② ③ ④ ⑤ 17. ① ② ③ ④ ⑤ 29. ① ② ③ ④ ⑤ 41. ① ② ③ ④ ⑤ 53. ① ② ③ ④ ⑤

6. ① ② ③ ④ ⑤ 18. ① ② ③ ④ ⑤ 30. ① ② ③ ④ ⑤ 42. ① ② ③ ④ ⑤ 54. ① ② ③ ④ ⑤

7. ① ② ③ ④ ⑤ 19. ① ② ③ ④ ⑤ 31. ① ② ③ ④ ⑤ 43. ① ② ③ ④ ⑤ 55. ① ② ③ ④ ⑤

8. ① ② ③ ④ ⑤ 20. ① ② ③ ④ ⑤ 32. ① ② ③ ④ ⑤ 44. ① ② ③ ④ ⑤ 56. ① ② ③ ④ ⑤

9. ① ② ③ ④ ⑤ 21. ① ② ③ ④ ⑤ 33. ① ② ③ ④ ⑤ 45. ① ② ③ ④ ⑤

10. ① ② ③ ④ ⑤ 22. ① ② ③ ④ ⑤ 34. ① ② ③ ④ ⑤ 46. ① ② ③ ④ ⑤

11. ① ② ③ ④ ⑤ 23. ① ② ③ ④ ⑤ 35. ① ② ③ ④ ⑤ 47. ① ② ③ ④ ⑤

12. ① ② ③ ④ ⑤ 24. ① ② ③ ④ ⑤ 36. ① ② ③ ④ ⑤ 48. ① ② ③ ④ ⑤

Skills Survey Answer Sheets

Writing Skills Survey, Part I

Name: _____

1. ① ② ③ ④ ⑤ 7. ① ② ③ ④ ⑤ 13. ① ② ③ ④ ⑤ 19. ① ② ③ ④ ⑤ 25. ① ② ③ ④ ⑤

2. ① ② ③ ④ ⑤ 8. ① ② ③ ④ ⑤ 14. ① ② ③ ④ ⑤ 20. ① ② ③ ④ ⑤ 26. ① ② ③ ④ ⑤

3. ① ② ③ ④ ⑤ 9. ① ② ③ ④ ⑤ 15. ① ② ③ ④ ⑤ 21. ① ② ③ ④ ⑤ 27. ① ② ③ ④ ⑤

4. ① ② ③ ④ ⑤ 10. ① ② ③ ④ ⑤ 16. ① ② ③ ④ ⑤ 22. ① ② ③ ④ ⑤

5. ① ② ③ ④ ⑤ 11. ① ② ③ ④ ⑤ 17. ① ② ③ ④ ⑤ 23. ① ② ③ ④ ⑤

6. ① ② ③ ④ ⑤ 12. ① ② ③ ④ ⑤ 18. ① ② ③ ④ ⑤ 24. ① ② ③ ④ ⑤

Social Studies Skills Survey

Name: _____

1. ① ② ③ ④ ⑤   8. ① ② ③ ④ ⑤   15. ① ② ③ ④ ⑤   22. ① ② ③ ④ ⑤   29. ① ② ③ ④ ⑤

2. ① ② ③ ④ ⑤   9. ① ② ③ ④ ⑤   16. ① ② ③ ④ ⑤   23. ① ② ③ ④ ⑤   30. ① ② ③ ④ ⑤

3. ① ② ③ ④ ⑤   10. ① ② ③ ④ ⑤   17. ① ② ③ ④ ⑤   24. ① ② ③ ④ ⑤   31. ① ② ③ ④ ⑤

4. ① ② ③ ④ ⑤   11. ① ② ③ ④ ⑤   18. ① ② ③ ④ ⑤   25. ① ② ③ ④ ⑤   32. ① ② ③ ④ ⑤

5. ① ② ③ ④ ⑤   12. ① ② ③ ④ ⑤   19. ① ② ③ ④ ⑤   26. ① ② ③ ④ ⑤

6. ① ② ③ ④ ⑤   13. ① ② ③ ④ ⑤   20. ① ② ③ ④ ⑤   27. ① ② ③ ④ ⑤

7. ① ② ③ ④ ⑤   14. ① ② ③ ④ ⑤   21. ① ② ③ ④ ⑤   28. ① ② ③ ④ ⑤

Science Skills Survey
Name: _____

1. ① ② ③ ④ ⑤ 6. ① ② ③ ④ ⑤ 11. ① ② ③ ④ ⑤ 16. ① ② ③ ④ ⑤ 21. ① ② ③ ④ ⑤

2. ① ② ③ ④ ⑤ 7. ① ② ③ ④ ⑤ 12. ① ② ③ ④ ⑤ 17. ① ② ③ ④ ⑤ 22. ① ② ③ ④ ⑤

3. ① ② ③ ④ ⑤ 8. ① ② ③ ④ ⑤ 13. ① ② ③ ④ ⑤ 18. ① ② ③ ④ ⑤

4. ① ② ③ ④ ⑤ 9. ① ② ③ ④ ⑤ 14. ① ② ③ ④ ⑤ 19. ① ② ③ ④ ⑤

5. ① ② ③ ④ ⑤ 10. ① ② ③ ④ ⑤ 15. ① ② ③ ④ ⑤ 20. ① ② ③ ④ ⑤

Interpreting Literature and the Arts Skills Survey

Name: _____

1. ① ② ③ ④ ⑤   6. ① ② ③ ④ ⑤   11. ① ② ③ ④ ⑤   16. ① ② ③ ④ ⑤   21. ① ② ③ ④ ⑤

2. ① ② ③ ④ ⑤   7. ① ② ③ ④ ⑤   12. ① ② ③ ④ ⑤   17. ① ② ③ ④ ⑤   22. ① ② ③ ④ ⑤

3. ① ② ③ ④ ⑤   8. ① ② ③ ④ ⑤   13. ① ② ③ ④ ⑤   18. ① ② ③ ④ ⑤   23. ① ② ③ ④ ⑤

4. ① ② ③ ④ ⑤   9. ① ② ③ ④ ⑤   14. ① ② ③ ④ ⑤   19. ① ② ③ ④ ⑤

5. ① ② ③ ④ ⑤   10. ① ② ③ ④ ⑤   15. ① ② ③ ④ ⑤   20. ① ② ③ ④ ⑤

Mathematics Skills Survey
Name: _____

1. ① ② ③ ④ ⑤ 7. ① ② ③ ④ ⑤ 13. ① ② ③ ④ ⑤ 19. ① ② ③ ④ ⑤ 25. ① ② ③ ④ ⑤

2. ① ② ③ ④ ⑤ 8. ① ② ③ ④ ⑤ 14. ① ② ③ ④ ⑤ 20. ① ② ③ ④ ⑤ 26. ① ② ③ ④ ⑤

3. ① ② ③ ④ ⑤ 9. ① ② ③ ④ ⑤ 15. ① ② ③ ④ ⑤ 21. ① ② ③ ④ ⑤ 27. ① ② ③ ④ ⑤

4. ① ② ③ ④ ⑤ 10. ① ② ③ ④ ⑤ 16. ① ② ③ ④ ⑤ 22. ① ② ③ ④ ⑤ 28. ① ② ③ ④ ⑤

5. ① ② ③ ④ ⑤ 11. ① ② ③ ④ ⑤ 17. ① ② ③ ④ ⑤ 23. ① ② ③ ④ ⑤

6. ① ② ③ ④ ⑤ 12. ① ② ③ ④ ⑤ 18. ① ② ③ ④ ⑤ 24. ① ② ③ ④ ⑤

Diagnostic Charts for *Passing the GED*

Writing Pretest

Subtopic	Question Numbers	Number Correct	Instructional Pages
Sentence combining	1, 5, 6, 7, 9, 12, 14, 16, 17, 18, 22, 23, 25, 26	/14	157–59, 165–67, 173–74, 182–83, 190–91
Spelling	2, 15, 20	/3	160–61, 168–69, 180–81, 188–89
Capitalization	3, 24	/2	164, 176, 179, 192
Verb tense	4, 10, 21	/3	162–63
Verb agreement	11, 19, 28	/3	170–71, 175, 178

Writing Posttest A

Subtopic	Question Numbers	Number Correct	Instructional Pages
Sentence combining	7, 8, 12, 13, 14, 18, 25, 26, 27, 30, 31, 35, 36, 37, 38, 43, 45, 47, 48, 50, 51, 52	/22	157–59, 165–67, 173–74, 182–83, 190–91
Spelling	6, 20, 32, 34, 42, 55	/6	160–61, 168–69, 180–81, 188–89
Capitalization	11, 28, 40, 54	/4	164, 176, 179, 192
Verb tense	5, 10, 16, 21, 22, 24, 33, 46	/8	162–63
Verb agreement	2, 3, 4, 23, 39, 49	/6	170–71, 175, 178
Pronouns	9, 17, 44, 53	/4	172, 184–86, 193–94

Writing Posttest B

Subtopic	Question Numbers	Number correct	Instructional Pages
Sentence combining	1, 2, 5, 9, 11, 12, 13, 14, 18, 19, 20, 21, 22, 25, 27, 29, 32, 34, 39, 41, 44, 47, 51	/23	157–59, 165–67, 173–74, 182–83, 190–91
Spelling	3, 7, 17, 26, 30, 37, 45, 48, 49	/9	160–61, 168–69, 180–81, 188–89
Capitalization	6, 24, 33	/3	164, 176, 179, 192
Verb tense	8, 16, 23, 28, 40, 43, 46	/7	162–63
Verb agreement	4, 10, 36, 53, 55	/5	170–71, 175, 178
Pronouns	31, 42, 54	/3	172, 184–86, 193–94

Social Studies Pretest

Subtopic and Instructional Pages	Comprehension Question Numbers	Application Question Numbers	Analysis Question Numbers	Evaluation Question Numbers	Total Number Correct
Geography (261–68)	8, 14	9, 15	16, 17, 18	19	/8
Behavioral Sciences (269–77)	25	5, 6, 7			/4
Economics (278–87)	10, 20, 30	32	11, 21, 31		/7
Political Science (288–97)	13, 22, 26, 28	12, 23, 29	4, 24	3, 27	/11
U.S. History (298–311)	1		2		/2

Social Studies Posttest A

Subtopic and Instructional Pages	Comprehension Question Numbers	Application Question Numbers	Analysis Question Numbers	Evaluation Question Numbers	Total Number Correct
Geography (261–68)	23, 24, 32, 33	14, 25	31	13, 25	/9
Behavioral Sciences (269–77)	29, 34	7, 49, 50, 51, 52	35	30, 36, 37	/11
Economics (278–87)	3, 5, 8, 9, 16, 26, 41, 42	28	10, 11, 12, 17, 20, 27, 40, 44, 48, 53	4, 6, 18, 54	/23
Political Science (288–97)	38, 45, 56, 61, 62	39, 63	19, 55	46, 47, 64	/12
U.S. History (298–311)	1, 21	57, 58, 59, 60	43	2, 22	/9

Social Studies Posttest B

Subtopic and Instructional Pages	Comprehension Question Numbers	Application Question Numbers	Analysis Question Numbers	Evaluation Question Numbers	Total Number Correct
Geography (261–68)	9, 50, 54	13, 52, 57	10, 11, 51, 55, 56	12	/12
Behavioral Sciences (269–77)	7, 8, 40, 58	38, 39, 59		60	/8
Economics (278–87)	1, 2, 26, 27, 29, 64	33	28, 30, 32, 41, 42	31, 63	/14
Political Science (288–97)	47, 49, 62	3, 4, 5, 6, 53, 61	48		/10
U.S. History (298–311)	14, 17, 21, 34, 35	18, 22, 23, 43, 44, 45, 46	19, 24, 36	15, 16, 20, 25, 37	/20

Science Pretest

Subtopic and Instructional Pages	Comprehension Question Numbers	Application Question Numbers	Analysis Question Numbers	Evaluation Question Numbers	Total Number Correct
Biology (340–59)	8, 9, 16	10, 27	17, 18, 23, 26, 28	11	/11
Earth Science (360–70)	1, 22		2, 3, 4	5	/6
Chemistry (371–78)	19, 20, 30	6, 29	7, 31	21, 32	/9
Physics (379–86)	24, 25	12, 13, 14, 15			/6

Science Posttest A

Subtopic and Instructional Pages	Comprehension Question Numbers	Application Question Numbers	Analysis Question Numbers	Evaluation Question Numbers	Total Number Correct
Biology (340–59)	1, 21, 34, 40, 41, 44, 63, 64	2, 11, 12, 13, 14, 15, 16, 35	3, 22, 24, 33, 36, 42, 54, 61	23, 43, 55, 65, 66	/29
Earth Science (360–70)	7, 8, 9	10	29, 30		/6
Chemistry (371–78)	17, 18, 38, 39	4	6, 19, 30, 31, 32, 37, 48, 60	5, 20, 62	/16
Physics (379–86)	25, 26, 45, 46, 56, 57, 59	49, 50, 51, 52, 53	27, 47, 58	28	/16

Science Posttest B

Subtopic and Instructional Pages	Comprehension Question Numbers	Application Question Numbers	Analysis Question Numbers	Evaluation Question Numbers	Total Number Correct
Biology (340–59)	13, 26, 44, 45, 46, 59, 61	21, 29, 30, 31, 32, 33, 55, 56	22, 27, 28, 42, 57, 58, 62, 63	34, 47, 48, 50, 54, 64, 66	/30
Earth Science (360–70)	7, 17		8, 9, 18, 19, 35, 65	20, 36	/10
Chemistry (371–78)	10, 15, 23, 24, 25, 38	1, 2, 3, 4, 5, 6, 16, 40	11, 37, 43	39, 41	/19
Physics (379–86)	51, 60	14	49, 52	12, 53	/7

Interpreting Literature and the Arts Pretest

Subtopic and Instructional Pages	Comprehension Question Numbers	Application Question Numbers	Analysis Question Numbers	Total Number Correct
Nonfiction (83–97)	1, 20, 22	21	2, 3, 4	/7
Commentary (98–105)		12	13	/2
Fiction (106–16)	9, 10, 14, 15, 16	11		/6
Drama (117–24)	17, 18, 19			/3
Poetry (125–32)	5, 6		7, 8	/4

Interpreting Literature and the Arts Posttest A

Subtopic and Instructional Pages	Comprehension Question Numbers	Application Question Numbers	Analysis Question Numbers	Total Number Correct
Nonfiction (83–97)	8, 30, 32, 33	10, 34	7, 9, 11, 12, 31, 35	/12
Commentary (98–105)	1, 3, 36, 37, 39, 40	2	4, 5, 6, 38	/11
Fiction (106–16)	17, 18, 19, 20		21, 22, 23	/7
Drama (117–24)	24, 25, 26, 27	28	29	/6
Poetry (125–32)	13, 14, 15, 41, 43		16, 42, 44, 45	/9

Interpreting Literature and the Arts Posttest B

Subtopic and Instructional Pages	Comprehension Question Numbers	Application Question Numbers	Analysis Question Numbers	Total Number Correct
Nonfiction (83–97)	29, 30, 31, 32, 33	34		/6
Commentary (98–105)	13, 14, 15, 24, 25, 26	16, 27	17, 18, 28	/11
Fiction (106–16)	1, 2, 3, 4, 5, 35, 36, 37, 40	6, 38	39	/12
Drama (117–24)	41, 42, 43, 44, 45			/5
Poetry (125–32)	7, 9, 10, 19, 20, 21, 22		8, 11, 12, 23	/11

Mathematics Pretest

Subtopic	Question Numbers	Number Correct	Instructional Pages
Arithmetic	1, 2, 3, 4, 5, 6, 7, 8, 9, 11, 12, 13, 14, 15, 16, 17, 18, 19, 20, 21, 26	/21	413–92
Geometry	22, 23, 24	/3	493–521
Algebra	10, 25, 27, 28	/4	522–44

Mathematics Posttest A

Subtopic	Question Numbers	Number Correct	Instructional Pages
Arithmetic	1, 3, 4, 5, 7, 8, 10, 11, 12, 13, 15, 19, 21, 23, 24, 28, 29, 30, 36, 37, 38, 39, 40, 41, 42, 43, 44, 45, 48, 49, 51, 53, 55, 56	/34	413–92
Geometry	2, 6, 16, 17, 18, 22, 31, 32, 33, 34, 35, 47, 50, 52	/14	493–521
Algebra	9, 14, 20, 25, 26, 27, 46, 54	/8	522–44

Mathematics Posttest B

Subtopic	Question Numbers	Number Correct	Instructional Pages
Arithmetic	1, 2, 3, 5, 6, 7, 9, 10, 11, 12, 13, 14, 15, 19, 20, 21, 23, 25, 26, 28, 29, 30, 31, 32, 33, 34, 35, 40, 48, 49	/30	413–92
Geometry	4, 8, 16, 17, 18, 22, 27, 36, 38, 41, 42, 44, 45, 46, 50, 51, 53, 54, 55, 56	/20	493–521
Algebra	24, 37, 39, 43, 47, 52	/6	522–44

Skills Survey Class Performance Charts and Posttest Skill Charts for the *Springboards*

Writing Skills Survey		Class Performance			
Question number	Number of incorrect answers	Percentage (total in col. 2)		Skill	Lesson
		$\left(\begin{array}{l}\text{no. of items} \\ \text{in col. 1}\end{array}\right) \times \left(\begin{array}{l}\text{no. in} \\ \text{class}\end{array}\right)$			
5, 9, 11, 13, 16, 17, 19, 21, 24, 26				Sentence structure	1–2, 5–9
2, 27				Subject-verb agreement	3, 20
1, 15, 20, 25				Verb forms and tenses	4, 18–19
6, 14				Pronouns	21
4, 8, 10, 12				Punctuation	5–7, 23
7, 22				Capitalization	22
3, 18, 23				Spelling	Spelling breaks

Writing Posttest A   Skill Chart

Question number	Number of incorrect answers	Percentage (total in col. 2) $\left(\begin{array}{l}\text{no. of items}\\\text{in col. 1}\end{array}\right) \times \left(\begin{array}{l}\text{no. in}\\\text{class}\end{array}\right)$	Skill	Lesson
4, 5, 8, 11, 13, 15, 16, 17, 21, 24, 25, 26, 28, 34, 35, 38, 41, 42, 47, 50, 53			Sentence structure	1–2, 5–9
10, 20, 45, 51, 55			Subject-verb agreement	3, 20
9, 18, 22, 33, 36, 40			Verb forms and tenses	4, 18–19
2, 37, 49			Pronouns	21
3, 23, 31, 32, 43, 44, 48, 52			Punctuation	5–7, 23
6, 12, 19, 30			Capitalization	22
1, 7, 14, 27, 29, 39, 46, 54			Spelling	Spelling breaks

Writing Posttest B   Skill Chart

Question number	Number of incorrect answers	Percentage (total in col. 2) $\left(\begin{array}{l}\text{no. of items}\\\text{in col. 1}\end{array}\right) \times \left(\begin{array}{l}\text{no. in}\\\text{class}\end{array}\right)$	Skill	Lesson
2, 6, 7, 11, 13, 14, 17, 18, 19, 28, 30, 41, 42, 44, 47, 48, 50, 51, 52			Sentence structure	1–2, 5–9
16, 20, 29, 31, 36			Subject-verb agreement	3, 20
8, 9, 23, 33			Verb forms and tenses	4, 18–19
12, 21, 34, 46, 53			Pronouns	21
3, 15, 25, 35, 37, 38, 39, 40, 43, 54			Punctuation	5–7, 23
26, 27, 49			Capitalization	22
1, 4, 5, 10, 22, 24, 32, 45, 55			Spelling	Spelling breaks

Social Studies Skills Survey   Class Performance

Question number	Number of incorrect answers	Percentage (total in col. 2) $\dfrac{\text{(no. of items in col. 1)}}{\text{(no. of items in col. 1)}} \times \text{(no. in class)}$	Skill	Lesson
1, 13			Inference	4
2, 7			Summarizing	14
3, 5, 19, 23			Restating information	2, 13
4, 22, 25			Cause and effect	9, 16, 27
6, 9, 10, 11, 12, 14, 18, 20, 21, 31			Application	5, 7, 19
8, 15, 26, 27, 30, 32			Conclusions	8, 10, 22, 24, 26
16			Identifying assumptions	6, 21, 25
17			Beliefs and decision making	18, 23, 29
24, 28, 29			Facts and opinions	11, 17, 20

Social Studies Posttest A — Skill Chart

Question number	Number of incorrect answers	Percentage (total in col. 2) $\left(\begin{smallmatrix}\text{no. of items}\\\text{in col. 1}\end{smallmatrix}\right) \times \left(\begin{smallmatrix}\text{no. in}\\\text{class}\end{smallmatrix}\right)$	Skill	Lesson
2, 3, 5, 15, 19, 29, 33, 35, 38, 56, 59, 60			Inference	4
1, 23, 30, 37, 39			Summarizing	14
4, 7, 14, 17, 22, 28, 40, 41, 44, 46, 51, 54, 58, 61, 62, 63			Restating information	2, 13
10, 16, 36, 57			Cause and effect	9, 16, 27
9, 20, 21, 24, 25, 26, 27, 31, 32, 34, 47, 48, 49, 50			Application	5, 7, 19
11, 13, 43, 45, 52			Conclusions	8, 10, 22, 24, 26
12, 53, 64			Assumptions	6, 21, 25
6, 8, 18, 42, 55			Facts and opinions	11, 17, 20

Social Studies Posttest B — Skill Chart

Question number	Number of incorrect answers	Percentage (total in col. 2) $\left(\begin{smallmatrix}\text{no. of items}\\\text{in col. 1}\end{smallmatrix}\right) \times \left(\begin{smallmatrix}\text{no. in}\\\text{class}\end{smallmatrix}\right)$	Skill	Lesson
3, 7, 8, 14, 15, 16, 17, 19, 28, 30, 32, 34, 35, 38, 43, 46, 47, 48, 49, 53, 54, 57			Inference	4
9, 18			Summarizing	14
4, 6, 10, 21, 22, 31, 45, 58, 61, 62, 64			Restating information	2, 13
2, 56			Cause and effect	9, 16, 27
12, 23, 24, 29, 40, 41, 51			Application	5, 7, 19
1, 11, 20, 25, 33, 37, 39, 60, 63			Conclusions	8, 10, 22, 24, 26
52			Assumptions	6, 21, 25
27, 55			Beliefs and decision making	18, 23, 29
5, 13, 26, 36, 42, 44, 50, 59			Facts and opinions	11, 17, 20

Science Skills Survey — Class Performance

Question number	Number of incorrect answers	Percentage (total in col. 2) $\left(\begin{array}{l}\text{no. of items}\\\text{in col. 1}\end{array}\right) \times \left(\begin{array}{l}\text{no. in}\\\text{class}\end{array}\right)$	Skill	Lesson
1, 13, 22			Cause and effect	5, 15, 25
2, 7, 8, 9, 10			Application	6, 19, 24
3, 5			Restating information	2, 12
4			Beliefs and decision making	18, 23
6, 21			Fact, opinion, hypothesis	8, 20, 26
11, 17, 19			Conclusions	7, 14, 21
12, 18			Evaluation	10, 22, 27
14, 20			Summarizing	4, 13
15			Identifying assumptions	9, 16
16			Faulty logic	11, 17, 28

Science Posttest A — Skill Chart

Question number	Number of incorrect answers	Percentage (total in col. 2) $\left(\begin{array}{l}\text{no. of items}\\\text{in col. 1}\end{array}\right) \times \left(\begin{array}{l}\text{no. in}\\\text{class}\end{array}\right)$	Skill	Lesson
12, 15, 19, 20, 34, 36, 41, 51, 52, 65			Cause and effect	5, 15, 25
1, 2, 3, 4, 5, 6, 10, 18, 24, 26, 28, 29, 30, 31, 35, 48, 49, 59, 64			Application	6, 19, 24
9, 13, 14, 42, 53, 62			Restating information	2, 12

(continued)

Science Posttest A   Skill Chart

Question number	Number of incorrect answers	Percentage (total in col. 2) $\left(\begin{array}{l}\text{no. of items}\\\text{in col. 1}\end{array}\right) \times \left(\begin{array}{l}\text{no. in}\\\text{class}\end{array}\right)$		Skill	Lesson
22, 33, 56				Beliefs and decision making	18, 23
8, 11, 21, 25, 38, 46, 55, 57				Fact, opinion, hypothesis	8, 20, 26
17, 43, 45, 50				Conclusions	7, 14, 21
7, 16, 32, 40, 44, 66				Evaluation	10, 22, 27
23, 37, 47, 60, 63				Summarizing	4, 13
27, 39, 54, 61				Identifying assumptions	9, 16
58				Faulty logic	11, 17, 28

Science Posttest B   Skill Chart

Question number	Number of incorrect answers	Percentage (total in col. 2) $\left(\begin{array}{l}\text{no. of items}\\\text{in col. 1}\end{array}\right) \times \left(\begin{array}{l}\text{no. in}\\\text{class}\end{array}\right)$		Skill	Lesson
5, 12, 44, 46, 47, 51				Cause and effect	5, 15, 25
2, 3, 13, 14, 15, 16, 24, 26, 28, 29, 37, 38, 39, 40, 41, 42, 43, 49, 53, 62, 63, 64, 65, 66				Application	6, 19, 24
1, 7, 18, 25, 50, 52, 54, 60, 61				Restating information	2, 12
4, 22, 58				Beliefs and decision making	18, 23
6, 32, 33, 55, 59				Fact, opinion, hypothesis	8, 20, 26
8, 36				Conclusions	7, 14, 21
9, 10, 19, 23, 34				Evaluation	10, 22, 27
30, 35, 45, 57				Summarizing	4, 13
11, 17, 21, 27, 31, 48, 56				Identifying assumptions	9, 16
20				Faulty logic	11, 17, 28

Interpreting Literature and the Arts Skills Survey

Class Performance

Question number	Number of incorrect answers	Percentage (total in col. 2) $\left(\begin{array}{c}\text{no. of items} \\ \text{in col. 1}\end{array}\right) \times \left(\begin{array}{c}\text{no. in} \\ \text{class}\end{array}\right)$		Skill	Lesson
1, 13				Supporting details	2–3, 12
2, 6, 16, 21				Main idea	1–2, 11, 21, 26, 32
3				Seeing patterns	10
4, 11				Tone	15, 24
5, 10, 20				Technique/style	9, 17, 35
7, 9				Characterization	20, 29
8				Context clues	4, 13, 33
12				Figures of speech	5, 22, 34
14, 15				Application	8, 16, 23, 30
17				Setting	19, 28
18				Plot	18, 27
19				Conclusions	7, 14
22				Understanding consequences	6
23				Mood	25, 31, 36

Interpreting Literature and the Arts Posttest A   Skill Chart

Question number	Number of incorrect answers	Percentage (total in col. 2) $\left(\begin{array}{l}\text{no. of items}\\\text{in col. 1}\end{array}\right) \times \left(\begin{array}{l}\text{no. in}\\\text{class}\end{array}\right)$		Skill	Lesson
1, 3, 9, 36, 39, 41				Supporting details	2–3, 12
7, 16, 19, 32, 35				Main idea	1–2, 11, 21, 26, 32
10, 15, 37				Seeing patterns	10
11, 13, 14, 26, 40				Tone	15, 24
5, 6, 24, 29				Technique/style	9, 17, 35
20, 22, 23, 43, 44				Characterization	20, 29
2, 28, 38				Context clues	4, 13, 33
8, 12, 25				Figures of speech	5, 22, 34
4, 17, 27, 30, 33				Application	8, 16, 23, 30
31				Plot	18, 27
42				Concluions	7, 14
21				Understanding consequences	6
18, 34, 45				Mood	25, 31, 36

Interpreting Literature and the Arts Posttest B   Skill Chart

Question number	Number of incorrect answers	Percentage (total in col. 2) $\left(\begin{array}{l}\text{no. of items}\\\text{in col. 1}\end{array}\right) \times \left(\begin{array}{l}\text{no. in}\\\text{class}\end{array}\right)$		Skill	Lesson
9, 15, 20, 22, 27, 34, 40, 42				Supporting details	2–3, 12
1, 3, 7, 19, 26, 39				Main idea	1–2, 11, 21, 26, 32
44				Seeing patterns	10
10, 17, 24, 28, 45				Tone	15, 24
29				Technique/style	9, 17, 35
2, 13, 14, 16, 37				Characterization	20, 29

(continued)

Interpreting Literature and the Arts Posttest B   Skill Chart

Question number	Number of incorrect answers	Percentage (total in col. 2) $\begin{pmatrix} \text{no. of items} \\ \text{in col. 1} \end{pmatrix} \times \begin{pmatrix} \text{no. in} \\ \text{class} \end{pmatrix}$		Skill	Lesson
33				Context clues	4, 13, 33
25, 32, 41				Figures of speech	5, 22, 34
4, 8, 11, 21, 23, 30, 36, 43				Application	8, 16, 23, 30
12				Setting	19, 28
31				Plot	18, 27
6				Conclusions	7, 14
35				Understanding consequences	6
5, 18, 38				Mood	25, 31, 36

Mathematics Skills Survey   Class Performance

Question number	Number of incorrect answers	Percentage (total in col. 2) $\begin{pmatrix} \text{no. of items} \\ \text{in col. 1} \end{pmatrix} \times \begin{pmatrix} \text{no. in} \\ \text{class} \end{pmatrix}$		Skill	Lesson
1, 4, 21, 22				Whole numbers	2–7
2				Decimals	8–11
5, 6, 9				Fractions	12–18
7, 8, 23, 28				Percents	19–21
3, 15, 16, 19, 20				Data analysis	22–25
10, 11, 18				Number relationships	26–28
27				Measurement	29–32
12, 13, 14				Geometry	33–42
17, 24, 25, 26				Algebra	43–50

Mathematics Posttest A   Skill Chart

Question number	Number of incorrect answers	Percentage (total in col. 2) $\left(\begin{array}{l}\text{no. of items}\\\text{in col. 1}\end{array}\right) \times \left(\begin{array}{l}\text{no. in}\\\text{class}\end{array}\right)$	Skill	Lesson
1, 2, 22			Whole numbers	2–7
5, 9, 10, 13, 21, 27, 28			Decimals	8–11
4, 6, 17, 18, 26			Fractions	12–18
3, 11, 12, 15, 16			Percents	19–21
7, 8			Data analysis	22–25
20, 23, 25, 43, 55			Number relationships	26–28
14, 19, 29, 30, 32, 36			Measurement	29–32
31, 33, 34, 35, 37, 38, 39, 40, 56			Geometry	33–42
24, 41, 42, 44, 45, 46, 47, 48, 49, 50, 51, 52, 53, 54			Algebra	43–50

Mathematics Posttest B   Skill Chart

Question number	Number of incorrect answers	Percentage (total in col. 2) $\left(\begin{array}{l}\text{no. of items}\\\text{in col. 1}\end{array}\right) \times \left(\begin{array}{l}\text{no. in}\\\text{class}\end{array}\right)$	Skill	Lesson
1, 16			Whole numbers	2–7
3, 4, 7			Decimals	8–11
2, 5, 6			Fractions	12–18
8, 9, 10, 11			Percents	19–21
12, 13, 14, 23, 24, 25, 26, 27			Data analysis	22–25
17, 18, 19, 20, 39			Number relationships	26–28
15, 21, 22, 28, 32			Measurement	29–32
29, 30, 31, 33, 34, 35, 36, 37, 38, 40, 46			Geometry	33–42
41, 42, 43, 44, 45, 47, 48, 49, 50, 51, 52, 53, 54, 55, 56			Algebra	43–50

Scope and Sequence—Writing Skills *Springboard*

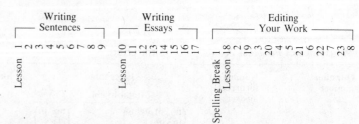

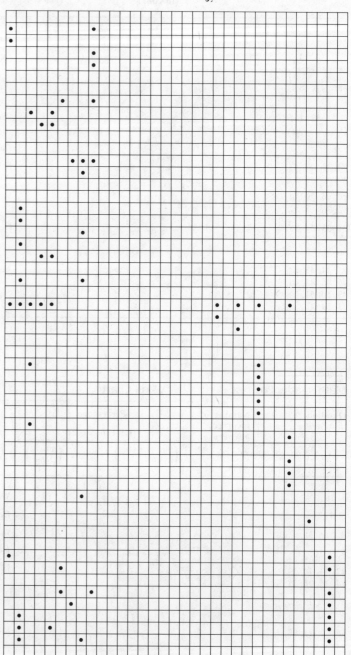

	Writing Sentences									Writing Essays								Editing Your Work													
	1	2	3	4	5	6	7	8	9	10	11	12	13	14	15	16	17	SB1	18	2	19	3	20	4	5	21	6	22	7	23	8
Sentences																															
Complete sentences	•							•																							
*Fragments	•																														
Run-ons								•																							
Comma splices								•																							
Coordination																															
Compound sentences					•			•																							
Compound subjects			•	•																											
Compound predicates				•	•																										
Subordination																															
Complex sentences						•	•	•																							
Relative clauses							•																								
Modification																															
Adjectives		•																													
Adverbs		•																													
Appositives						•																									
Placement		•																													
Parallelism				•	•																										
Nouns		•					•																								
Verbs	•	•	•	•	•														•		•		•		•						
Tenses																			•												
Forms																							•								
Subject-verb agreement																															
Noun-verb pairs			•																				•								
Interrupting phrase																							•								
Inverted structure																							•								
Expletives																							•								
Connectives other than *and*																							•								
Neither-nor/either-or			•																												
Pronouns as subjects																									•						
Pronouns																															
Agreement w/antecedent																									•						
Pronoun consistency																									•						
Clear reference																									•						
Relative pronouns							•																								
Capitalization																											•				
Punctuation																															
End punctuation	•																													•	
Semicolons				•																										•	
Commas																															
Between independent clauses				•		•																								•	
After introductory dependent clauses					•																									•	
After introductory elements		•																												•	
Between items in series		•	•																											•	
Around appositives, parenthetical ideas		•					•																							•	

Spelling

Process of writing
  Prewriting
  Writing first draft
  Revising
  Editing

Structure of essay
  Organization of ideas
  Beginning and ending
  Transitions

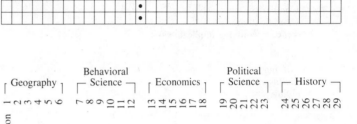

Column headings: Writing Sentences (Lesson 1–9) · Writing Essays (Lesson 10–17) · Editing Your Work (Spelling Break 1, Lesson 18–...)

Vocabulary Development
  Word structure
  Context clues

Skimming

Comprehension
  Paraphrasing (restating)
  Determining main idea
  Summarizing
  Understanding organization of ideas
    Chronological order
    Classification
    Comparison/contrast
  Inference (identifying implications)

Application
  Classifying
  Extrapolating
  Applying

Analysis
  Relating ideas
    Sequential
    General vs. specific
    Similarity vs. difference
  Recognizing assumptions
  Cause-effect
  Distinguishing fact and opinion
  Distinguishing fact and hypothesis
  Distinguishing conclusion from support

Evaluation
  Detecting faulty logic
  Assessing support for conclusions
  Recognizing role of values

*Boldface entries are GED skills.

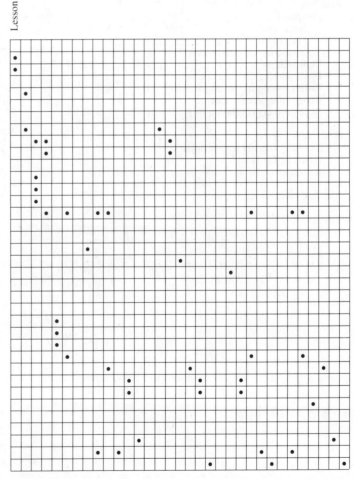

Column headings: Geography (Lesson 1–6) · Behavioral Science (7–12) · Economics (13–18) · Political Science (19–23) · History (24–29)

Visual Materials
  Reading visual materials is introduced in the opening section "Answering Questions Based on Graphics" and reinforced throughout the book.

Scope and Sequence—Science *Springboard*

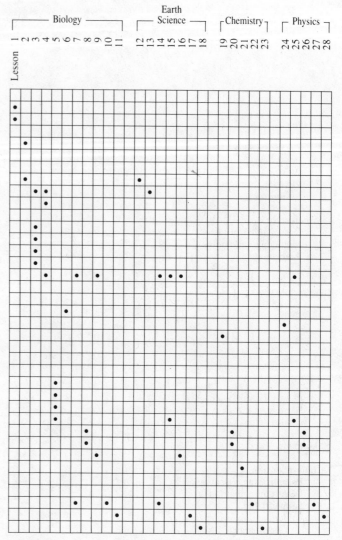

Skills chart. Lessons 1–28 grouped as Biology (1–11), Earth Science (12–18), Chemistry (19–23), Physics (24–28). A dot (•) indicates the skill is taught in that lesson.

Skill	Subject area / Lessons with a mark
Vocabulary Development	
Word structure	Biology 1
Context clues	Biology 1
Skimming	Biology 3
Comprehension	
*Paraphrasing (restating)	Biology 3; Earth Science 13
Determining main idea	Biology 4, 5; Earth Science 14
Summarizing	Biology 5
Understanding organization of ideas	
Chronological order	Biology 4
Order of importance	Biology 4
Comparison-contrast	Biology 4
Classification	Biology 4
Inference (identifying implications)	Biology 5, 8, 9; Earth Science 15, 16, 17; Physics 26
Application	
Classifying	Biology 10
Predicting	Physics 25
Applying	Chemistry 22
Analysis	
Relating ideas	
Sequential	Biology 6
General vs. specific	Biology 6
Similarity vs. difference	
Cause-effect	Biology 6; Earth Science 17; Physics 24
Distinguishing fact and opinion	Biology 8; Chemistry 20; Physics 26
Distinguishing fact and hypothesis	Biology 8; Chemistry 20; Physics 26
Recognizing assumptions	Biology 9; Earth Science 16
Distinguishing conclusion from support	Chemistry 21
Evaluation	
Assessing support for conclusions	Biology 7, 9, 11; Chemistry 20; Physics 24, 27
Detecting faulty logic	Biology 10; Earth Science 18; Physics 28
Recognizing role of values	Earth Science 17; Chemistry 22

*Boldface entries are GED skills.

Visual Materials
  Reading visual materials is introduced in the opening section "How to Read Scientific Diagrams, Tables, and Graphs" and reinforced throughout the book.

	Nonfiction									Commentary								Fiction								Drama						Poetry				
Lesson	1	2	3	4	5	6	7	8	9	10	11	12	13	14	15	16	17	18	19	20	21	22	23	24	25	26	27	28	29	30	31	32	33	34	35	36
Comprehension																																				
Vocabulary																																				
Word structure				•																																
Context clues				•									•																				•			
Figurative language						•																•													•	
Determining main idea																																				
Stated	•																																			
Implied		•										•								•					•							•				
Supporting details	•	•	•										•																							
Summarizing												•																								
Inference		•					•					•			•	•		•	•	•	•			•		•	•	•	•							
Understanding organization of ideas																																				
Classification												•																								
Chronological order												•																								
Comparison/contrast												•																								
Cause-effect												•																								
Literary elements																																				
Plot																			•							•										
Character																					•							•								
Setting																				•							•									
Application								•							•						•								•							
Analysis																																				
Cause-effect						•					•																									
Author's style																																				
Purpose										•						•																		•		
Tone														•															•							
Mood																															•		•			•

*Boldface entries are GED skills.

Scope and Sequence—Mathematics *Springboard*

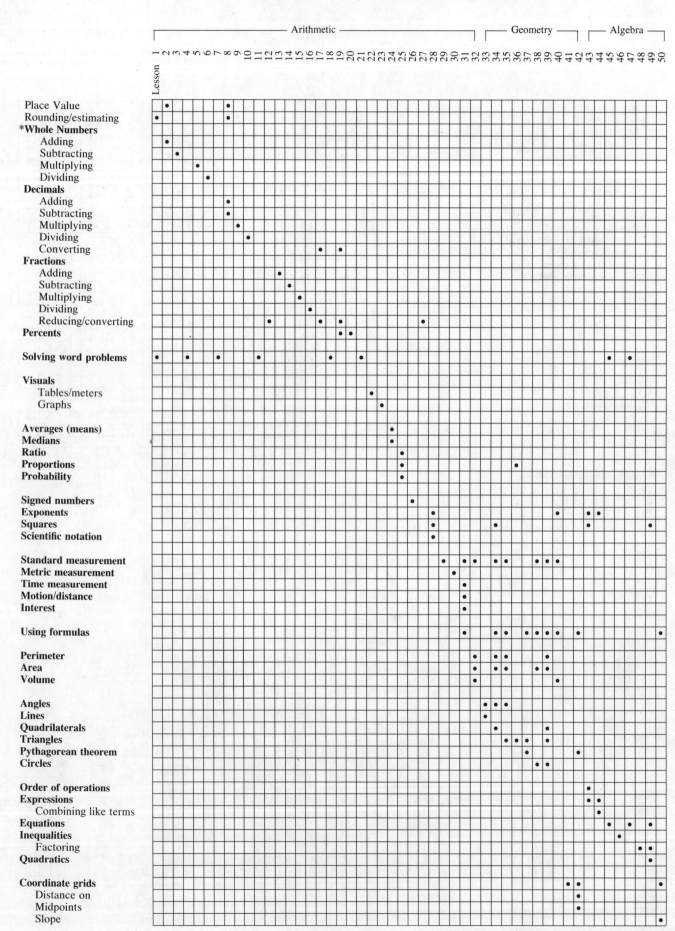

Columns represent Lessons 1–50, grouped as: Arithmetic (Lessons 1–32), Geometry (Lessons 33–42), Algebra (Lessons 43–50).

Topic	Lessons with entries
Place Value	2, 8
Rounding/estimating	1, 8
*Whole Numbers	
Adding	2
Subtracting	3
Multiplying	5
Dividing	6
Decimals	
Adding	8
Subtracting	8
Multiplying	9
Dividing	10
Converting	17, 18
Fractions	
Adding	13
Subtracting	14
Multiplying	15
Dividing	16
Reducing/converting	12, 17, 19, 27
Percents	20, 21
Solving word problems	1, 4, 7, 10, 18, 21, 45, 47
Visuals	
Tables/meters	23
Graphs	24
Averages (means)	25
Medians	26
Ratio	26
Proportions	26, 39
Probability	26
Signed numbers	27
Exponents	29, 41, 44, 45
Squares	29, 35, 44, 49
Scientific notation	29
Standard measurement	30, 32, 33, 35, 36, 40, 41, 42
Metric measurement	31
Time measurement	31
Motion/distance	31
Interest	32
Using formulas	30, 33, 35, 37, 38, 39, 41, 50
Perimeter	33, 35, 36, 40
Area	33, 35, 36, 40, 41
Volume	31, 40
Angles	33, 34
Lines	33
Quadrilaterals	35, 40
Triangles	34, 35, 36, 39
Pythagorean theorem	38, 42
Circles	38, 39
Order of operations	43
Expressions	43, 44
Combining like terms	44
Equations	45, 46, 47
Inequalities	46
Factoring	48, 49
Quadratics	49
Coordinate grids	41, 42, 50
Distance on	42
Midpoints	42
Slope	50

*Boldface entries are GED skills.